Library of Congress Cataloging-in-Publication Data

Newman, John, 1942-
    Vietnam War Literature : an annotated bibliography of
imaginative works about Americans fighting in Vietnam / by
John Newman, with Ann Hilfinger. -- 2nd ed.
        p.   cm.
    Includes indexes.
    ISBN 0-8108-2155-9
    1. American literature--20th century--Bibliography.
2. Vietnamese Conflict, 1961-1975--Literary collections--
Bibliography.   3. American literature--20th century--
Stories, plots, etc.   4. Vietnamese Conflict, 1961-1975--
Literature and the conflict.   I. Hilfinger, Ann.
II. Title.
Z1227.N49 1988
[PS228.V5]
016.81'08'0358--dc19   88-15747

DEDICATION

This book is dedicated to the Americans
who fought their country's war in Vietnam.

ACKNOWLEDGMENTS

This bibliography was compiled with the
assistance from friends and colleagues at
Colorado State University Libraries and at
other universities in this country and
abroad. Much of the research and writing
was done during a sabbatical leave granted
to Newman by the governing board of Colorado
State University. Con Woodall, Brian
Albright and Karen Cagle helped manage the
text and index on the computer.

TABLE OF CONTENTS

FOREWORD TO THE FIRST EDITION

John Clark Pratt
Vietnam/Thailand/Laos   August 1969 - August 1970

For a Vietnam veteran, to read through John Newman's bibliography is to relive the war. As are the literary works themselves, the significant events, sights, and feelings are documented here: the trauma, the internal conflicts, the atrocities, the heroism, the misunderstandings, the loves, the losses, and yes, even the humor. John has combined sincere scholarship with unusually dispassionate insight, and this first annotated guide to Vietnam fiction and poetry is not only a significant contribution to literary history but also an important documentation of the breadth of writing done about America's longest war.

In 1975, when John and I first discussed the possibilities of such a collection, we knew of about fifty novels, quite a few poems, and some short stories. One has only to look at the publication dates noted in this bibliography to realize how ignorant we, along with so many other Americans, were. An incident that occurred soon afterward is an example: for a 1976 talk I was preparing on Vietnam War literature, I queried major U.S. publishers about their offerings. One leading editor-in-chief replied that his firm had published no Vietnam War fiction; nor did he intend to, because it would not sell. Subsequent investigation showed that his company had already published three novels about the war. It is as if this editor had done what so many other Americans have done: simply block out the facts of this most unpopular war.

Thanks to John Newman, as well as a few others who have been working quietly to preserve what the Vietnam War really was, those authors who wrote about the war can now have their voices heard. Readers can now start with the annotations in Newman's work. His summary comments, resulting from months of immersion in the literature, indicate mainly

what the work is about, and, as an annotated bibliography
should do, abstain remarkably from editorial bias (except in
a few instances where the work in question is unmitigated
trash whose relevance to Vietnam is purely exploitative).
Knowing John Newman as I do, I had expected far more subjective analyses. I was wrong, and I would suggest that future
readers for whom this bibliography will provide a necessary
starting point profitably emulate the careful, sincere
attention to objectivity. Perhaps for the first time since
the outbreak of hostilities (whenever that really was), an
analysis of Vietnam-related material has been made without
overweening bias.

This bibliography accordingly stands as a work of scholarship to which all that follow will be mere revisions and
addenda. Certainly, there have been omissions, particularly
in regard to poetry, where many of the original fugitive
pieces were never cataloged. Information about and especially copies of any missing literary publications would be
welcomed, because the Vietnam War Literature Collection at
Colorado State University is an ongoing project.

Finally, I would like to echo John Newman's dedication of
this work to those who served. Now, years after the official ending of hostilities, only by reading about the way it
seemed to those who wrote about it can Americans perhaps
finally understand how the Vietnam War really was.

J.C.P.
12 January 1982

FOREWORD TO THE SECOND EDITION

Now that authors writing fiction about the war in Vietnam
have received two National Book Awards (Tim O'Brien for
Going After Cacciato in 1978 and Larry Heinemann for Paco's
Story in 1987) and that since 1982, hundreds more works on
Vietnam have been published or reprinted, it's appropriate
that this new edition of John Newman's premier bibliography
be issued.

Reversing their earlier apathy, publishers have flooded (not
all of them responsibly) the marketplace with war-related
material in observance of the 1985 tenth anniversary of
Saigon's fall to the North Vietnamese. There are now, for
instance, more than 400 published novels about Americans
fighting in Vietnam, as well as numerous others about the

consequences of the war. Sadly, not all are first- or even
second-rate, but Newman must be commended for including all
of them here--even those for which sexual exploitation is
primary and those (especially the series publications) whose
glorification of combat bears little relation to the
actuality of Vietnam. To be complete, a bibliography cannot
consciously exclude.

For all of these more recent works, Newman has devoted
voracious research and unsparing comments. Because this
book is bibliography and not literary criticism, a reader
looking for experimental or advanced literary techniques
might not agree with John that some books are "difficult to
follow," but his statements that other works are "superficial," "tedious," "trash," or "an embarrassment" are
usually right on target.

That the first edition of Vietnam War Literature has been
invaluable is attested to by many of the participants in the
growing number of international conferences on the war: The
Asia Society Conference in New York, 1985; the Macquarie
University Conference, Sydney, Australia, 1987; the EVAC
Conference at Manchester Polytechnic, U.K., 1987; and the
Vietnam and the West Conference at the University of Wales,
Swansea, U.K., 1988. Future scholars, I am sure, will be
just as indebted to this new edition and the additional
perspectives that it provides.

J.C.P.
1 February 1988

Three of John Clark Pratt's eight books are about the
Vietnam War: The Laotian Fragments (Avon, 1985); Vietnam
Voices (Viking Penguin, 1984); and (with Tim Lomperis)
Reading the Wind: The Literature of the Vietnam War (Duke,
1986).

Background

Like the first edition in 1982, this annotated bibliography
is based primarily on the Vietnam War Literature Collection
at Colorado State University. That collection was begun in
1975 after a survey of large research libraries revealed
that none had a collection of fiction, poetry, drama and
other creative works about the Vietnam War.

The collection is now much larger than the 226 items that
were listed six years ago. Its holdings, catalogs and
databases are a resource for scholars, writers, dealers and
others interested in the literature. In turn, holdings and
knowledge here at Colorado State have been enriched by the
informed good will of these and other persons.

Scope

The great increase in Vietnam writing and associated criticism and scholarship has made this study much more active
and interesting now than at any time during the past fifteen
years. There is a healthy variety of opinions among everyone involved with Vietnam literature as to the proper scope
and content of the field. The compilers, for example, have
made their own subjective decisions about what to include
here.

This bibliography includes novels, short stories, poetry
collections, plays and such miscellaneous works as humor,
sketchbooks and anthologies published in English. There is
no nonfiction material. Some personal narratives, diaries
and so-called "nonfiction novels" have much to say about the
war, but they are not in this guide to purely creative
works. The locale is Vietnam, but there are other settings
during the war including Laos, Cambodia and imaginary
countries clearly meant to represent Vietnam. There is
nothing here that focuses only on the French in Indochina,

nor are there any of the fantastic postwar adventures to
rescue POWs or destroy the Southeast Asian drug trade. Much
of the war protest literature refers to Vietnam, but it is
included only if it is set there. Comic books and audio-
visual media are excluded as a practical matter.

The Vietnam veteran is a popular character in modern American fiction, and many books about veterans have preliminary
chapters or flashbacks set in Vietnam. The practice here is
to include novels in which the Vietnam segment is substantial enough to tell its own story and is also important
to the main plot.

The essential goal has been to present works that describe
the Vietnam War as it was experienced firsthand by relatively few people and watched on television by a great many
more.

This bibliography was compiled in late 1987, so most, but
not all, material for that year has been found and there are
as well some early 1988 publications.

Even within these limits of scope and time, it has not been
possible to see everything. Some items simply could not be
purchased, borrowed or even read on-site. There are books
that seem, from bibliographic or critical information, to
belong here, but the editorial decision has been to include
only those works that could actually be read and annotated.
Realistically, this bibliography can only make a contribution to the literature, not express the final word on it.

Arrangement

The chronological arrangement was suggested by several
persons who used the first edition. The intention is to
reflect something of the historical development of the
literature. In the case of drama, the copyright may be much
earlier than the date of the published script. Attention,
too, should be given to internal dates which are often
different from the time of publication.

Entries

The entries are intended to be straightforward and complete.
Publishers' full names, taken from title pages, are helpful
in identifying those enterprises that are not well known.
Pagination conveys something of a work's size and provides
precise information for ordering copies of material from
periodicals. Library of Congress card numbers are supplied
when they are known. In lieu of LC numbers, International

Standard Bibliographic Numbers are given if they are available. The entries list as many variant editions of books and reprints of stories as could be seen or reliably identified from secondary sources.

Annotations

The annotations have been prepared after a complete reading of every work. With very few exceptions, that has been the first edition of a book or the original appearance of a story. Each item has been approached as a unique literary effort, separate from the others and separate, for the most part, from the actual history of the Vietnam War. These works are imaginative; it would be unfair and limiting to evaluate them as history.

If the information is available in the original work, most annotations include the dates of the story, the location, the rank and duties of the characters, the plot and sometimes an opinion of the work's literary or other qualities. It is worth emphasizing that these are annotations written by a librarian, not reviews written by a critic or a professional student of literature. Numbers in parenthesis following titles refer to item numbers in this bibliography.

Compilers

For this bibliography, John Newman determined the scope, identified appropriate titles and wrote the annotations. Ann Hilfinger managed the database on a microcomputer, prepared the bibliographic entries and produced the camera-ready copy.

VIETNAM WAR LITERATURE

1964

1. Carter, Nick. <u>Saigon</u>. NY: Award Books, 1964.
    157 pp.
    London: Tandem, 1969. 156 pp.

There is just enough American military presence to
qualify this as a Vietnam War novel. Nick Carter, an
American spy, makes use of American uniforms, military
convoys, and helicopters as he pursues his secret
mission from Saigon into North Vietnam. The story is
both lurid and superficial. Carter is armed with all
manner of inappropriate devices, including a killer
fingernail! With American military help, he manages
to complete his mission, which involves rescuing a
beautiful French woman from the hands of North Vietnamese torturers and retrieving a secret message that
reveals the names of Vietcong agents in South Vietnam.

1965

2. Ballinger, Bill S. <u>The Spy in the Jungle</u>. NY: New
    American Library, Signet Books, 1965. 127 pp.

When secret agent Joaquin Hawks sets out from Saigon
for a clandestine run into North Vietnam, he is ably
supported by a substantial American military presence,
which is already running the war. The settings are
worked out in detail, including some highly inaccurate
background about Oriental martial arts. Moreover,
Hawks is indestructable. His mission deep into North
Vietnam in search of a secret missile installation is
implausible. Even so, this is an interesting early
book because it shows the results of so much research.

Hawks survives for more novels, beyond the scope of
this bibliography.

3.   Moore, Robin. The Green Berets. NY: Crown, 1965.
          341 pp. 65-15849.
          Taiwan: n.p., 1965. 341 pp.
          NY: Avon, 1965. 334 pp.
          NY: Crown, for the Green Beret Holding Corp.,
          1969. 341 pp.
          NY: Ballantine, 1983. 339 pp. 65-15849.

One of the earlier novels about Americans fighting in
Vietnam, this enthusiastic account of Special Forces
adventures is the basis for the motion picture of the
same name. Captain Steve Kornie and his team are
clearly the good guys, and the Vietcong and North
Vietnamese are just as clearly and wholly bad. The
plot is actually a series of separate stories, which
includes the brilliant defense of a Special Forces
camp and a clandestine operation inside North Vietnam.
Moore is convinced, it seems, that the Special Forces
will win the war, despite only lukewarm assistance
from the South Vietnamese and restrictions imposed by
higher military and civilian command.

4.   Morrison, C.T. The Flame in the Icebox. NY: Exposi-
          tion Press, 1965. 112 pp.

This brief novel offers an unfortunate and unusual
combination of florid descriptive prose and over-
simplified characters and action. An American infantry squad (which is led, implausibly, by a lieutenant) spends a day in heavy combat with the
Vietcong. After ambush and counterambush, most of the
men are killed. Two enlisted men are captured and
taken to a camp in the nearby jungle. During their
captivity, the men are treated reasonably well, and
some attempt is made by their captors to indoctrinate
them. After one or two halfhearted attempts at escape
fail, the men are told that they will be released soon
in any case. Then American forces attack the camp and
kill everyone, including the prisoners. The book
concludes with the helpful explanation that Vietnam is
the flame in the icebox of the Cold War. The review
copy is badly made; the stitching on the spine is
incomplete.

5.   Tran Van Dinh. No Passenger on the River. NY:
        Vantage, 1965. 243 pp.

        A firm command of idiomatic English is beyond the
        author, but his main character, a Vietnamese colonel,
        is unigue in Vietnam fiction. Colonel Minh graduates
        from the Command and General Staff College at Fort
        Leavenworth in 1963 at the top of his class. Return-
        ing to Vietnam, he is disheartened by governmental
        duplicity and corruption. After some combat with
        American advisors, Minh is drawn into a coup plot.
        Senior Vietnamese generals hijack the coup and murder
        Minh. He leaves behind a pregnant American
        girlfriend.

                                1966

6.   Blacker, Irwin R. Search and Destroy. NY: Random
        House, 1966. 274 pp. 66-21492.
        London: Cassell, 1966. Published as The Valley
        of Hanoi.
        NY: Dell, 1967. 237 pp.

        The American title is a bit misleading, for this is an
        account of a commando-type raid into North Vietnam.
        After learning of the construction of an airfield, a
        dam and fuel storage facilities near Hanoi, an
        American President determines that bombing them would
        run too great a risk of war with Russia and China.
        Instead, he sends in a small group of men on the
        ground. Their background and training are recounted
        completely, but details about military procedures and
        weapons are not always accurate. At one point, a
        general commanding a secret national military agency
        flies into North Vietnam to assist. The team com-
        pletes its mission and destroys the facilities, but
        nearly all of its members are killed. The Vietnamese
        appear hardly at all in this story; it is essentially
        a military adventure.

7.   Carter, Nick. Hanoi. NY: Award Books, 1966. 156 pp.

        Nick Carter, who first appeared in the 1964 novel,
        Saigon, is back in Vietnam again. He performs
        numerous feats of derring-do, including impersonating
        a Vietnamese peasant, capturing a renegade scientist
        in North Vietnam and then returning in disguise to
        penetrate a secret installation there. What is

interesting is the support he draws from Special
Forces units. They have what amounts to a permanent
installation not far from Hanoi. In this author's
imagination, the Special Forces also has its own
aircraft and pilots.

8.   Derrig, Peter. <u>The Pride of the Green Berets</u>. NY:
         Paperback Library, 1966. 288 pp.

In the early part of the war, the Special Forces
caught the imagination of some Americans, and they
were fitting subjects for such books as this. A
twelve-man Special Forces team is active primarily in
the Mekong Delta in the early 1960s. There is a surprising amount of accurate military detail. Among the
plot elements are U.S.-Vietnamese feuds, struggles
with cowardly and venal American officers and the
inevitable love story between the team captain and a
lovely Vietnamese woman. In one of the many battles,
an ARVN unit outfights a larger Vietcong force.
Another time, an American staff colonel stalks and
kills two Vietcong machine gunners with a knife. In
line with this sort of patriotic optimism, the book
ends when the team commander is promoted to major and
awarded the Congressional Medal of Honor.

9.   Elegant, Robert S. <u>A Kind of Treason</u>. NY: Holt,
         Rinehart & Winston, 1966. 284 pp.
         NY: Avon, 1967. 239 pp. 66-13099.
         Great Britain: Judy Piatkus Ltd., 1980.
         NY: Penguin, 1982. 249 pp.

This sophisticated novel demonstrates Elegant's
familiarity with Asia as well as his mature writing
talent. It also touches on the ease with which an
accredited journalist might undertake an intelligence
mission. Gerry Mallory, an old Asian hand, visits
Saigon in 1964, ostensibly as a magazine feature
writer, but actually as a C.I.A. agent looking for an
intelligence leak. He has standard U.S. military
briefings and goes out on operations. He also makes
contact with the South Vietnamese resistance and the
National Liberation Front. Busy as he is, he finds
time to fall in love with a beautiful Vietnamese
woman. While pursuing his journalistic and intelligence missions, Mallory encounters individuals and
situations that suggest the war is already lost.
Futility emerges from the three standard sources:

South Vietnamese corruption, American ineptitude and
NLF commitment.

10.   Field, Della. <u>Vietnam Nurse</u>. NY: Avon, 1966.
          126 pp.

Nurse Lee Knight finds military service in Vietnam to
be exciting and romantic, not squalid and dangerous.
She arrives in Saigon as an ensign in the Navy Nurse
Corps. Her fiance is a Green Beret officer, missing
in the jungle, and one of the purposes in coming to
Vietnam is to find him. Lee Knight gives some
perfunctory attention to her nursing duties, which are
described in the most general way, but most of her
attention must go to resisting the advances of strong,
handsome young men. When they are not busy "dropping
from parachutes and fighting hand-to-hand," they just
cannot leave Lee alone. After learning that her
fiance has been killed, Lee transfers her affections
to another Special Forces trooper and accompanies him
on several adventures, including intense combat. Her
new lover is eventually wounded, but not so badly that
they cannot live happily ever after.

11.   Garfield, Brian. <u>The Last Bridge</u>. NY: David McKay,
          1966.   277 pp.   66-23423.
          NY: Avon, 1967.   224 pp.
          NY: Dale Books, 1978.   285 pp.   78-69544.

This novel of high adventure is difficult to believe,
but easy and interesting to read. In the span of a
few days, a small team of Americans and South Vietnamese plans and executes a mission into North Vietnam
to rescue an American prisoner and to destroy a vital
railroad bridge. They complete both goals successfully. Along the way, they steal a great deal of
North Vietnamese equipment; kill a number of people
with explosives, small arms, knives and bare hands;
and outwit all opposing forces that have the ill luck
to meet them. Some scenes of torture are effective.
The characters are all solid military types.

12.   Hempstone, Smith. <u>A Tract of Time</u>. Boston: Houghton
          Mifflin, Riverside Press, 1966.   271 pp.
          66-11226.
          Greenwich, CT: Fawcett, 1966.   224 pp.

In a preface, the author sets his story in 1963,
before and during the fall of the Diem government.
Diem is one of the characters, and the coup that led
to his fall is a major feature of the novel. Harry
Colart is a CIA operative working with mountain
tribesmen against the Vietcong. Colart's men are as
much opposed to the South Vietnamese government as
they are to the enemy. Theirs is only one dilemma
among the mix of confusion and conflicts in the book.
Colart and other characters are caught up in events
out of their control as the war widens almost from
pressure of its own. They are sensitive and thoughtful individuals, and they dwell at length on a cause
that they suspect may already be lost.

13.   Krueger, Carl. Wings of the Tiger. NY: Frederick
            Fell, 1966. 285 pp. 66-27604.

In lengthy prefatory material, Krueger recounts his
long association with the Air Force as a novelist and
screenwriter. He explains that Wings of the Tiger
began life as a screenplay. The novel, written in
superlatives, certainly reflects its origin. Aircraft
are described in very great detail, both at rest and
in battle. The human characters are bantering,
courageous pilots, bent on their mission to destroy an
airfield north of Hanoi. Subplots include romance,
spies and a look at the lives of some amazingly
simpleminded North Vietnamese living near the intended
target. In view of subsequent events, Krueger's
bright enthusiam for the war seems naive, but his
skill as a writer holds the story together.

14.   Newhafer, Richard. No More Bugles in the Sky. NY:
            New American Library, 1966. 306 pp. 66-22216.
            NY: New American Library, Signet Books, 1966.
            288 pp. Published as The Violators.

Like other Air Force novelists, Newhafer suffers from
no lack of imagination and enthusiasm. His hero, Dan
Belden, is a World War II and Korean War ace on a
semisecret mission for the Director of the CIA in
1964. Belden's job is to use air power to widen the
Vietnam War! Only then can enough American troops be
brought in to win it. Belden's adventures are
numerous. Often he is in the cockpit, flying against
an old Chinese foe from Korea. Finally, Belden is
successful, and the President authorizes the dispatch

of one hundred thousand American troops to Vietnam.
In view of the subsequent developments in the Vietnam
War, Newhafer's ideas of 1966 are unfortunately
prophetic.

15.   Roberts, Suzanne.   <u>Vietnam Nurse</u>.   NY: Ace, 1966.
         142 pp.

This view of Vietnam as the locale for a sort of
extended prom date is certainly unusual, even in a
varied and unconventional body of literature.   Nurse
Katie arrives in Vietnam with the personality of a
high school virgin.   The settings in Vietnam and
indeed in the Army are perfunctory and entirely
notional.   The war appears as occasional bursts of
machine gun fire from bothersome snipers.   These may
interrupt Katie and her beau of the moment, but they
represent no real danger.   Several other novels about
nurses by the same author are listed on one of the
preliminary pages.   This one reveals little or nothing
about medical care in Vietnam.

16.   Runyon, Charles.   <u>Bloody Jungle</u>.   NY: Ace, 1966.
         157 pp.

Lieutenant Clay Macklin is a one-man army.   A Green
Beret stationed in Vietnam in the early 1960s, he
survived the destruction of his camp, escapes through
the jungle with the help of a Vietnamese woman, saves
the wife of a French plantation owner from a gang rape
by the Vietcong and makes his way alone to another
Special Forces camp.   Macklin is evacuated to Saigon,
where he receives a Silver Star, engages in some
freehanded spying, survives another terrific fight in
the jungle, destroys the secret headquarters of the
Vietcong and rescues some prisoners in the process.
To achieve all this, Lt. Macklin triumphs over the
jungle, the enemy, the corrupt South Vietnamese, inept
officers in his own army and the world press.
Everything happens in less than one month.

17.   Seran, Val.   <u>Vietnam Mission to Hell</u>.   NY: Bee-Line
         Books, 1966.   155 pp.

Unquestionably <u>Vietnam Mission to Hell</u> is among the
worst novels read for this bibliography.   A group of
nine American soldiers is sent into North Vietnam to

lead a tribe of Montagnards in various attacks and
raids against military and civilian targets. Subplots
include a long standing feud between the two officers
and a love affair one of them has with a native woman.
None of this makes any sense. The plot, characters,
settings and action are all superficial. Among other
problems, the author knows nothing about soldiers or
infantry weapons. Two of the original nine men
survive to be evacuated, but the specifics of that
event, like the rest of the book, ring utterly untrue.

18.   Stone, Scott C.S. The Coasts of War. NY: Pyramid,
          1966. 157 pp.

In addition to being one of the few Navy novels of
Vietnam, this excellent little book is also one of the
earliest, apparently set in 1964. One of the principal events, for instance, is the first combat air
strike by U.S. Navy jets in Vietnam. The story has to
do with Lt. Eriksen, a Navy officer advising a
Vietnamese small-boat patrol force in the Mekong
Delta. Eriksen is a competent and enthusiastic
professional officer, and the Vietnamese he advises
are capable patriots. In keeping with this positive
tone, they are usually successful in military and even
political action against the Vietcong. This is not,
however, a foolish book. The characters and situations are believable, and the writing is able.

19.   Wilson, William. The LBJ Brigade. Los Angeles, CA:
          Apocalypse, 1966. 124 pp. 65-28536.
          NY: Pyramid, published in cooperation with
          Parallax Publishing, 1966. 141 pp.
          London: MacGibbon & Kee, 1966. 135 pp.

For such an early book, the antiwar message here is
overwhelming. The narrator, who is not named, tells
of his service as an Army infantryman in the present
tense. Settings and actions are simplified. Upon
arriving in Vietnam, the hero meets Sace, an
experienced sergeant who tries to teach him how to
stay alive. However, he disobeys the sergeant's
instructions and as a result Sace is killed and he is
captured by the Vietcong. After some time observing
the superior tactics of the enemy, the narrator is
killed in an air strike.

1967

20. Archibald, Joseph. Special Forces Trooper. NY: David
         McKay, 1967. 186 pp. 67-26862.

     The most notable aspect of this book for boys is its
     industrial strength binding. The story is full of
     patriotism and adolescent good intentions. Stan
     Rusat, a failed West Point cadet, goes through
     extensive Special Forces training in the U.S. before
     he is sent to a camp near the Cambodian border. The
     soldiers he joins there never swear and almost never
     drink. Rusat is involved in some ambush and counter-
     ambush operations before the final Vietcong assault on
     the camp. In that battle, one hundred sixty of the
     enemy are killed. Rusat survives and looks forward to
     his remaining months in Vietnam.

21. Butterworth, W.E. Air Evac. NY: Norton, 1967.
         211 pp. 67-18675.

     The first and largest portion of this novel describes
     the family, social relationships, college career and
     ideas of a young man named Ken Maddox. It is set in
     the mid-1960s, and Maddox must face the draft after
     college. As a near pacifist, he is unwilling to kill,
     but he manages to be assigned to training as a medical
     helicopter pilot in Alabama. Near the end of the
     book, Maddox goes to Vietnam, where he firms up his
     personality and ideas. The reader is left with
     impression that Maddox may become a competent profes-
     sional officer. This novel is almost juvenile. The
     characters seldom drink, curse or fornicate. Their
     motives and ideas are always completely clear (and
     simple). There is a wealth of information about
     helicopters and military training, but little about
     Vietnam.

22. Calin, Harold. Search and Kill. NY: Belmont Books,
         1967. 173 pp.

     Mistakes abound in this disjointed story about an
     infantry company near the Cambodian border. Weapons
     nomenclature and other military terms are confused,
     people speak into radio receivers, not transmitters,
     and they violate the most fundamental practices of
     communications security. The Americans are beset by

cowardly and corrupt ARVN colleages, but they manage
to outwit and outfight both the Vietcong and North
Vietnamese regulars. Characterization and dialog are
shallow; hardly anyone uses profanity. The action is
virtually impossible to follow, but American arms are
successful. At the end, the characters are confident
that they have learned enough to win the rest of the
war.

23.   Daniels, Norman. Operation VC. NY: Pyramid, 1967.
          157 pp.

John Keith, an agent of a secret American agency, is
sent to destroy two artillery pieces and their atomic
shells that the enemy has hidden outside Saigon.
Keith makes everything easy. He outwits and outfights
both the Vietcong and various Chinese soldiers and
spies. He survives torture with virtually no ill
effects and he accomplishes his mission. Keith also
enjoys a relationship with a beautiful Eurasian woman.
So as not to leave Southeast Asia with too little
done, Keith finishes by setting the Laotian economy on
a sure path toward future prosperity.

24.   Derrig, Peter. Battlefield. NY: Paperback Library,
          1967. 287 pp.

Major Dave Cunningham and his team of Green Berets
move even further away from reality in this third book
by Derrig. A few months after his adventures in The
Glory of the Green Berets, Cunningham is assigned by
his patron general officer to shape up a poor-quality
U.S. infantry regiment stationed on the southern coast
of South Vietnam. Combining the talents of superb
infantrymen, training cadre, detectives and secret
agents, Cunningham and his men infuse the regiment
with fighting capacities, destroy a major enemy base
and capture or kill members of a black market ring.
They have the company of several beautiful women as
they succeed on all fronts.

25.   Derrig, Peter. The Glory of the Green Berets. NY:
          Paperback Library, 1967. 288 pp.

Major Dave Cunningham is newly promoted to major and
decorated with the Congressional Medal of Honor for
exploits in The Pride of the Green Berets (8), a

marginally better book. Cunningham leaves his job as
a general's aide to return to Vietnam with remnants of
his old Special Forces team and a bewildering array of
Australian, Korean, Thai, Laotian, Filipino and ARVN
troops. There is also a beautiful Asian American
woman. Cunningham's new mission is to plant electronic sensing devices along enemy supply trails in
Laos. Despite intrusion by obnoxious, self-serving
reporters and incompetent soldiers of several nationalities, he manages to get the job done.

26.   Dexter, John. <u>No Virgins in Cham Ky</u>. San Diego, CA:
          Corinth Publications, 1967. 159 pp.

It is hard to imagine what reason there would be to
fictionalize Vietnam in this book, but the country is
Cham Ky and the enemy are the Cham Cong. Pat Killane,
a former serviceman, works for Dragon Air, a company
much like Air America . Against the background of
incompetent national army, French halfcastes, brave
mountain tribesmen and a confused American military
effort, Killane has several physical and sexual
adventures. This is blow by blow adventure, without
much context or meaning.

27.   Dexter, John. <u>Vietnam Vixens</u>. San Diego, CA: Phenix
          Publications, 1967. 159 pp.

This shallow aggregation of words fails even as
pornography. Although noted on the cover as "adult
reading" and "A Late-Hour Library Book," the relativly
few scenes of sexual activity are as general and
meaningless as the rest of the book. The story is
about an Australian nurse and her missionary father
who try to meet the North Vietnamese in the jungle in
order to promote a peace plan. This effort is
supported by American military authorities and shows
some promise of success. Barely legible printing adds
to the problems of an already poor book.

28.   Ford, Daniel. <u>Incident at Muc Wa</u>. Garden City, NY:
          Doubleday, 1967. 231 pp. 67-12876.
          London: Heinemann, 1967. 231 pp.
          NY: Pyramid, 1968. 192 pp.
          NY: Jove, 1979. 192 pp. Published as <u>Go Tell It</u>
          <u>to the Spartans</u>.

A motion picture based on this novel bears the same
name as its more recent title. Although locations and
units are nominally disguised, this describes the
Special Forces in the Vietnam highlands in 1964. The
establishment and subsequent loss of a fortified camp
at Muc Wa proceed from the military politics of
careerist officers who are unbelievable fools. The
men on the ground are more credible, although they
include such standard characters as a foolish second
lieutenant and a wise old sergeant. Details of locale
and military matters are convincing.

29.   Halberstam, David. <u>One Very Hot Day</u>. Boston: Hough-
          ton Mifflin, 1967. 216 pp. 67-27510.
          NY: Avon, 1969. 192 pp.
          NY: Warner Books, 1984. 230 pp.

This competent early novel of the war is set in a
time prior to the arrival of large numbers of American
troops. Captain Beaupre is old for his rank and
somewhat tired. Assigned as an adviser to a Vietnamese unit in the Mekong Delta, he finds the heat as
much of an enemy as the communists. He fights the
heat throughout the entire day in which this story
takes place. Among Beaupre's other enemies are the
Vietnamese he advises. He cannot understand or accept
their passive and lackadaisical approach to the war.
Thuong, a Vietnamese officer, views events and
personalities differently from the American adviser.
Scenes of combat, especially at the end of the book,
are fast-paced; the author is an able journalist.
Halberstam manages to convey, even in 1967, a sense of
the vast complexity and hopelessness of Vietnam.

30.   Hall, Ken. <u>Flesh or Fantasy</u>. Aquora, CA: Pad
          Library, 1967. 191 pp.

Air Force Lieutenant Charles Kelly is an ace who has
shot down seven enemy aircraft. As he is exploited
for favorable publicity in South Vietnam, he has
countless unimaginative sexual adventures. There is
no plot worth mentioning in this pornographic,
ungrammatical novel.

31.   Hennesey, Hal. <u>The Midnight War</u>. NY: Pyramid, 1967.
          172 pp.

This bizarre technological fantasy also includes
elements from a typical spy thriller of the 1950's or
early 1960's. Paul Partridge, a civil engineer and
occasional secret operative, has designed a huge
telescoping tank/bulldozer combination. He first
tries it out in Panama, where there are adventures
with Russians and Red Chinese spies. Then, under Army
and CIA auspices, he goes to Vietnam. He serves for a
few months as a freelance spy and commando, leading a
very exciting life in and around Saigon and having a
great deal of sex. Then, after an unusual ride on an
armored train from Saigon to Hue, he and some others
take the tank/bulldozer on a raid into North Vietnam.
The story at this point, and indeed throughout, shows
a marvelous ignorance of the relationship between
military explosives and military armour. Partridge
and many of his cronies are alive after the raid. The
book ends on a high note. Things are looking up
because it seems more Americans will soon be joining
the war.

32.   Hershman, Morris. <u>Glory in Hell</u>. NY: Lancer, 1967.
         223 pp.

An attempt to create a meaningful and poignant story
of a young man growing to maturity in combat fails for
several reasons, not the least of which is inaccuracy
about most things military and Vietnamese. Jud
Pachewik joins a cavalry unit that fights only as
infantry. The men often engage the enemy hand-to-
hand. Jud wears shoes, not boots, in combat, and
another soldier suffers a wound from a wire-operated
punji stake. Jud is taken under the wing of Raven, an
experienced soldier. By the time the book ends, Raven
is dead and Jud, now a wise old soldier, assumes
responsibility for the guidance of another
newly-arrived man. Hershman is clearly motivated to
praise American soldiers in Vietnam, and he can write
fluent dialog, but in this instance he seems
unfamiliar with his subject and setting.

33.   Kolpacoff, Victor. <u>The Prisoners of Quai Dong</u>. NY:
         New American Library, 1967. 214 pp. 67-25937.
         Canada: Canada General Publishing, 1967.
         NY: NAL, Signet, 1968. 160 pp.

Biographical material at the end of the book
establishes that Kolpacoff has not been to Vietnam,

and there is no mention of his having had military
service. That may account for the minor inaccuracies
in his novel about soldiers in Vietnam. Kreuger, a
former infantry lieutenant, is imprisoned at Quai
Dong, on the South China Sea, for refusing to fight.
After a year at hard labor, he is told to use his
Vietnamese language skill to question a Vietcong
suspect. The interrogation and ancillary torture of
the suspect occupy most of the book. Kreuger struggles with the prisoner, the other Americans and with
himself and his values. In the end, he stops the
torture with an inspired lie, claiming that the
prisoner named a location for enemy supplies. By
utter accident, when troops are sent they draw fire
and find supplies. Kreuger is released from the
stockade as a reward for his supposed good service.

34.   Michaeles, M.M. <u>Suicide Command</u>. NY: Lancer, 1967.
          158 pp.
       NY: Prestige Books, n.d. 158 pp.

The dramatic title does not fit this elementary and
superficial story of an infantry captain in Vietnam.
Harry Angel is a West Point graduate who left the
service for civilian life, then returned in time for
the Vietnam War to command a company under a former
classmate who is now a lieutenant colonel. Early
tension between the two men and between Angel and his
experienced subordinates is resolved when he
heroically saves a wounded sergeant under enemy fire.
There are three battles in the book, and, although the
author has some familiarity with military activities,
none evokes a realistic sense of jungle combat. This
is particularly true at the end, when Harry and some
of his men are captured by the Vietcong. He has
civilized conversations with an enemy officer, and is
generally treated quite well before he and his men
escape in a hail of bullets.

35.   Michaels, Rand. <u>Women of the Green Berets</u>. New York:
          Lancer, 1967. 223 pp.

There is not much of a plot here. Numerous Green
Berets rattle around Vietnam, serving sometimes as
shock troops and on other occasions in their more
traditional role as trainers of local forces. The
battle scenes appear to be taken from situations more
common in World War II than Vietnam. Some are clearly

from the author's imagination. In Saigon, a
relatively peaceful civilian city, the women of the
title have such adventures as performing plastic
surgery on a Vietcong leader, driving around in open
cars and enduring rape. To add confusion to an
already unfocused book, new characters are introduced
as late as eight pages from the end.

36.   Moore, Gene D. <u>The Killing at Ngo Tho</u>. NY: Norton,
         1967. 242 pp. 67-12445.
      NY: Pyramid, 1968. 223 pp.

Like his hero, Scott Leonard, Moore is a regular Army
colonel with service in Vietnam. Leonard is assigned
as an adviser to the Vietnamese chief of a province on
the Cambodian border. There is a bit of internal
trouble with dates, but this seems to be set in the
mid-1960s, just after the termination of the Diem
government. There is not as much pessimism and
cynicismhere as in later novels. Leonard has the
motives and talents of an ambitious professional
officer. Some of his Vietnamese counterparts are
capable patriots, the peasants are loyal and the cause
is not yet lost. Colonel Leonard's particular
adventure has to do with the location and destruction
of a concealed Vietcong headquarters. He also feuds
with an irrational superior officer. The ending, like
the whole book, is optimistic.

37.   Murdoch, Gus. <u>Saigon Sex Trap</u>. North Hollywood, CA:
         Brandon House, 1967. 190 pp.

Despite its title, this is not another piece of
Vietnam pornography. Rather, it is a spy story with
graphic sex scenes. Army Major Milo Ross, a Special
Forces combat veteran, returns to Vietnam in the mid-
1960s in the guise of a civilian supply expert. His
job is to stop the theft of medical supplies.
Corruption is everywhere, and several of the villains
are Americans. With only a few delays to sleep with
beautiful women, Ross performs his mission with
suitable intelligence and brutality.

38.   Olemy, P.T. <u>The Transgressors</u>. NY: Caravelle Books,
         1967. 192 pp.

Quite unlike any other Vietnam novel, <u>Transgressors</u> is

set among the entourage of Phil Mosconi, well-known
singer and comedian, who flies to Vietnam in 1967 to
entertain the troops. The dialog is stilted, and the
writing generally is thin and awkward, but the real
value of the book lies in its look at Vietnam from the
perspective of a visiting group of entertainers.
Olemy appears to have no firsthand knowledge, and some
of the military situations are outrageous. He is more
successful in conveying the straightforward patriotism
of the World War II generation. In a transport
aircraft over Vietnam, Mosconi is confronted by his
bastard son, conceived in rape in an earlier war, and
the plot works its way to an uninspired end.

39.   Taylor, Thomas. A-18. NY: Crown, 1967. 273 pp.
         67-26244.

Taylor, an Army officer and Vietnam veteran, offers
the rather fanciful tale of a Special Forces team sent
to North Vietnam to kill or capture two important
politicians. The greater part of the book has to do
with the background, selection and training of the
team. This takes place in Hawaii, Okinawa and
Formosa. The characters are professional, long-
service soldiers. They and their dialog seem sometimes to belong in World War II, but they make quite a
contrast to the unmotivated draftees who populate so
many Vietnam novels. The mission into North Vietnam
occupies only the last thirty or so pages, and it is
described in a relatively spare and hurried manner
when compared with the earlier and very full accounts
of Special Forces procedures, equipment and training.
What is most apparent throughout is Taylor's sincere
admiration of the Special Forces.

40.   Tully, Andrew. The Time of the Hawk. NY: Morrow,
         1967. 335 pp. 67-11637.

Set at a time in the near future, this early novel
describes a Vietnam much as it may actually have been
in the early 1950s. A cease-fire has ended the
fighting, but American troops still occupy the country
as a bewildering array of politicians and factions
seek control of the government of Vietnam. The forces
of Peking are a particularly sinister and strong
element. Order is brought out of this chaos by U. S.
Senator Baldwin, who secretly represents a hawkish
American president. The middle-aged, sedentary

senator performs activities that would tax the
abilities of a soldier, athlete, spy and youthful
lover. Despite the implausibility of its parts, the
whole book comes together as a coherent story.

41.   Whittington, Harry. <u>Doomsday Mission</u>. NY: Banner,
          1967. 160 pp.

Unfamiliarity with military terminology and equipment
is an unhappy characteristic for any war novel. In
this one, it is combined with some phrases, such as,
"90 degree perimiter" and "nylon trip wire" that
simply make no sense. The story has to do with a
patrol of some forty Vietcong defectors and a few
American enlisted men led by a green lieutenant. The
military action and dialog are not convincing,
although some of the characters, surprisingly, are
quite well developed. At the end of many adventures,
including frequent hand to hand combat, the destruction of a huge tunnel complex and the capture of a
beautiful Vietcong female, most members of the patrol
are casualties.

                              1968

42.   Anderson, William C. <u>The Gooney Bird</u>. NY: Crown,
          1968. 306 pp. 68-20458.
          NY: Paperback Library, 1969. 256 pp.

The use of an antiquated, slow-flying, transport plane
as a platform for machine guns is tactically fascinating. In addition to describing that innovation, this
book offers a certain look at the attitudes and
practices of military pilots. Unfortunately, the
characters are rather shallow and quite similar to one
another. If this book is to be believed, the air war
in Vietnam was fought by enthusiatic, wisecracking
officers, every one of whom was a memorable personality. The wounded and dying are heroic and quiet,
and the survivors return home with minor wounds and
much glory. The pilots are essentially indifferent to
the ground beneath them. The story happens to be set
in Vietnam, but there is little background description
and no significant Vietnamese characters appear.

43.   Bassett, James. <u>The Sky Suspended</u>. NY: Delacorte,
          1968. 326 pp. 68-12197.

Vietnam is "Thietvanne" and the enemy are the "kong,"
but the thinness of the literary disguise here is
probably deliberate. In Bassett's story, the Americans have withdrawn, leaving the South Thietvannese to
fight the North and the kong alone. Frederick Peter
Cragg, a WWII PT boat commander, is hired to reconsti-
tute his old crew and lead a raid on shipping in North
Thietvannese waters. Amid much adventure and political intrigue, Cragg is successful in destroying so
many military supplies that he affects the course of
the war and the composition of the government. Of
course, he finds time to make love to a couple of
beautiful women whenever the bullets are not actually
flying.

44.   Biersach, Frank J. Jr. So Cruel World. N.p., 1968.
          183 pp.

The paper, typeface and method of construction suggest
that this book may have been manufactured in Asia.
Reproduction is especially bad. Many letters are
illegible, and some corrections appear to have been
made in the review copy with a typewriter. The story
has to do with the younger members of a Vietnamese
family and their association with an American officer
in Saigon in 1965. One of the sons of the family
becomes an independent newspaper editor; the other is
a Vietcong terrorist who is sent to kill him. The
narration and dialogue are stilted and awkward, and
there is much pontification about causes, rights and
wrongs of the Vietnam War. This book must have been
produced privately, and it clearly has not been edited
in any customary manner.

45.   Butterworth, W. E. Orders to Vietnam. Boston:
          Little, Brown, 1968. 162 pp. 68-15387.

Like Butterworth's earlier Air Evac (21), this is a
paean to the Army in general and to helicopter pilots
in particular. Bill Byers, the son of an Army general
and dropout from West Point, is trained as a helicopter pilot after being drafted. Byers is sent to
Pleiku, where he flies both unarmed craft and gunships
in numerous actions. The enemy hardly appear as
characters; they are just targets on the ground.
Vietnam and the South Vietnamese also have little to
do with the story. Aircraft and their battles are

described in exhaustive detail. To his credit,
Butterworth tries to convey the spirit and military
attitude of professional officer, but he is rather
heavyhanded in the attempt.

46.   Cameron, Lou. _The Dragon's Spine_. NY: Avon, c1968,
      1969. 191 pp.

The title is taken from a large ridge that is supposed
to exist in the Central Highlands. After an attack on
an enemy missile base there goes bad, the remnants of
a quite unlikely Special Forces team wander around in
the nearby mountains and jungle where they encounter
Montagnard tribesmen, a group of primitive native
hunters, a beautiful half-caste North Vietnamese woman
officer, some refugee French medical personnel and
other unlikely persons. An attempt to tell some of
the story from the natives' point of view is actually
quite interesting. There is a subplot having to do
with prejudice, but the most noteworthy aspect of the
book is its persistent mistakes about GI slang,
weapons nomenclature and other military matters.

47.   Cook, Kenneth. _The Wine of God's Anger_. Melbourne,
      Australia: Cheshire-Lansdowne, 1968. 155 pp.

Cook does not name the Southeast Asian country where
his story is set, but internal evidence definitely
identifies it as Vietnam. His story of a young
Australian volunteer at war is much affected by his
hero's Catholicism. The moral issues are pondered and
argued at length. There is quite a bit of realistic
infantry action, including the usual costly mistakes.
Finally, the hero deserts to Bangkok, still wondering
about right and wrong.

48.   Cortesi, Lawrence. _The Magnificent Bastards of Viet-
      nam_. NY: Tower Publications, 1968. 218 pp.

This is not presented as juvenile literature, but
there is a simplicity and naivete about the book that
suggests its intended audience may have been adolescent boys. The Marine infantrymen who operate in and
around Chu Lai see the goals and participants of the
war in black and white. They seldom use profanity,
speaking instead in patriotic platitudes. Some ideas
about the purposes of the war emerge from the discus-

sions between a Marine lieutenant and a civilian nurse
with whom he is romantically involved. In the field,
the men are able to outfight and outsmart the enemy,
and by the end of the book the future looks bleak for
the Vietcong.

49.   Dunn, Mary Lois. The Man in the Box: A Story from
         Vietnam. NY: McGraw-Hill, 1968. 155 pp.
         68-19488.

The subtitle may be a bit misleading, because there is
no evidence that the author based her book on any
first hand experience in Vietnam. An American Special
Forces man is wounded and captured by the Vietcong.
They place him in an exposed box or cage in a Montagnard village. A young boy, Chau Li, rescues the
soldier and helps him return to an American unit.
They are separated in a subsequent battle, and the
soldier is evacuated to Da Nang. The boy takes a
sampan and loyally sets off to follow him there. For
what might first be taken as a childen's story, the
descriptions of brutality and torture are quite
graphic.

50.   Elliott, Ellen. Vietnam Nurse. NY: Arcadia House,
         1968. 191 pp.
         Sydney, Australia: Calvert Publishing, n.d.   128
         pp. Published as Nurse in Vietnam, by Shanna
         Marlowe.

Except for the slight variation that Joanna Shelton,
the nurse heroine, is Australian, this differs little
from the other adolescent nurse novels of the Vietnam
War. The story is that Nurse Shelton's father, a
medical missionary greatly loved by the Vietnamese
people, has vanished on a peace mission. The nurse is
brought from Sydney on a B-52 bomber, personally
briefed by a four star general commanding U.S. forces
in Vietnam, then sent into the jungle to find her
father. She is accompanied by a handsome Special
Forces captain, one of a presumably standard model
issued to all heroines of Vietnam nurse novels. After
adventures that include capture by an unbelievably
kind group of Vietcong, Nurse Shelton finds her
father. Then he, she and her American boyfriend are
all set free by the Vietcong.

---

51.   Grantland, Scott. The Bamboo Beast. N.p.: Pompeii
       Press, 1968. 188 pp.

       There is a coherent plot in this pornographic novel.
       Janice Murphy is a secretary in a civilian construc-
       tion company in Saigon. She is kidnapped by a
       turncoat American and sold to the Vietcong. Among
       many sexual adventures, she observes the enemy at rest
       and in battle. Finally rescued after a Vietcong
       defeat, she returns to Saigon and becomes a
       prostitute.

52.   Hershman, Morris. Mission to Hell. NY: Pyramid,
       1968. 157 pp.
       Israel: Priory Books, [1970]. 157 pp.

       This Air Force novel is inaccurate in military
       details, and the setting in Vietnam is described
       unconvincingly. As the story follows the improbable
       career of a single air crew, it touches upon such
       matters as cowardice, homosexuality, racism and aging.
       The crew moves from one type of aircraft to another
       and to different sorts of missions nearly every week.
       Flying in support of a remote fortress, they are shot
       down and captured. After grim experiences in a North
       Vietnamese prison camp, most of them escape. They are
       helped in part by one of their number who establishes
       a homosexual liaison with one of the guards.

53.   Lanh Ba. The Secret Diary of Ho Chi Minh's Daughter.
       NY: Lancer, 1968. 254 pp.

       The heroine of this fictional autobiograpy is a Saigon
       prostitute whose madame advertises her as Ho Chi
       Minh's daughter in order to command a higher price
       from American customers. Among the incessant and
       boring sex scenes, the young woman makes astute and
       valid observations about her customers and life in
       general in Saigon during the early 1960's. After
       careful preparation to disguise her past, she is able
       to find an American to marry her and take her back to
       the U.S. with him. Once there, she discards the
       husband and resumes her former profession.

54.   Melaro, H.J.M. The Viet-Nam Story. Willingboro, NJ:
       Alexia Press, 1968. 309 pp. 68-20489.

The heroes of modern paperback potboilers have a
literary ancestor in Jerry DiMartino. Educated in
medicine, the law and virtually everything else,
DiMartino has a full life in French Indochina, Korea,
Europe and the United States before he joins the
Vietnam War in the mid-1960s. He is a civilian
contract pilot, hired by a mysterious Mr. X, to do
only the roughest jobs. Secondary characters include
several Asian beauties and a group of suitable
buddies. All of this is conveyed in a language whose
vocabulary and grammar is more exuberant and less
meaningful than standard English.

55.   Morris, Edita. Love to Vietnam. NY: Monthly Review
        Press, 1968. 92 pp. 68-22425.

What this Swedish author has to say, simply and rather
crudely, is that Americans burn Asians. The story
unfolds in letters written by a young Japanese man who
was disfigured and orphaned at Nagasaki. He writes
first to a young girl in Vietnam who has been burned
by American napalm. Then he visits her there and
descibes his adventures to a friend in Japan. These
are such loving and exquisite victims that they seem
to exist only to suffer from American bombing.

56.   Myrer, Anton. Once an Eagle. NY: Holt, Rinehart and
        Winston, 1968. 817 pp. 68-21746.
        NY: Dell, 1970. 1043 pp.
        NY: Berkley, 1976. 915 pp.

Myrer's "Khotiane" is a country very similiar to
Vietnam. Chapters relating to it appear at the end of
this lengthy novel about two career Army officers
between World War I and 1962. Sam Damon is clearly a
good guy, and Courtney Massengale is unquestionably a
bad one, yet both rise to be generals. Sam Damon is
called out of retirement to evaluate the military
situation in Khotiane, where Massengale commands
American advisors. Damon's honest appraisal does not
fit with Massengale's plans to bring in large numbers
of American combat troops and perhaps invade China.
In the end, however, it appears that evil triumphs
over good, because Damon is killed and Massengale is
left alive with his plans. The characters are a bit
too pure to be wholly believed, but Myrer offers an
intriguing suggestion of how the Vietnam War might
have been viewed by senior military officers.

57.   Rothberg, Abraham. <u>The Other Man's Shoes</u>. NY: Simon
      & Schuster, 1968. 507 pp. 69-12095.

      In a Saigon cafe, a newsman and a soldier sitting
      together are attacked with a hand grenade. At the
      cost of his life, the soldier smothers the grenade.
      After recovering from injuries, the newsman returns to
      California and investigates the soldier's family and
      friends. While doing so, he encounters Vietnam
      protesters, black revolutionaries and the spectrum of
      the California social scene of the late 1960s. Much
      of this excellent novel is set outside of Vietnam, but
      one of its values is that it provides an interesting
      view of the war from the perspective of a successful
      international journalist.

58.   Rowe, John. <u>Count Your Dead</u>. Sydney, Australia:
      Angus and Robertson, 1968. 223 pp.
      London: Corgi, 1975.

      Incompetent American and Vietnamese officers do a bad
      job of implementing a stupid strategy in this novel of
      an Army brigade in Duc Binh province. Bill Morgan, a
      staff major with recent combat experience, finds
      himself in constant conflict with his commanding
      officer, a colonel who is interested in his own
      career. Together with Vietnamese officers, the
      colonel involves the brigade in several pointless
      battles that cause heavy casualties. At one point,
      the colonel inflates an enemy body count of
      twenty-three to an improbable figure of five hundred.
      Morgan's colleagues have typically low opinions of the
      South Vietnamese and the American peace movement.
      Eventually, the colonel's "capacity to put an exag-
      geratedly favorable interpretation on events" brings
      him promotion to general, while Morgan is fired from
      his job and sent to a desk in Saigon.

59.   Sparrow, Gerald. <u>Java Weed</u>. London: Triton Books,
      1968. 160 pp.

      The narrator of this short, first-person novel is a
      British newspaper reporter in Vietnam. With two
      colleagues, an American and a Eurasian woman, he is
      captured by the Vietcong and taken to a jungle prison
      camp where conditions include debasement and torture.
      The reporters escape and hide in floating clumps of
      Java weed in the Mekong River. After many adventures,

and help from friendly Vietnamese, they finally reach
freedom. The prison camp sequences are unpleasant,
but like the entire novel, they lack convincing
detail.

60.   Tiede, Tom. Coward. NY: Trident Press, 1968.
          383 pp. 68-18311.
          NY: Pocket Books, 1968. 335 pp.

Tiede effectively expresses the tragedy and injustice
of the Vietnam War. His main character is Nathan
Long, an Army privite who begins a hunger strike at
his post in the United States to avoid going to
Vietnam. He is unsure of the rightness of the war,
but principally he is afraid and he admits it. Long
is court-martialed and assigned as a company clerk to
an infantry unit somewhere near Saigon. The time
seems to be the mid- or late 1960s. The Vietnamese
and their country are truly revolting to the young
man, who is simply terrified of the war. After his
friend is killed, Long volunteers for a patrol that
ends in his capture, torture and death. Scenes of
combat are not as effective as those set in military
rear areas.

61.   Whittington, Harry. Burden's Mission. NY: Avon,
          1968. 144 pp.

Like Whittington's other Vietnam novel, Doomsday
Mission (41), this one has so many technical errors
that it is difficult to believe the author knows
anything about the military. Adam Burden, an Army
captain who flies bombers, goes to a rural town in
Vietnam to search for his brother. The brother, a
drunk with personal problems, was a military courier
trusted with top secret documents which were lost.
After wildly improbable adventures among Vietnamese
villagers and French planters, Burden learns that his
brother is dead.

1969

62.   Baker, W. Howard. The Judas Diary. NY: Lancer,
          1969. 190 pp.

This "suspense thriller" unfolds as alternate extracts
from the diary of a spy and the report of the intel-

---

ligence agent who pursues him. What is fascinating is
Baker's view of the Vietnam War. There is an Australian Task Force with two battalions of infantry and
nine artillery batteries as well as an attached
company of New Zealand infantry. This unit is in
heavy World War II type combat with Vietcong. The
"Judas" of the title, a newspaperman turned spy, goes
into the jungle with a patrol and never returns.

63.   Beatty, David L. <u>Don't Tread On My Tire Rubber
      Sandals</u>. N.p.: Seven Oceans, 1969.
      203 pp.

Captain Fervent arrives in Saigon in 1966 as a rear
echelon intelligence officer. As he collates reports,
observes the city and reacts to the war, Fervent
emerges as an interesting man. The plot wastes this
character because it cannot settle whether it is
serious or comic, realistic or symbolic. When Fervent
enters on his first field assignment, the outcome is
amazingly successful, and the end to his war is a
comfortable flight home. That is an abrupt conclusion
to a novel that seems to have lost control of itself.

64.   Briley, John. <u>The Traitors</u>. NY: Putnam, 1969.
      441 pp. 78-81568.
      Toronto: Longmans Canada, 1969.
      NY: Popular Library, Eagle Books, 1969. 480 pp.

The subject of treachery is handeled well and at
considerable length in this novel by an American
living in England. A squad of American soldiers is
captured in South Vietnam, probably sometime in the
late 1960s. They are taken to North Vietnam, where
some of them are persuaded by a defector, Evans, to
assist a mission to rescue an important communist from
a South Vietnamese jail. The characters, including
some Vietnamese, have complete and complex
personalities, and their conversations are interesting
and plausible. Indeed, much of the book is given over
to talk about the rights or wrongs of the parties
participating in the Vietnam War. The lives and
military methods of the North Vietnamese appear in
very great detail. The rescue mission and ensuing
fight provide a climax in which many of the major
characters are killed.

---

65. Butterworth, W. E. Stop and Search: A Novel of Small
         Boat Warfare off Vietnam. Boston: Little, Brown,
         1969.

     Virtually a work of adolescent literature, this simple
     novel nonetheless conveys a great deal of apparently
     accurate information about small boat operations in
     Vietnam. The hero is Eddie Czernik, a modest,
     clean-living young man who graduates from college at
     the age of 20--too young to receive the officer's
     commission he had expected. Sent to Vietnam as a Navy
     enlisted man, he serves heroically in small boat
     combat. Upon returning from a hospital in the
     Philippines, Eddie is commissioned and given command
     of his own craft. No character in this novel uses
     profanity or talks about sex.

66. Clark, Alan. The Lion Heart. NY: Morrow, 1969.
         255 pp. 69-11569.

     Clark, an English historian, writes with impressive
     familiarity and accuracy about Americans. His story
     is set in Central Vietnam, near the Cambodian border,
     in 1967. Jack Lane, a Special Forces officer, is
     assigned to advise the newly arrived American 78th
     Division. Against Lane's advice, the general com-
     manding the division launches a classic military
     operation, which ends in disaster. Lane is killed,
     but the general manages to preserve his command and
     his reputation with consummate political skill. All
     the characters of any consequence are officers. While
     the book ends on a neutral note insofar as the future
     of the war is concerned, there is a good deal of
     emphasis on the corruption of the South Vietnamese and
     the commitment of the Vietcong. Clark provides a list
     of characters, a glossary of Vietnamese and military
     terms and frequent explanatory footnotes.

67. Crumley, James. One to Count Cadence. NY: Random
         House, 1969. 338 pp. 68-14518.
         NY: Bantam, 1970. 294 pp.
         NY: Vintage Contemporaries, 1987. 338 pp.

     The U.S. Army before Vietnam was certainly a much
     different organization from what it became at the
     height of the war. It is that Army of the early 1960s
     that Crumley describes so well in this competent and
     engrossing story. The characters are enlisted men and

junior officers in a security communications detachment in the Philippines in 1962. Slag Krummel, the
hero, returns to the Army after an academic interlude,
establishes personal relationships with other soldiers
and emerges eventually as a genuine leader. Near the
end of the book, when the detachment is sent to
Vietnam, Krummel's strong body and personality enable
him to survive a harsh baptism of fire.

68.   Dean, Nell M. Nurse in Vietnam. NY: Julian Messner,
            1969. 192 pp. 69-12111.

After her fiance is killed in Vietnam, Air Force nurse
Lisa Blake volunteers for duty in Southeast Asia.
She is stationed at Clark Air Force Base in the
Philippines and visits Vietnam on medical evacuation
flights. During one, her aircraft is shot down and
she has adventures in the jungle. A handsome Special
Forces captain is on hand in this "career-romance for
young moderns." There are more medical details here
than in some other adolescent nurse novels.

69.   Eastlake, William. The Bamboo Bed. NY: Simon &
            Schuster, 1969. 350 pp. 70-79630.
            London: Michael Joseph, 1970. 284 pp.
            NY: Avon, 1985. 394 pp.

This might well be the closest approach to a Catch-22
of the Vietnam War. Everything is symbolic and
complex. The "Bamboo Bed" of the title is a rescue
helicopter. Characters recline, rest and fornicate on
bamboo beds, and the bamboo bed probably also stands
for Vietnam. Among the most durable characters are
Captain Knightbridge and his female aide, who copulate
above battle zones in the helicopter. Eastlake
certainly manages to represent the chaos and ambiguity
of Vietnam.

70.   Ehrlich, Jack. Close Combat. NY: Pocket Books,
            1969. 180 pp.
            Richmond Hill, Ontario: Simon & Schuster of
            Canada, 1969.

The reader is asked to believe that a suprise military
combat patrol into a neutral country in 1966 would be
led by a superman, staffed with an ad hoc assortment
of military types from various services and improperly

suplied. Major Hogan and his boys walk hundreds of
miles into Cambodia to destroy a super radar set that
is causing extraordinarily high casualties among all
U.S. aircraft in Vietnam. Hogan accomplishes his
mission in the first half of the book and then
extracts his men and himself back to Vietnam in
several different and unlikely ways. This is an
archtype of later series literature about teams of
superheros in Vietnam, and Hogan is so relentlessly
capable that he is charming.

71.   Hunter, Evan. <u>Sons</u>. Garden City, NY: Doubleday,
          1969. 396 pp. 78-79415.
          NY: New American Library, Signet, 1970. 383 pp.
          London: Constable, 1970. 396 pp.

The story of Wat Tyler alternates, chapter by chapter,
with those of his father and grandfather as each man
fights the war of his generation--World War I, World
War II and Vietnam. Wat is in high school in 1963,
and the portions of the novel that deal with him take
him through entering college at Yale, a romance and
involvement with the peace movement before he is
drafted in 1965 and sent to Vietnam as an infantryman.
There are scenes set in Saigon, in the jungle and
elsewhere. Tyler's buddies represent typical Vietnam
soldier's backgrounds and attitudes, and their varying
fates are also typical. This war-by-war comparison
is an effective, but somewhat mechanical, method to
illustrate the attitudes of American soldiers over the
course of this century.

72.   Larson, Charles. <u>The Chinese Game</u>. Philadelphia:
          Lippincott, 1969. 236 pp. 69-11308.
          NY: Pocket Books, 1970. 172 pp.

The central character in this complicated and somewhat
vague novel is Belgard, a Special Forces captain who
commands a Montagnard camp in 1963. Wounded in
battle, he is evacuated to a hospital. Belgard's main
interest seems to be to protect his camp from both the
Vietcong and the South Vietnamese military politicians. In pursuit of this, he is drawn into a
conflict between Diem and the Buddhists and into a
love affair with a Vietnamese woman. Elements of
dreams or hallucinations are woven into the story.
Belgard finally ends up in the city of Hue, where his
story ends in a curious and unsatisfying fashion.

73.   Linn, Edward and Pearl, Jack. Masque of Honor. NY:
         Norton, 1969. 235 pp. 78-77410.
      NY: Macfadden-Bartell, 1970. 222 pp.

      Several excellent Vietnam novels touch on racial
      issues. This one has the latter quality, but not the
      former. David Walsh, a forty-five year old, black
      infantry captain leads American and Vietnamese troops
      to capture a mountain near the Cambodian border in
      1968. Through the efforts of a self-seeking journal-
      ist, the event is dramatized out of proportion, and
      Walsh is nominated for a Congressional Medal of Honor.
      Back in the U.S., Walsh is pressured by his family,
      business opportunities, the press and black civil
      rights organizations to accept and exploit the award
      for varies reasons, but in the end, he declines it.
      This correct and honorable decision does not, however,
      work to his advantage. The book suffers from repeti-
      tive conversations and reflections about morality.
      Moreover, the authors appear to have no familiarity
      with the Army of the Vietnam War. Military ranks from
      World War II are used, and a sergeant serves as a
      helicopter pilot.

74.   Porter, John B. If I Make My Bed in Hell. Waco, TX:
         Word Books, 1969. 165 pp. 69-20234.
         Minneapolis: Jeremy Books, 1979. 297 pp.
         79-84346.

      In a prefatory note, Porter explains his own experien-
      ces as an Army chaplain in Vietnam as a basis for his
      novel. Chaplain Grayson is a character much like
      Porter. He serves both in the field and in camp with
      an airborne infantry unit near Saigon. He deals with
      soldiers' moral, psychological and religious problems
      and with his own doubts and fears. There is no
      question about Porter's sincerity. His writing
      ability is generally equal to his task, although
      characters and their conversations are rather obvious-
      ly constructed and the ending is rather abrupt. This
      thorough view of the life of an Army chaplain is
      unique among Vietnam War novels.

75.   Quinn, Adrian. Operation Poontang. Atlanta, GA:
         Pendulum Books, 1969. 191 pp.

      These are the explicit sexual adventures of a career
      Army sergeant. After a tour as an instuctor at Fort

Gordon, Georgia, he is sent to Vietnam in what is
probably 1966. His job is to sleep with Vietnamese
prostitutes in order to look for intelligence leaks to
the Vietcong. Along the way the sergeant encounters a
group called "Citizens for World Peace." In contrast
to most books that feature mostly sex, this one
reveals something of a sense of humor.

76.   Ross, William. <u>Bamboo Terror</u>. Rutland, VT: Charles
       E. Tuttle, 1969. 260 pp. 69-13506.

This adventure story might be set as early as 1961, or
perhaps a few years later, because at the time it
occurs, American Special Forces are on the scene in
Vietnam in large enough numbers to attract the
attention of the North Vietnamese. There are,
however, worries closer to home in the form of an
independent anticommunist mercenary group at a base
somewhere on the coastline of North Vietnam. Michael
Hazzard, a veteran of intelligence operations in World
War II and Korea, is recruited from his job as a
private detective in Japan and brought, by various
means, into association with the mercenaries. In
thrilling jungle adventures, he assists the mercenaries to locate a traitor in their midst and
survives a successful North Vietnamese assault on
their stronghold. Hazzard ends up in Paris, where one
has the impression that he is on the verge of new
adventures.

77.   Sellers, Con. <u>Where Have All the Soldiers Gone?</u>. NY:
       Pyramid, 1969. 174 pp.

Lee Boyd had been a war protester who chose service as
a medic rather than jail. When he arrives at a line
unit of the 1st Infantry Division, he learns about war
very quickly and changes his ideas in order to stay
alive. Boyd comes to respect the professional soldiers
who lead the company, especialy a senior sergeant who
is killed near the end of the story. Boyd finally
becomes an infantryman and an NCO himself, and he
survives because he has learned to adapt. The
characters' thoughts are rendered better than their
words. The dialog does not seem authentic, especially
in the important areas of profanity and GI slang.

78.   Spetz, Steven N. <u>Rat Pack Six</u>. Greenwich, CT:

Fawcett, 1969. 206 pp.

A note on the cover explains that this is a fictionalized account of the battle of Ap Bau Bang, part of
Operation Junction City II. The time is proably late
1967. A large number of enemy troops attacks a well
organized American position and suffers hundreds of
casualties from superior firepower and air strikes.
Spetz, a former captain in a mechanized infantry unit,
describes the military aspects of the battle clearly
and accurately. He is less successful with his
characters, who include members of an American squad
and a number of the North Vietnamese and Vietcong who
oppose them. The dialog is particularly restrained.
The letters FTA, for instance, do not stand for "frig
the Army".

79. Toni A.M. The Buffalo Doctor. Philadelphia:
      Dorrance, 1969. 76-94254. 151 pp.

The strangely named author is a woman and her first-
person narrator is a man. Clint Amundson, a civilian
physician, goes to Vietnam in 1955 and remains for
over ten years, observing the growth of the war and
American participation in it. Clint sees the best in
every person and situation. He survives many unlikely
adventures, including captivity by the Vietcong. When
the book ends, about 1966 or 1967, he is optimistic
about the future. The simple characters and action
combine with stilted dialog to limit severely the
impact of this short novel.

1970

80. Baber, Asa. The Land of a Million Elephants. NY:
      Morrow, 1970. 152 pp. 71-103886.

In contrast to real life, this tale of the mythical
kingdom of Chanda describes its people in their
successful attempt to resist importation of a general
Southeast Asian war. Chanda can be reached by air
from Saigon, and it is clearly an artificial analog to
Laos. The country is host to military advisers,
diplomats and spies from major European and Asian
nations. After these individuals manage to introduce
the beginnings of a war, the inhabitants of Chanda
flee to the Plain of Elephants, where their folk magic
protects them from both Russian tanks and American

atomic bombs. In this story of what might have been,
the peaceful life endures. The style, which is
similar to that of a folk story or children's tale,
enhances literary quality and sustained humor without
becoming wearing or tedious. This is a sophisticated
and successful piece of writing.

81.   Collingwood, Charles. The Defector. NY: Harper &
         Row, 1970. 313 pp. 77-103133.
         NY: Ace, n.d. 318 pp.

Not surprisingly, the hero of this novel is a television correspondent. During the Paris peace negotia-
tions, Bill Benson is recruited by the Cental Intelligence Agency to assist with the escape of a North
Vietnamese government official who wishes to defect.
The descriptions of Hanoi, based on the author's visit
there in 1968, are fascinating, as are observations
throughout about the toughness and commitment of the
North Vietnamese people. The defector is eventually
escorted south to the Demilitarized Zone by Benson,
and the escape is made in a hail of gunfire. Once
inside South Vietnam, the escapee is murdered, and the
explanation emerges as a story of plots within plots.
Collingwood essentially ignores the ethical issues
that might be expected to confront a journalist
working for the CIA.

82.   Gentry, Claude. Love and War in Vietnam. Baldwyn,
         MS: Magnolia Publishers, 1970. 65 pp.

It is difficult to determine the intended audience for
this book. It's length and simplicity would suggest
adolescents, but the language is a bit strong for
that. The story is about John Scruggs, a soldier who
arrives in Vietnam in 1965 and almost immediately sets
out on a trek through the jungle with a beautiful
Vietnamese girl. Together, they travel vast dis-
tances, endure much hardship and inflict many casualties on the enemy.

83.   Maitland, Derek. The Only War We've Got. London:
         New Authors Limited, 1970. 269 pp.
         NY: Morrow, 1970. 270 pp. 70-128764.
         NY: Paperback Library, 1971. 269 pp.
         London: Arrow Books, 1971. 270 pp.

Maitland is a British journalist who worked in Vietnam
prior to the 1968 Tet Offensive. Representations of
that offensive and other major battles provide much of
what plot there is in this humorous and ironical book.
In thin disguises, the major personalities, groups,
institutions, and events of the Vietnam War of that
time appear here, and they are all portrayed as being
without a sense of honor. Favorite targets of
ridicule are Americans, but all characters, including
the Vietcong and a British newspaperman, are touched
by Maitland's consistently acid wit. An important
battle at the end of the book takes place in a huge
American Post Exchange where everyone involved is more
interested in loot or profit than in military victory.
Realistic scenes of bloody death occur occasionally as
abrupt surprises amid the otherwise unrelenting
satire.

84.   Sisco, Sam and Sisco, Bert. The Littlest Enemy. San
          Diego: Greenleaf, 1970. 192 pp.

Captain Rainwater of the Special Forces has equal
amounts of contempt for his Vietnamese counterpart, a
colonel, and for the M-16 rifle. Both are weak and
unreliable, and he rages against them incessantly.
Rainwater, and a few others, including a beautiful
female doctor, attempt to evacuate Montagnard villages
before they are bombed in a scorched-earth policy. In
this effort, he is several times impeded by Vietnamese
children, some as young as seven, who poison and shoot
his men and on one occasion eliminate a helicopter
with a hand grenade on a string. In this case two
authors by no means assure doubled literary quality.

85.   Taylor, Thomas. A Piece of This Country. NY: Norton,
          1970. 192 pp. 70-105739.
          Toronto/NY: PaperJacks, 1984. 192 pp.

The central problem with this story is that Taylor, a
white officer, is writing about a black main character, Jackson, an NCO. From the advantageous perspective of eighteen years after the book was published,
it is reasonable to guess that many blacks would find
the character of Jackson patronizing. The plot
centers on the defense of a small Vietnamese outpost
near the Laotian border in 1965. Jackson, an outstanding soldier, is induced to extend his stay in
Vietnam and to replace a deceased captain as senior

advisor to the Vietnamese garrison. Jackson deals
with the military and personnel situation at the camp
and effects an improvement in its fighting potential.
The difference in outlook between American and
Vietnamese soldiers is presented with convincing
force. Also, scenes of combat are fast paced and
expert. In the end, Jackson emerges as a sort of hero,
but Taylor conveys the impression that the North
Vietnamese and Vietcong will be the final victors.

86.   Williams, Alan. _The Tale of the Lazy Dog_. London:
           Anthony Blond, 1970. 287 pp.
           NY: Simon & Schuster, 1970. 315 pp. 78-132203.
           London: Panther Books, 1971. 272 pp.
           NY: Pocket Books, 1973. 246 pp.

Murray, an Irish writer and old hand in Southeast
Asia, learns of occasional shipments of large amounts
of American currency from the Tan Son Hut airbase back
to the United States. With the help of numerous
persons from many countries in Southeast Asia, he
arranges a plan to steal one of the shipments. Among
his assistants is the Algerian-French wife of an
American CIA oficial, and part of the plot involves a
staged Vietcong attack on the airbase, so credibility
is not high. There are several rather offhand
murders, as the conspirators simply kill everyone who
gets in their way. The crime is successful, but the
writer and his colleagues soon find themselves and
their loot in the hands of the North Vietnamese, who
had been the secret sponsors of the plan all along.

                              1971

87.   Brossard, Chandler. _Wake Up. We're Almost There_. NY:
           Richard W. Baron, 1971. 540 pp. 76-125552.
           NY: Harper & Row, Harrow Books, 1972. 756 pp.

With some effort, it is possible to locate three
sections of this large and complex novel that are set
in Vietnam. In the two shorter passages, Cedric, a
black homosexual, serves as a typical infantryman,
involved in an ambush in the Central Highlands and in
the subsequent occupation of a village. In the third
(and largest) section, Bosworth Horn, a lieutenant of
Cherokee Indian background, joins the Vietcong to bomb
two American installations in Saigon. It is in no way
clear how these incidents relate to each other or to

the remainder of the book, whose plot seems to
transcend time, space and reality. Brossard is a
noted and experienced novelist, but in this work the
Vietnam sections are physically and contextually lost.

88.   Carver, James. <u>The Shadows in Go-Yeu</u>. NY: Walker,
          1971.   307 pp.   79-142838.

This interesting and sophisticated novel is set in a
remote village shortly after the 1968 Tet Offensive.
A few Americans advise ARVN troops, and soldiers of
both armies interact regularly with the villagers.
This is a much different war from that of large
American units engaged in major operations. Most of
the villagers are Vietcong, and they conduct what
amounts to a cottage industry stealing American
supplies for their own use. The American effort is
obstructed by the commanding officer, an unusually
stupid captain. Vietcong activities are finally
discovered by a recently arrived lieutenant who speaks
both French and Vietnamese. A problem with the novel
is the author's apparent uncertainty about military
life and weapons.

89.   Davis, George. <u>Coming Home</u>. NY: Random House, 1971.
          208 pp.   78-140699.
          NY: Dell, 1975.   185 pp.
          Washington, DC: Howard University Press, 1984.
          215 pp.

This novel is notable for an exploration of the
relationships between black and white Air Force pilots
based in Thailand. No dates are given, but the action
takes place during the attacks on Haiphong harbor.
The plot is sketchy, and narration moves from one
person to another in each chapter. The scenes of
combat flying are not as numerous as in most Air Force
novels. The characters are intriguing, however, and
the setting in Thailand is described in detail.

90.   Dibner, Martin. <u>The Trouble with Heroes</u>. Garden
          City, NY: Doubleday, 1971.   365 pp.   74-131071.
          Los Angeles: Pinnacle, 1980.   372 pp.

Novels about naval service during the Vietnam War are
all too rare. This one has an interesting premise.
Paul Damion, the commanding officer of the nuclear

cruiser <u>Chesapeake</u>, is a genuine hero, a holder of the
Navy Cross from the Korean War. In 1968, Damion is
ordered to shell a Vietnamese coastal vilage. When
Damion learns from a prisoner that the village has a
peaceful civilian population, he tries unsuccessfully
to have his orders changed. Troubled by conscience,
he turns command of the vessel over to the executive
officer, who completes the mission. These events
occur early in the book, and the remainder of the
story has to do with the consequences. They include
the machinations of an opportunistic congressman and
activities of various other persons leading up to a
naval court of inquiry into the incident. Dibner
deals sympathetically with antiwar sentiment in the
United States.

91.   Fick, Carl. <u>The Danziger Transcript</u>. NY: Putnam,
         1971. 295 pp. 75-174634.
      NY: Dell, 1974. 286 pp.

Peter Danziger is a newspaperman who has recently
returned to the United States after an assignment in
Vietnam. It seems to be about 1969. During his time
in Vietnam, Danziger made contact with the Vietcong
and North Vietnamese Army and visited their base camps
and logistical areas in Cambodia and elsewhere. He
noted military aspects of their operations and had
conversations on political topics with enemy officers
up to the rank of general. After returning to the
United States, Danziger has a voluntary conversation
with Major Pike, an intelligence officer. The
transcript of that conversation, as well as cor-
respondence and memoranda, constitute much of the
book. This fragmentary material is not integrated as
well as it might be, and the story requires some
effort to follow.

92.   Higgins, Jack. <u>Toll for the Brave</u>. NY: Fawcett,
         1971. 208 pp. 0-449-14105-5.

Approximately the first third of this superficial
adventure novel is set in a North Vietnamese prison
camp. The hero, Ellis Jackson, is an Englishman
serving in an American airborne unit. After capture,
he is sent to a camp run by Red Chinese, where he is
tortured and brainwashed. The time is 1967 or 1968.
In the camp, he meets a heroic American general who
helps him endure the treatment and ultimately leads

him in an escape. Living in England in the early
1970s, Jackson again encounters the general as well as
the former Chinese camp commandant. The plot at that
point becomes an improbable spy thriller.

93.   Keith, Jeff. A Child's Crusade. NY: Vantage, 1971.
           92 pp.

A considerable lack of familiarity with military
matters is the most notable characteristic of this
superficial but occasionally interesting book. At
loose ends after high school, Jason Bates joins the
Army in 1967 and is sent, improbably, to a combat unit
in Thailand. Bates has a relatively easy tour and
returns to the United States where he cannot get along
with his parents or anyone else. Reenlisting, he is
sent to Vietnam and wounded in the leg. While there,
he murders his Thai girlfriend but escapes punishment.
Wounded again, he leaves the Army and tries college,
but his old problems emerge again. At the end, it
seems that he will kill his mother.

94.   Kumar, P.J. Roll Call of Death. NY: Manyland Books,
           1971. 248 pp. 76-153369.

This unusual novel has a unique Indian perspective on
the Vietnam War that, surprisingly, is pro-American.
Kishore, an Indian journalist and karate expert, is
hired by the CIA in 1967 to replace another Indian,
whom he resembles, on a trip to visit captured
American pilots. After adventures in Bangkok, Kishore
reachs the Vietcong prison camp. It is thirty miles
from Khe Sanh and contains five hundred American
prisoners kept in unspeakable conditions by twenty
thousand guards. Kishore engineers an escape, but he
is recaptured and tortured to death before Americam
Marines raid the camp and free the prisoners. Like
the story, the dialogue is unusual, but the straightforward support of America's role in the war is
refreshing in a book written by an Asian.

95.   Phou Louang. The Men of Company 97. N.p.: Neo Lao
           Haksat Publications, 1971. 61 pp.

The men of Company 97 carry the true revolutionary
spirit in their hearts. They fight the Yankee
aggressors and their Lao lackeys with commitment,

skill and inevitable success. They love their
homeland and have an excellent relationship with the
peasants. Subordinate fighters are prompt and alert
to take correct political and military instructions
from their superiors. When not actually fighting or
engaging in political discussions, the men have time
for a hint of romance and even a song or two about the
revolution. Physically, the book reflects rather
primitive origins and a certain unfamiliarity with
common English usage.

96.   Moore, Robin with Collins, June. The Khaki Mafia.
           NY: Crown, 1971.   284 pp.   79-168317.
           NY: Avon, 1972.   351 pp.

Corruption of high ranking Army sergeants who ran
recreational clubs in Vietnam and elsewhere among
American forces became known to the public in the late
1960s and early 1970s. This fictionalized account of
those events reflects Moore's close familiarity with
the U.S. Army. Although the plot is simplistic,
the details and dialogue ring true, and the extent of
fraud and theft is staggering. June Collins enter-
tained in clubs in Vietnam and gained firsthand
experience at a number of activities that must have
enhanced her contribution to the book. Little in this
novel reveals the anguish and doubts about the war
that are so common in other works.

97.   Moore, Robin and Rothblatt, Henry. Court Martial.
           Garden City, NY: Doubleday, 1971.   410 pp.
           75-139048.
           NY: Dell, 1972.   442 pp.

This story of the killing of a suspected Vietnamese
double agent by Army Special Forces officers is set
both in Vietnam and Washington, D.C. Details of the
alleged crime emerge in chapters and sections that
alternate with those describing the investigation and
other subsequent events. Rivalries between regular
Army officers and the Special Forces play an important
part in the novel, as do conflicts between American
and Vietnamese political factions. The hero is Hank
McEwan, an attorney, and much of the second half of
the book describes a military trial in which he
ultimately succeeds on behalf of the accused officers.

98.   Mossman, James. <u>Lifelines</u>. Boston: Little, Brown,
            1971.   256 pp.   76-154950.

        Like the author, the main character, Dan Fenwick, is a
        newspaper correspondent with a long career in South-
        east Asia.   He and his colleagues in Hong Kong seem
        either just to have arrived from Vietnam or to be just
        about to return to the war.   On a trip to Vietnam,
        Fenwick covers a brutal Marine assualt and baptizes a
        dying infantryman.   Later, he covers the
        self-imolation of a Buddhist monk.   Returning to Hong
        Kong, Fenwick essentially fails to work out the
        meaning of his own life and loves; the image of the
        dying Marine remains with him.

99.   Pollock, Lawrence. <u>Xin Loi (Sorry About That) Doc!</u>
            NY: Vantage, 1971.   379 pp.

        These anecdotes about the 55th Evacuation Hospital
        near Qui Nhon are set at a time when American troops
        are on hand in large numbers.   The author is clearly
        not a conventional novelist.   There are numerous
        curiosities of format and style.   The medical action
        is fascinating and realistic, although somewhat
        brutal.   There is also an oppressive vulgarity in the
        characters' action and language.   In a body of
        literature notable for awful people and scenes, this
        book stands out.   One doctor, for instance, extracts
        his payment for a nurse's abortion in the form of
        intercourse in advance on the operating table.   More
        editing or an able joint author could have turned this
        potent material into a much more readable book.

100.   Sloan, James Park. <u>War Games</u>. Boston: Houghton
            Mifflin, 1971.   186 pp.   77-124357.
            NY: Avon, 1973.   190 pp.

        When a first-person novel takes the form of a diary,
        it usually has the advantages of a simple chronolog-
        ical progression, a consistant point of view and some
        insight into at least one of the characters (the
        diarist).   In this story, the chronology is steady,
        but the point of view and the personality of the chief
        character are elusive.   The hero is assigned to an
        Army unit in the Mekong Delta, which apparently
        symbolizes, rather than describes, the real Army.   The
        persons he encounters are classic Vietnam types--a
        career sergeant, a bar girl, a flashy and heroic

helicopter pilot, etc. The sparse dialogue is
ungainly, with no general conversations among groups
of persons. The hero is first given clerical duties.
When he later goes into combat, he murders a number of
allied Vietnamese servicemen. After that and other
adventures, he flies home to resume civilian life.
The book does not reach a conclusion in any customary
literary sense; it just stops.

101. Van Heller, Marcus. Jungle Fever. NY: Ophelia Press,
         1971. 179 pp.

In July, 1967, Chris Halsman is a British freelance
reporter in Saigon. He joins with a colleague, a
black Canadian woman, for an adventure into Cambodia.
They find and interview three Caucasians imprisoned by
the Cambodian rebels. The men are accused of being
CIA agents, but they deny it to the reporters.
Halsman and his companion are then captured and
tortured by pro-government agents at Angkor Wat.
Eventually they escape and return to Saigon. Throughout the story there is incessant, ugly sex.

102. Vaughan, Robert and Lynch, Monroe. Brandywine's War.
         N.p.: Bartholomew House, 1971. 249 pp.
         77-155027.
         Greenwich, CT: Fawcett, 1972. 224 pp.

By manipulating the essential stupidity of all wars,
the authors manage to write a funny book about
Vietnam. Chief Warrant Officer W. W. Brandywine is a
recovery-and-supply officer in a helicopter unit where
everone, it seems, is either a fool or a scoundrel.
Brandywine is skilled at finding supplies and equipment through all sorts of means, and he is also an
adept practical joker. The unit is commanded by a
publicity-seeking general whose life is run by a PFC,
the self-proclaimed son of the Secretary of Defense.
Amid the humor generated by such characters, men
occasionally fight and die in the real war. These
scenes of combat and death appear as rather abrupt
surprises in the text. Unlike most Vietnam novels,
this one begins and ends with almost all the main
characters still in place.

103. Williams, Bill. The Wasters. NY: Macfadden-Bartell,
         1971. 192 pp.

This fictionalized account of the My Lai Massacre
follows actual events so closely that at one point the
author slips and uses the actual name for the village,
rather than the one he has invented for the story.
The William Calley character, who is called Neal
Gilbert here, is an unstable young officer who has a
relationship of mutual mistrust and dislike with the
Mexican-American captain who commands his company.
Gilbert also has a drinking problem. During a sweep
through a group of hamlets known to be sympathetic to
the Vietcong, some of Gilbert's men are ambushed and
one is taken prisoner and mutilated. In a rage,
Gilbert personally slaughters a group of civilian
prisoners. As the story ends, he is awaiting the
result of his court martial.

1972

104. Atkinson, Hugh. The Most Savage Animal. London:
         Rupert Hart-Davis, 1972. 373 pp. 71-139615.
         NY: Simon and Schuster, 1972. 349 pp.

An unusual and interesting international perspective
on the Vietnam War emerges in this novel of the
International Committee of the Red Cross. It is set
both in Europe and in Vietnam around 1969, and the
numerous characters include executives, doctors and
volunteers for the Red Cross, as well as Americans and
Vietnamese fighting the war. The plot has two main
threads. One is an attempt by International Red Cross
officials to politicize the organization in an anti-
American fashion, and the other is a scheme to smuggle
plague-infested rats into the United States aboard
transport aircraft. There are numerous subplots.
Several battle scenes are chilling and convincing, but
the book seems to have no central focus as a story.
It does provide, however, a view of the humanitarian
effort in Vietnam and of European manners and
attitudes that is not often found in books about this
war.

105. Bosse, M. J. The Incident at Naha. NY: Simon &
         Schuster, 1972. 221 pp. 72-179588.
         London: Macmillan, 1972.

The narrator is a young white woman living in New York
with her black lover, Virgil. He is a man of
unbelievable beauty, strength, courage, intellect,

integrity and philosophical depth. Virgil served as a
lieutenant in a unit that had been remotely involved
in a massacre of civilians in Vietnam. When another
former member of the unit is murdered, Virgil and his
lady begin a search through the man's papers. These,
reproduced at great length in the text, have to do
with Commodore Perry's mission to Japan. The murder
is finally solved, and the Vietnam connection is one
of many historical threads drawn together to achieve a
solution.

106. Boulle, Pierre. Ears of the Jungle. Translated by
        Michael Dobry and Lynda Cole. NY: Vanguard
        Press, 1972. 224 pp. 72-83350.

Boulle, the author of a number of realistic novels set
in Southeast Asia, turns here to broad parody. With
an overwhelming faith in military technology, the
Americans plant sound sensors, disguised as vegeta-
tion, along the Ho Chi Minh Trail. The North Vietnamese, who already have penetrated American intelligence
headquarters, begin in the early 1970s to play the
sensors back against the Americans. Using recordings
of truck sounds and other technical measures superior
to what the Americans have, the North Vietnamese guide
planes to false targets. Growing ambitious, they are
able to trick Americans into blasting the roadway for
a Ho Chi Minh superhighway to be built after the war.
Finally, the North Vietnamese cause the Americans to
bomb and destroy their own headquarters.

107. Bunting, Josiah. The Lionheads. NY: Braziller,
        1972. 213 pp. 78-188356.
        London: Sidgwick & Jackson, 1973. 143 pp.
        NY: Popular Library, n.d. 205 pp.

There is often a considerable distance between the
views of generals who plan battles and the lower-rank-
ing men who must fight them. Bunting's touching and
cynical story, set in the Mekong Delta in March of
1968, has to do with an attempt by an American brigade
to destroy a North Vietnamese main force battalion.
Most of the characters are officers, including a
careerist general who fights a battle to advance his
own prospects. The general is successful, but the
battle is terribly costly to Americans. Bunting
describes the Mekong Delta with accuracy and detail,
and he clearly explains the problems of Americans

fighting there, especially the high reliance upon
complicated equipment that does not always work.
There is no real attempt to personalize the enemy or
to describe his tactics, although he is perceived by
all the characters as being much more able than they
to operate in the difficult terrain of jungle and
swamp.

108. Crawford, William. The Marine. NY: Pinnacle Books,
          1972. 186 pp.

An account of American prisoners of war emerges in the
testimony at a military court martial in the United
States. Frank Garrison, a Marine pilot, is charged
with attempted murder of another prisoner, an Army
officer, who collaborated with the enemy. In this
account, Marine Corps prisoners are credited with much
better behavior than those from other services. Like
the hero in other novels by Crawford, Garrison is an
extremely stubborn and determined individual. There
is a good deal of chilling detail about the inhuman
and illegal treatment meted out to American prisoners
of war by their North Vietnamese captors. A problem
is that Crawford, through his characters, makes
unwarranted judgments about men's behavior in such
circumstances.

109. Graham, Gail. Cross-Fire: A Vietnam Novel. Illus-
          trated by David Stone Martin. NY: Pantheon
          Books, 1972. 135 pp. 71-175953.

Its style suggests that this book might almost be
meant for children. An American infantryman, Harry,
and four Vietnamese children survive together for
several days in the jungle. Although Harry can
neither speak to the children nor understand their
language, they gradually become sensitive to one
another. After this rather gentle mood is established, the book ends surprisingly.

110. Grey, James. Soldiers & Whores. London: D.H.L.,
          1972. 192 pp.

Thinly disguised as a work of sociology, this is an
aggregation of accounts of soldiers' sexual activities, including some from Vietnam. There is even less
plot here than in most pornography.

111. Haldeman, Joe W. War Year. NY: Holt, Rinehart and
          Winston, 1972. 121 pp. 77-182778.
      NY: Pocket Books, 1978. 127 pp.
      NY: Avon, 1984. 108 pp.

      John Farmer, a nineteen-year-old draftee, is sent to
      the central highlands of Vietnam as a combat engineer
      with the 4th Division. Farmer describes his experi-
      ences with an innocent, but not childlike, simplicity.
      He makes friends, engages in battle and is wounded.
      After recovering from his wounds, Farmer is assigned
      as a supply clerk in a rear area, but he fails to
      salute the jeep of a brigadier general and is sent
      back to try to clear a landing zone for a helicopter.
      Throughout, Farmer is almost bewildered by his role in
      the war. He is put into combat and later given
      considerable responsibility with surprisingly brief
      training and experience. In different editions of the
      book, Farmer either survives the war or becomes one of
      its permanent casualties.

112. Honig, Louis. For Your Eyes Only: Read and Destroy.
          Los Angeles: Charles Publishing, 1972. 249 pp.
          72-83313.
      NY: Bantam, 1973. 245 pp.

      In a preface, the author explains that a private plan
      for peace in Vietnam in the late 1960s did, in fact,
      exist. In his novel, the plan is offered by Peters,
      an important international political columnist. This
      individual manages to enter the secret underground
      headquarters of the National Liberation Front in South
      Vietnam to present his ideas. On the way out, he is
      ambushed by agents of the CIA and of the Communist
      Chinese intelligence service, each acting separately.
      Along with this sort of action, the book offers
      discussions of the views and positions of the numerous
      parties to the Vietnam War in the 1960s.

113. Maggio, Joe. Company Man. NY: Putnam, 1972. 222
          pp. 76-175267.
      NY: Pinnacle Books, 1974. 220 pp.

      Company Man purports to be the barely fictionalized
      biography of a CIA mercenary soldier in the 1960s. If
      so, the country was served then by silly incompetents
      in the clandestine forces. Nick Martin, a Marine
      veteran, joins the CIA. After adventures in training

and at the Bay of Pigs, Martin performs military
duties in Vietnam that were typically done by the
Special Forces or Seal personnel. He fights along the
Cambodian border using "Indian knife tactics" then
baits the North Vietnamese into the attack on U.S.
destroyers that leads to the Tonkin Gulf Resolution,
bringing U.S. forces directly into the war. Later,
against orders, Martin extracts an intelligence team
fron North Vietnam and suffers a great deal of
brutality from the CIA in consequence. The book
leaves him on a merchant ship, having barely escaped
from sure death in Africa. Thankfully, there appears
to be no sequel.

114.   Pelfrey, William. The Big V. NY: Liveright, 1972.
          158 pp.   78-167289.
          NY: Avon, 1984.   182 pp.   83-91196

This is one of the most touching and complete novels
of the Army infantry in the Vietnam War. The hero,
Henry Winsted, is a draftee assigned as a radio
operator with the 4th Division in the Central Highlands of Vietnam. The action takes place at the
height of American involvement in the war. Winsted
has typical experiences in training, in base camp and
in combat. The other characters, mostly enlisted men
and junior officers, are complete and convincing.
Pelfrey writes dialogue well, and the conversations
are spontaneous and natural. Senior NCOs and officers
contend with the poor morale of draftees, but all of
the soldiers have a measure of pride in their fighting
ability. The first edition has a very small typeface,
a bothersome mechanical flaw in a fine novel.

115.   Pollard, Rhys. The Cream Machine. Sydney, Australia:
          Angus & Robertson, 1972.   161 pp.   0-207-12495-7.

Based on the author's experiences in 1968 and 1969,
this choppy, difficult account of Australian conscript
infantry depicts characters that are every bit as
confused and incompetent as the worst American
draftees. The novel conveys very little of how the
Australian army or its component units went to battle.
It is filled with the impressions of the narrator, his
reflections about his situation and his conversations
with other private soldiers. Among their concerns are
the antiwar movement back home in Australia and the
differences between themselves and the protesters.

Anti-Semitism, almost unknown in Vietnam fiction, occurs here.

116. Proud, Franklin M. and Eberhardt, Alfred F. <u>Tiger in the Mountains</u>. Hong Kong: Defral, 1972. 334 pp. NY: St. Martin's, 1976. 333 pp. 76-25849.

American prisoners of war in North Vietnam figure in relatively few Vietnam novels, and none is as imaginative as this one. Courtney Palmer, a wealthy former Air Force officer, devises a bizzare plan to rescue an old friend and other prisoners from North Vietnam. With a few associates, he hijacks an Air France jetliner and forces it to land in Hanoi. There he negotiates with the North Vietnamese to trade the passengers, who include several important persons, for 117 American prisoners. The Vietnamese agree, and Palmer manages to get the aircraft with the prisoners aboard to safety in Hong Kong. The minute-by-minute action is interspersed frequently with flashbacks describing Palmer's early life, including his Air Force service in Southeast Asia.

117. Smalley, Peter. <u>A Warm Gun</u>. London: Andre Deutsch, 1972. 233-96172-0. 183 pp.

In an unnamed war that must be Vietnam, everything is insane, especially the characters. Events include an invasion of the North, a failed nuclear bombing and an eventual enemy victory. Nonsensical characters rush about on ridiculous errands. In particular, a crazy general attempts to conceal the death of an enlisted man. If the author's goal is to express the essential lunacy of war, he makes his point relentlessly.

118. Williams, John A. <u>Captain Blackman</u>. Garden City, NY: Doubleday, 1972. 336 pp. 75-171328. NY: Bantam, 1974. 311 pp.

Abraham Blackman serves as the typical black American soldier from the Revolution through Vietnam, where he is the Captain Blackman of the title. Vietnam scenes are a relatively small part of the book, but they touch upon the growing role of blacks in the Army and upon the racial tension that was certainly a fact of life in the Army in the 1960s. Throughout the book, in all historical eras, Blackman must continually

fight the racial prejudice of the Army establishment.
A tendency to see all things black as good and all
things white as evil hurts the credibility of an
otherwise effective story.

1973

119. Browne, Corrine. Body Shop. NY: Stein & Day, 1973.
         180 pp. 73-79226.

Most of the characters in this sensitive novel are
patients in the amputation ward of San Francisco Army
Hospital. The time is between 1970 and 1972, and
there are numerous, lengthy flashbacks that describe
how several of the amputees grew up, joined the
military, fought in Vietnam and were wounded. The
stories are often poignant, and the men respond
thoughtfully to the loss of one or more limbs. In the
hospital, they smoke dope frequently, enjoy good
relationships with one another and with the staff and
seem self-aware. A few have given up hope entirely,
but the novel focuses on one man, Woody, who makes a
good and aggressive adjustment to civilian life. With
all its sensitivity and apparent veracity, the book
suffers from occasional proofreading errors, and it
would seem that the author is not completely familiar
with military terms and initialisms.

120. Chandler, David. Captain Hollister. NY: Macmillan,
         1973. 207 pp. 72-90548.
         NY: Popular Library, 1973. 222 pp.

Ernest Hollister, a Vietnam veteran and college
professor, rejoins the Army and returns to Vietnam
after a six-year absence. The time seems to be around
1970. Hollister is assigned to a graves registration
unit and finds himself writing letters of condolence
to survivors of dead men. Driven by motives that are
not completely clear, Hollister begins to write
letters describing the true circumstances of deaths.
After a brief experience in the field, Hollister joins
with a group of enlisted men to ship heroin back to
the United States in the bodies of dead servicemen.
There is some intimation that the heroin will somehow
be used to destabilize American society, but Hollister
is killed before he can see the plan through.
Chandler is an able novelist, but his point is not
quite understandable.

121.   Crawford, William.   Gunship Commander.   NY: Pinnacle
       Books, 1973.   184 pp.

       Colonel Joe Brown, an Army helicopter pilot, is just
       too contentious to be believed.   On his fifth tour in
       Vietnam, near the end of the war, he is assigned to
       bring effective leadership to an incompetent helicop-
       ter company.   He does so by beating men with his
       fists, assaulting them in various other ways and
       transferring or demoting virtually everyone he does
       not attack.   This behavior extends to military
       colleagues and superiors.   In forays against the
       enemy, Brown is characteristically bellicose.   When he
       finally leaves his command in a fury and returns to
       the U.S., Brown vents his rage on a senior general.

122.   Dennis, Charles.   Stoned Cold Soldier.   London:
       Bachman & Turner, 1973.   214 pp.

       This self-indulgent aggregation of printed words is
       supposed by the publisher to be a novel.   The author,
       a Canadian who lives in London, could apparently find
       no better subject than the Vietnam War about which to
       try to make a book-length joke.   Locations in Vietnam
       are mentioned for the activities of characters who
       babble meaninglessly to one another.   There is a
       British reporter, a crazy priest, an Oriental bandit
       and a platoon that thinks it is a sports team.   Amoung
       the events that are not a plot is a military trial.
       This is not, as the jacket claims, "a brilliantly
       satirical novel"; it is an embarrassment.

123.   Downs, Hunton.   The Opium Stratagem.   NY: Bantam,
       1973.   245 pp.   73-8514.

       Lee Kopit, a former Special Forces captain, returns to
       Vietnam in what seems to be 1973 as a contract
       employee in a secret U.S. military unit.   Directed by
       a legendary tough Army colonel, the unit is sent from
       Vietnam into the Golden Triangle, where Kopit becomes
       involved in internecine fighting among the numerous
       groups and factions that seek control of the opium
       trade.   Twists of the plot are extremely complicated,
       and the loyalties of characters shift on almost every
       page.   The U.S. government, represented by the State
       Department, the CIA and uniformed military services,
       is deep in every plot.   Among all these confusing

elements, Kopit is somehow able to survive--at least for a while.

124. Edgar, Ken. As If. Englewood Cliffs, NJ: Prentice-
      Hall, 1973. 317 pp. 73-7962.

In 1972, Tom Welland temporarily leaves his job as a
civilian weapons engineer to rejoin the Air Force and
fly a mission over North Vietnam. Welland is a former
Korean War fighter pilot who must observe a new bomb
in action in order to correct a flaw in it. During
the first half of the book, Welland takes painful
leave of friends and family. When he finally arrives
in Vietnam, he is shot down on his mission, wounded
and captured. With the help of a bellicose pilot, he
escapes, is captured again, and escapes again. Then
he returns to the U.S. and resumes his civilian life.
There are pointless digressions throughout, including
the correct recipe for a Margarita and a verbatim
conversation with a cabdriver about football.

125. Giovanitti, Len. The Man Who Won the Medal of Honor.
          NY: Random House, 1973. 211 pp. 73-5003.
          NY: Popular Library, 1976. 224 pp.

Giovanitti does not convey a sense of assured familiarity with the area in which his story is set.
Private David Glass is drafted and sent to Vietnam in
1968 after growing up in an orphanage. He sees
Americans murder Vietnamese prisoners and he kills the
Americans in turn. There are no effective witnesses,
and he manages to get away with it and return safely
to the United States. Later, he is notified that he
will receive a Congressional Medal of Honor (for an
act he did not perform). At the awards ceremony, he
assaults the President and murders a military aide.
Glass is tried and found guilty, and as the book ends
he is in prison awaiting sentence. It is certainly in
order to point out the dehumanizing and ambivalent
aspects of the war, but this attempt is rather
heavy-handed.

126. Huggett, William Turner. Body Count. NY: Putnam,
          1973. 445 pp. 72-97297.
          NY: Dell, 1978. 445 pp.

Because of its superior literary quality and histori-

cal accuracy, Body Count must be among the very best
novels of Marines in Vietnam. The hero is Lieutenant
Chris Hawkins, an infantry platoon leader who learns
his profession at Khe Sanh, Da Nang and elsewhere.
Woven into one long, able story are such matters as
morale, race relations, military professionalism and
careerism and the hostile countryside of Vietnam.
Other members of Hawkins' platoon and company appear
as interesting, individualized characters, and their
actions and dialogue are credible. At the end of the
book, Hawkins leads and survives his greatest battle
and he appears to be in line for promotion to company
commander.

127. Jackson, Blyden. Operation Burning Candle. NY: Third
      Press, 1973. 221 pp. 73-82639.
      NY: Pyramid, 1974. 253 pp.

While several pages here and there take the characters
back to Vietnam, this is much more a novel of veterans
than of the war. The special reason to include it
here is that the Vietnam scenes have mostly to do with
a military police assault, using tanks and automatic
weapons, against a section of Saigon populated by
large numbers of black deserters. This is very much a
period piece, not least because the characters are
either evil white people or good black ones. Aaron
Rogers, a black psychologist, joins the Special Forces
and learns skills in Vietnam that he puts into the
black revolutionary struggle when he returns to the
United States. At the climax of the book, he and his
followers commit some spectacular political murders at
what is probably the 1972 Democratic political
convention.

128. Roth, Robert. Sand in the Wind. Boston: Little,
      Brown, 1973. 498 pp. 73-8768.
      NY: Pinnacle, 1974. 624 pp.

Murder, rape, cannibalism, racial tension, war
resistance and startling humor appear in this long
novel along with the more traditional aspects of
Marine infantry at war. The action is set in and
around Hue in what is clearly the 1968 Tet Offensive.
The main characters are Kramer, a lieutenant, and
Chalice, an enlisted man. The relationships between
them and the other characters are realistic and well
written. Characters have convincing personal man-

nerisms, personalities, and conversations. There are
many scenes of small unit action, and the entire book
seems credible and convincing. Roth's literary style
is able enough to maintain a reader's interest and to
convey and sustain the emotional environment of war.

129. Stone, Tom. Armstrong. NY: Warner Paperback Library,
     1973. 173 pp.

Walker Armstrong is a young Army sergeant involved in
the secret war in Laos, called Phoutain here. The
time seems to be around 1970. Armstrong kills a
double agent and his sister. Then his commanding
officer is killed in a separate incident. Deprived of
command guidance, Armstrong suffers a breakdown, then
babbles about the crime to virtually everyone he
meets until a new commander arrives and tells him to
shut up. With military authority in place once more,
Armstrong looks to his own survival and kills a
Phoutainese whore to whom he had confessed the crime.

130. Trowbridge, James. Easy Victories. Boston: Houghton
     Mifflin, 1973. 214 pp. 72-9018.

Knox, an American intelligence agent, is both amoral
and lucky. Assigned to Vietnam prior to the 1968 Tet
Offensive, he talks his way out of a dangerous posting
in the field and arranges instead to do relatively
safe work in Saigon. Among the rear area military
men, war profiteers, bar girls and civilians, Knox
manages to find a place and to enjoy himself. He
acquires a mistress and begins to make money in
illegal currency manipulations. The impression conveyed is that intelligence officers and indeed most
other people in Saigon are fools, traitors, alcoholics
or worse. Finally, Knox is nearly killed during Tet,
his mistress kills herself, and he decides it is time
to get out. Lucky until the end, Knox manages to
break his contract with the intelligence service and
find a first-class seat on a plane back to the United
States.

131. Wolfe, Michael. Man on a String. NY: Harper & Row,
     1973. 224 pp. 73-4166.

Michael Keefe makes a smooth transition from Signal
Corps officer to civilian cameraman near the end of

the war. Drawn into a scheme involving a missing Army
payroll, corrupt Vietnamese officers and an independent Montagnard force, Keefe has more adventures in an
average day than most men ecounter in a lifetime. At
the end, he is back in the Army again, working for a
secret agency that steps in to bring order out of the
chaos of the plot. Wolfe's skill as a writer is more
apparent in his ample descriptions of Saigon and the
Vietnamese countryside at a time when nearly all the
Americans have departed.

                                  1974

132. Boatman, Alan. Comrades in Arms. NY: Harper & Row,
         1974. 229 pp. 73-4139.

      Boatman is an able novelist. His characters are
      subtle and believable, and their thoughts, words and
      actions are interesting. In the first part of the
      book, a Marine corporal, Harding, is shot in the back
      by a black Marine. The motive could be attempted
      murder or simple incompetence; the reasons are vague.
      In any case, Harding's friends later murder the
      assailant. Harding is evacuated from Vietnam, and he
      awaits medical discharge at Marine bases in California
      and North Carolina. Like many of his friends, Harding
      is a draftee who chose the Marine Corps instead of
      flight from the war. Conversations among these
      characters are revealing. Among his other literary
      talents, Boatman is well able to evoke the sleazy
      atmosphere of military camp towns, with their bars,
      whores and greedy streets.

133. Charles, Robert. Sea Vengeance. NY: Pinnacle Books,
         c1974, 1976. 182 pp. 0-523-00946-1.

      In an interesting variation on Vietnam War fiction,
      this story is about a Vietcong hijack of a British
      merchant ship in Vietnamese waters. With some troops
      disguised as passengers and others stowed away, the
      Vietcong take control of a British tramp steamer, kill
      several of the crew and order the chief mate to take
      them first to one island, where they load artillery
      pieces, then to another island, which they assault.
      From the second island, they remove many Vietcong
      prisoners and kill the garrison. When the ship
      returns to the open sea, it is first buzzed by
      American aircraft, then attacked by South Vietnamese

Skyhawks. A very few of the survivors of this bloody
adventure live happily ever after.

134. Just, Ward. <u>Stringer</u>. Boston: Little, Brown, 1974.
        199 pp. 73-13682.
        Port Townsend, WA: Graywolf Press, 1984. 165 pp.

Vietnam is not named, but it is obviously the locale
where Stringer, a civilian, and Price, an Army
officer, are sent far into enemy territory to plant
electronic sensors along an infiltration route. There
is friction between the two men because of their
different backgrounds and attitudes. Descriptions of
their equipment, movements and the surrounding jungle
are minute. After their sensors guide in an air
strike, Price is killed and Stringer begins to walk
out. At this stage, about halfway through, there is a
marked change in the literary style as the meaning of
the novel becomes much more elusive. Stringer
encounters the enemy and his old friends in scenes
that may be hallucinatory, and the conclusion is
vague. Dialogue is sometimes indicated by dashes
rather than quotation marks, and there is a minor
technical error in which "clip" is used incorrectly
for "magazine." Nonetheless, Just is a good writer,
and this is a provocative view of the actions and
motives of men at war.

135. Karl, Terry. <u>Children of the Dragon</u>. San Francisco:
        People's Press, 1974. 51 pp. 0-914-750003.

The principal characters in this children's book are
eight and ten years of age. They live in the countryside of North Vietnam in 1972 where they and their
families and friends suffer from American bombing.
Excellent illustrations, some in color, combine with
the text to convey the message that Vietnam should be
peaceful and united. Near the end of the book, the
characters learn of the treaty between the United
States and North Vietnam. The book ends with a
suitably inspiring quotation from Ho Chi Minh.

136. Kingry, Philip. <u>The Monk and the Marines</u>. NY:
        Bantam, 1974. 182 pp.

The title character, a former novice at a monastery,
is a Navy corpsman serving with Marine infantry near

Chu Lai. The time is 1966, and nobody wants to be
there. Chris, the narrator, does his job with
modesty, courage and professional competence, as do
the Marines with whom he serves. Theirs is a terrifying life of combat patrols, sweeps and defense of
their base from mortar and rocket attacks. The
Marines' principal task is to stay alive, and at one
point Chris arranges the murder of an officer who has
too often put his men in danger. In fine, simple,
understated prose, Kingry recounts combat at a level
where the enemy is often close enough to see and
occassionally close enough to smell.

137.   Klose, Kevin and McCombs, Philip A.   The Typhoon
          Shipments. NY: Norton, 1974.   280 pp.
          NY: Pyramid, 1976.   222 pp.

       Bodies of deceased American servicemen are used to
       convey heroin from South Vietnam to the United States
       in this fast-paced thriller. The principal characters
       are customs agents in pursuit of the smugglers. Some
       of the action is set in Washington, D.C. and else-
       where, but there are many scenes in Saigon and one
       account of an improbable combat assault. Belief is
       also strained by the prospect of the body of a U.S.
       senator's son, full of heroin, lying in the Capitol
       Rotunda. This is followed by a wild gunfight in
       Arlington National Cemetery. While the essential
       story is not believable, the characters and their
       dialogue are.

138.   Littell, Robert.   Sweet Reason. Boston: Houghton
          Mifflin, 1974.   210 pp.   73-12079.
          NY: Popular Library, 1976.   221 pp.
          NY: Bantam, 1986.   226 pp.

       During only three days off the coast of Vietnam, the
       World War II destroyer Eugene F. Ebersole sinks both
       an innocent junk and a ditched aircraft; it attacks a
       school of whales with depth charges and causes the
       destruction of a friendly village. The characters are
       formed in a way that suggests the author has anti-
       military attitudes. Regular officers and loyal
       sailors are incompetent fools; pacifists among the
       officers and crew are portrayed as interesting,
       sincere idealists. "Sweet Reason," an anonymous
       pamphleteer, urges resistance to military authority,
       and eventually the men at the guns refuse to fire.

Shortly afterward, the Ebersole collides with an
aircraft carrier and sinks with half the men aboard.
Littel's humor is often effective, as when he exag-
gerates the hostile posturing of black militants among
the crew, but the short chapters and subchapters tend
to divide the text awkwardly.

139. Lockridge, Ernest. Prince Elmo's Fire. NY: Stein &
        Day, 1974. 346 pp. 73-82112.
        NY: Pocket Books, 1975. 341 pp.

In this first-person story of a man's entire life, his
service in Vietnam is only a part. Thus, the book is
realistic in a way that escapes most Vietnam novels.
Prince Elmo Hatcher grows up in poverty, but never
despair, in rural Indiana. When his family dissolves,
he is taken into a foster home where his talent as an
artist develops. After being expelled from college,
he is drafted and sent to Vietnam. The account of his
service as a combat infantryman there is more allegor-
ical and symbolic than earlier portions of the book,
which are often moving. Ridiculous characters and
events are introduced with the object, no doubt, of
ridiculing war. Hatcher and some others are captured
by an unlikely Vietcong women, Susie Q. After rescue,
he returns as a wounded hero to resume his life in the
United States.

140. McCarry, Charles. The Tears of Autumn. NY: Saturday
        Review Press/E.P. Dutton, c1974, 1975. 276 pp.
        74-7419.
        Great Britain: Hutchinson, 1975.
        Toronto: Clark, Irwin, 1975.
        London: Arrow Books, 1984. 276 pp.

The premise of this unusual novel is that the assassination of President John Kennedy was arranged by the
extended family of Vietnamese leader Diem in
retaliation for Kennedy's presumed complicity in the
1963 coup that led to Diem's death. The hero is Paul
Christopher, a senior and romantic American intelligence agent. He works out the puzzle as he travels
through Europe, Africa and Southeast Asia. Christopher pursues leads, questions other agents and
tortures informants. He learns, among other things,
that the Russians had Lee Harvey Oswald killed by Jack
Ruby because they feared unjustified blame for
Kennedy's assassination. When Christopher presents

his conclusions and supporting documentation to aides
of President Johnson, they suppress the information
because they fear its release would undermine popular
American support for the war. The settings all appear
accurate, and the novel contains information about the
Vietnamese kinship system.

141. Meyer, Nicholas. <u>Target Practice</u>. NY: Pinnacle
        Books, c1974, 1975. 186 pp.

This detective story set in the early 1970s touches
upon several Vietnam issues. A former prisoner of war
commits suicide after being charged with collaboration
by another prisoner. A private detective is hired to
investigate the charges. He learns of the dead man's
training, combat experience and imprisonment through
interviews with former soldiers. There is one
chilling session in a veterans' hospital with an
armless, legless survivor. The story that emerges is
that the former prisoners had been involved in a
massacre of innocent civilians prior to their capture
by the North Vietnamese.

142. Pratt, John Clark. <u>The Laotian Fragments</u> NY:
        Viking, 1974. 245 pp. 73-2499.
        NY: Avon, 1985. 240 pp. 84-91206.

The "fragments" of the title are fictitious letters,
memoranda, military reports, diaries, orders and
transcriptions that comprise the book and tell the
story of U.S. Air Force "civilian" pilots in Laos in
the mid-1960s. The epistolary style presents some
problems; readers familiar with military communications will be able to follow the story, but others may
not. The main character, Major William Blake, is one
of several American pilots who appear to be running
the Laotian Air Force in its battles with communist
forces and various political armies. The plot,
characters and action sequences are not overdone, as
is so often the case in Air Force novels, but are
vivid and convincing. The author, a former Air Force
pilot in Laos, has been instrumental in building the
Vietnam War Collection at Colorado State University
upon which this bibliography is based.

143. Rubin, Jonathan. <u>The Barking Deer</u>. NY: Braziller,
        1974. 335 pp. 73-88042.

NY: Avon, 1982.   335 pp.

Rubin describes a situation so confused, corrupt and
tragic that it would be unbelievable in any modern
context other than that of the Vietnam War. His story
is set among Montagnard tribesmen and an American
Special Forces team during the mid-1960s. Most of the
action and conversations occur among the Montagnards,
and the impression is conveyed that they are separated
from Americans by cultural differences too great to
understand, much less to breach. The complexity of
characters, spirit relationships and folk activities
is difficult and sometimes burdensome to follow. The
American characters are officers and enlisted men of
the Special Forces team, and at the end of this
extremely involved novel, they are among the many
dead.

144.   Stone, Robert. Dog Soldiers. Boston: Houghton
              Mifflin, 1974. 342 pp. 74-114411.
              NY: Ballantine, 1975. 339 pp.
              London: W.H. Allen, Star, 1979. 339 pp.
              NY: Penguin, 1987. 86-22659. 342 pp.

This story of the illegal narcotics trade is set for
the most part in California, but the initial chapters
describe action in Viietnam. Many of the characters
are either military veterans or civilians associated
in some capacity with the war effort. They are
accordingly somewhat brutalized, embittered, and fully
familiar with small arms and individual tactics. The
book points out the corruption in Vietnam that
facilitated the narcotics trade during the war. It is
a credible story that provided the basis for the
motion picture, Who'll Stop the Rain?

145.   Vaughan, Robert. The Valkyrie Mandate. NY: Simon &
              Schuster, 1974. 287 pp. 73-16880.
              London: New English Library, 1974.
              NY: Pocket Books, 1975. 254 pp.

Into the background of the coup that will overthrow
the Diem government, the author inserts fictional
characters and events. Lt. Colonel Justin Barclay is
an able military adviser with years of experience in
Vietnam and the unusual ability to speak and understand the language. Barclay is ordered to offer
American aid to one group of plotting Vietnamese

officers, but he decides on his own initiative to deal
with another group instead. Barclay picks his
conspirators well, and the coup is successful.
However, the end, among convolutions of Vietnamese
politics, is not to the planned advantage of any of
the Americans involved.

1975

146. Crowther, John. Firebase. NY: St. Martin's, 1975.
        206 pp. 75-9489.
        London: Constable, 1975. 206 pp.

Military combat and the enemy barely appear in this
account of racial tension and violence at a remote
Army firebase. Instead of fighting the communists,
the black and white Americans kill one another. The
hero, Lt. Mather, works out the conflict between his
loyalties to the Army and to his fellow blacks as he
attempts to mitigate the actions of a racist commanding officer. The problems with this novel include
mistakes about military details and a rather florid
style, but the exploration of racial matters is
interesting.

147. Grossbach, Robert. Easy and Hard Ways Out. NY:
        Harper's Magazine Press, 1975. 245 pp. 74-4863.
        NY: Warner Books, 1976. 238 pp.
        NY: Carroll & Graf, 1984. 245 pp. Published as
        Best Defense.

Settings both in Vietnam and in the United States
provide simultaneous looks at the lives of engineers
working on a part for a new fighter bomber and of a
pilot flying the airplane over North Vietnam. The
character and life of the pilot are in marked contrast
to those of the engineers, who are portrayed as weak
people doing easy jobs. When the engineers in the
United States allow an electronic countermeasure
device to go into production with a design flaw, the
pilot is killed over North Vietnam as a direct
consequence. The different points of view hold the
reader's attention, but the choppy chapters and
frequent shifting of perspective make this a difficult
book to read.

148. Kirkwood, James. <u>Some Kind of Hero</u>. NY: Thomas Y.
          Crowell, 1975. 399 pp. 75-5725.
          NY: New American Library, Signet, 1976. 294 pp.

Eddie Keller is a long-suffering hero. As a child,
Eddie is abandoned by his father to the care of an
alcoholic mother. Later, he is drafted into the Army
and sent to Vietnam, leaving behind his new, pregnant
wife. Eddie is captured and held prisoner in Hanoi
for five years. The lengthy prison camp sequences
deal fluently with physical and mental torture,
homosexuality, betrayal and death, yet they lack a
hard edge of realism. Eddie returns home to find that
his wife has squandered his back pay and moved in with
her former lover. His mother has had a stroke, and he
must face her medical bills. After an attempted
reconciliation with his father fails, Eddie turns to
crime and eventually becomes a competent armed robber.
Throughout it all, he maintains an amazing equanimity.

149. Little, Loyd. <u>Parthian Shot</u>. NY: Viking, 1975. 278
          pp. 74-30250.
          NY: Ivy Books, 1987. 289 pp. 0-8041-0004-7.

This sensitive and somewhat gentle novel is written by
a former Special Forces medic with service in Vietnam.
It is set among a Buddhist sect in the Mekong Delta in
1964. Several members of a Special Forces team are
lost on official Army records and temporarily stranded
in their area of operations by seasonal floods. They
decide to stay on and work for the local political and
military leader. The characters are credible, even
the old-time sergeant and the incompetent lieutenant.
In contrast to novels set later in the war, relations
between Americans and Vietnamese are excellent. There
are fine elements of humor, including the formation of
a joint stock company with the Vietcong as both
customers and shareholders and the implementation of a
Rand Institute recommendation that the Buddhists
survive the war by pretending to support both sides.
Action is somewhat slow for a war story, and combat is
confined to patrol skirmishes. Eventually, some of
the soldiers decide to return to the Army and to the
U.S. while others remain in the village. In a final
chapter, almost an afterword, the village is destroyed
by an air attack some years after the main action
occurs.

150. Nagle, William. The Odd Angry Shot. Sydney,
          Australia: Angus & Robertson, 1975.
          London: Angus & Robertson, Arkon ed., 1979.
          98 pp. 0-207-14208-4.

The Australian contribution in Vietnam is not well
known to Americans. As portrayed here, their soldiers
had much the same experiences and attitudes as ours.
The narrator and his comrades are members of the
Australian Army's elite SAS unit, similar to American
Special Forces or Rangers. Their attitudes about the
war and their part in it are cynical and sarcastic.
The Australians have generally friendly encounters
with the Americans they meet. They detest both the
South Vietnamese and the peace demonstrators back
home. There are a few errors missed in proofreading
and an unusual physical layout. This edition has
still photographs from a motion picture based on the
novel.

151. Nahum, Lucien. Shadow 81. NY: Doubleday, 1975.
          London: New English Library, 1976. 285 pp.
          NY: A Drum Book, 1986. 287 pp. 74-17770.

This is an account of an imaginative crime committed
in the context of the Vietnam War. An Air Force
general conspires with the pilot of an experimental
fighter bomber to fake a crash during an exciting
mission over Hanoi. The pilot then transports the
plane on a specially constructed ship to North
America, where he uses it to threaten a commercial
airliner and extort a large ransom. The pilot returns
to Vietnam and arranges to be captured by the North
Vietnamese. After enduring five months of captivity,
the pilot is released at the end of the war, and he
and the general escape with their loot. Almost like
human characters, airplanes and their capabilities are
described in loving detail.

152. Smith, Steven Phillip. American Boys. NY: Putnam,
          1975. 435 pp. 74-16619.
          NY: Avon, 1984. 435 pp. 0-380-67934-5.

The characters in this long, thoughtful novel are Army
enlisted men in an air mobile infantry unit in the
Central Highlands of Vietnam. The time appears to be
1966 or 1967. Four men transfer to Vietnam from
Germany and serve as riflemen and helicopter door

gunners. There is much combat action, and the book offers a full picture of helicopter warfare in support of infantry. The men suffer variously. One, a former football star, begins to murder prisoners. He is later badly wounded. Another man is killed, and the two survivors struggle with fatalism, narcotics and alcoholism. At the end of the novel, only one of the four boards the airplane to return home. In contrast to many accounts of Vietnam, the soldiers here are professionally competent and proud of their ability to fight. There are, however, the usual conflicts between low-ranking enlisted men and professional officers and NCOs.

153. Wolfe, Michael. The Two-Star Pigeon. NY: Harper & Row, 1975. 244 pp. 74-5804.

This fascinating but implausible story has to do with an attempt to restore the Vietnamese monarchy in the person of a child emperor. Much of the action takes place in Dalat, and there are full descriptions of that town and of the Vietnamese military academy located there. Among the would-be monarchists are an American major general and various Vietnamese soldiers and politicians. Their goals are to unify the country against the North Vietnamese and to secure benefits for themselves. An unqualified but inspired Army intelligence agent foils the plot by kidnapping the proposed emperor, and it develops that the child is an impostor without imperial lineage. These events occur after 1968 but at a time when Americans are still fully in charge of the war.

1976

154. Brooke, Dinah. Games of Love and War. London: Jonathan Cape, 1976. 190 pp.
NY: Harcourt, Brace, Jovanovich, 1976. 148 pp.
75-37524. Published as Death Games.

Like its title this book is almost a game. After the withdrawal of American troops and before the victory of communist forces in Vietnam, there was a confused and ambivalent period. Into this environment come Elspeth, a spoiled European girl, her businessman father and his mistress. Descriptions of Saigon, Udorn and other Southeast Asian locations, made from a European point of view, constitute the best parts of

the book. American and Asian characters are minor
stereotypes, and the plot seems as pointless as tthe
luxurious lives of the main characters. The difficulty in understanding the action is increased by
frequent changes between first- and third-person
narration and by the use of the present tense, and
imagined action. Also, quotation marks are absent.

155. Carter, Nick. The Vulcan Disaster. NY: Award Books,
       1976. 187 pp.

Sometime between Hanoi (7) and this novel, the Nick
Carter series changed from third-person to first-
person narration. The hero, however, is as universal-
ly capable as ever, and the action characteristically
implausible. The Vulcan Disaster begins in Saigon
just as the city is falling to the North Vietnamese.
Carter has a lifetime's worth of action in the doomed
city, killing a double agent and subduing a beautiful
woman spy, before he departs for the American embassy.
As it happens, he is attacked on the way and finally
leaves the country for Hong Kong on the aircraft of a
South Vietnamese drug seller. The remainder of the
novel, thankfully, takes place elsewhere.

156. Chalker, Jack L. A Jungle of Stars. NY: Ballantine,
       1976. 217 pp. 76-15209.
       NY: Ballantine, Del Rey, 1980. 217 pp.

On a pointless patrol in the Vietnamese jungle in
1969, Lieutenant Paul Savage is murdered by one of his
own men. Immediately after death, he is brought into
contact with a telepathic mentality that offers him
rebirth if he will enlist as a fighter in a galactic
war. Savage agrees and his further adventures in this
interesting novel are pure science fiction.

157. Cunningham, Ben. Green Eyes. NY: Ballantine Books,
       MCMXXVI [sic; probably 1976]. 167 pp.

Dubeck, a black Vietnam veteran, returns to Saigon in
1971 in order to find his former girlfriend and a baby
son he has never seen. After a variety of experiences, he locates the woman, only to find that she has
married someone else and that his son has died.
Dubeck decides to adopt a half-black Vietnamese orphan
and take him to America.

158. Durden, Charles. <u>No Bugles, No Drums</u>. NY: Viking,
        1976. 287 pp. 76-91.
        NY: Charter, 1978. 287 pp.
        NY: Avon, 1984. 287 pp. 84-90964.

Identified on the dust wrapper as a first novel, this
account of Army enlisted men at the notional Song My
Swine Project frequently attempts humor and often
achieves it. The first-person narrative is cynical
and adolescent, told by the hero, Jamie Hawkins, a
young private from Georgia. The dialogue and settings
are realistic; the characters include standard
military types--an innocent private, a tough old
sergeant and an incompetent second lieutenant. Among
the other characters are a best buddy who is killed
and a black soldier who turns traitor. After much
action and inaction, Hawkins, hardened and embittered
by the war, murders the black turncoat and tries to
walk home to Atlanta. Of course, he only makes it to
the coast. He is finally discharged from the Army
with nothing remaining but his "unshakable bad
attitude."

159. Hancock, J. Robert. <u>Memoirs of a Combat Corpsman</u>.
        Santee, CA: Blueboy Library, 1976. 182 pp.

In this explicit homosexual paperback, the two main
characters, Guy and David, are caught behind enemy
lines sometime near the end of the war. The setting
and plot are incidental to the extensive and rather
unimaginative sexual passages.

160. Hynd, Noel. <u>Revenge</u>. NY: Dial, 1976. 274 pp. 75-
        34127.
        NY: Dell, 1978. 255 pp.

Only the first ten pages of this gripping novel are
set in Vietnam, but they are enough, for they describe
the brutal torture that was a feature of imprisonment
in North Vietnam. Richard Silva, an Air Force
lieutenant, is tormented, and his friends are killed,
by a European guard. They believe he is French.
After release in 1973, Siva begins a hunt for the man,
which involves several interesting subplots and
eventually takes him to Paris. It develops that the
guard is a French intelligence agent, and Silva has
the satisfaction of killing him before a final

surprise at the book's end. The very short chapters
do not enhance readability.

161.   Kempley, Walter. The Invaders. NY: Dutton, Saturday
       Review Press, 1976. 263 pp. 0-8415-0393-1.
       Toronto: Clarke, Irwin, 1976.
       NY: Dell, 1979. 288 pp.

The continental United States becomes an extended
theater of operations for the Vietnam War in this mass
market paperback. A gang of black Army deserters in
Saigon is recruited by a fanatical North Vietnamese
major to launch unauthorized rocket and mortar attacks
on targets in the U.S. They are pursued by Lt. Gerald
Skilling, the commander of an improbably independent
Army unit assigned to track deserters. The deserters
are paid in heroin, and some of the action takes place
in the French criminal underground. These descriptions of black market and smuggling activities are
interesting, but they are written so simply that they
defy belief. For example, in the nine pages after he
is introduced, Eddie Palmer, a deserter, joins a
criminal gang in Saigon, singlehandedly salvages their
inept hijacking of a truck, sells its contents to a
Vietnamese thief he meets by accident, kills the gang
boss with one shot in the chest, and takes over as
leader. Most other action is similarly compressed in
a story that seems to take place between 1968 and
1971. The end comes after a gunfight in New York
City.

162.   Larteguy, Jean. Presumed Dead. Translated by Leonard
       Mayhew. Boston: Little, Brown, 1976. 459 pp.
       76-5209.

Larteguy is best known for his superb novels of French
colonial parachute infantry in Indochina and North
Africa. Here, he returns to a country he knows well
to tell the story of Hans Brucker, a Swiss banker who
journeys to Vietnam in 1970 to search for Ron Clark, a
Swiss-American journalist who may have been killed
near the Cambodian border. The story is extremely
complicated, but it has a unique European perspective.
For Brucker amd many other characters, Saigon is a
civilian city, and the American military is a doomed,
ineffective force whose private soldiers are being
ruined by narcotics. Larteguy manages to work into
his story substantial, realistic descriptions of

military operations and to convey a sense of how the
"American" Vietnam War fits into the larger history of
the country and region.

163. Malek, Parma. <u>Viet Cong Defilers</u>. Chatsworth, CA:
     Stag, 1976. 192 pp.

     With even less of a plot than most Vietnam pornog-
     raphy, this book is little more than one long sex
     scene. Torture, bestiality and death also figure in
     the experiences of WAC Corporal Sandra Harte's capture
     and ill-use by the Vietcong.

164. Wolfe, Michael. <u>The Chinese Fire Drill</u>. NY: Harper
     & Row, 1976. 247 pp. 75-6380.
     NY: Lorevan, 1986. 247 pp.

     The durable Michael Keefe, back from two earlier
     Vietnam novels, recruits a private army in Saigon and
     has various adventures. There, a beautiful Vietcong
     female spy, American prisoners who might be turncoats,
     a rich U.S. senator and a Vietnamese "third force" in
     the background. The setting for these bold but
     improbable doings is Vietnam after the U.S. military
     withdrawal but before the communist takeover. Saigon
     and other locations have just recently been full of
     Americans, and the sense in this story is that
     communist victory is not yet complete. As always,
     Wolfe's great strength is his ability to evoke his
     settings.

                            1977

165. Harper, Stephen. <u>Live Till Tomorrow</u>. London:
     Collins, 1977. 195 pp. 0-00-222405-4.

     The chaotic conditions during the fall of Saigon in
     1975 provide the setting for this story. Two former
     American servicemen, Barber and Ledger, have settled
     in Saigon to run a successful business. As the city
     falls, Ledger vanishes. Barber takes the man's large
     Vietnamese family through the harrowing and compli-
     cated evacuation to Guam. This last exit of America
     from Vietnam is told convincingly, with several
     anecdotes of escape by Americans and Vietnamese.
     Barber finally locates his lost partner in Singapore,
     but Ledger is killed in a criminal gun fight. The

plot is not too plausible, but the setting and
background are described well.

166. Heinemann, Larry. Close Quarters. NY: Farrar,
     Strauss, Giroux, 1977. 335 pp. 77-2245.
     NY: Popular Library, 1977. 316 pp.
     NY: Warner Books, 1983. 316 pp.
     NY: Penguin, 1986. 335 pp. 86-9466.

Armored personnel carriers are used as light tanks in
this long and realistic novel about an Army cavalry
unit in and around Tayninh City in 1967. The hero,
Philip Dosier, is an APC driver who describes events
fully and well. The other main charactes are hardened
combat soldiers with utter contempt for officers and
rear-area "housecats." They hate the enemy and fight
with bravado and some success. At rest, they despise
and brutalize the South Vietnamese. A period of
recreation in Japan is also described in full detail.
Unusually, this novel follows the hero home to his
family and friends. Once there, he learns of his best
friend's death back in Vietnam. Heinemann maintains
his pace and holds the reader's interest throughout.

167. Joss, John. Sierra Sierra. Los Altos, CA: Soaring
     Press, 1977. 200 pp. 77-82561.
     NY: Morrow, 1978. 235 pp.

On the surface, this is a first-person, present-tense
novel about a record attempt glider flight from Mount
Olympus, Washington, to Yuma, Arizona. The pilot,
Mark Lewis, is a retired Marine aviator who served in
Vietnam. As the glider journey progresses, Lewis
recalls in great detail a combat mission in Vietnam
during which his best friend was killed. This
description of the employment of carrier-based F4
Phantom fighters against hostile ground targets is
complex, but Joss manages all the technical infor-
mationin a lucid and understandable manner. He is
equally convincing in developing the character of
Lewis as a career military pilot. Other parts of the
book not specific to Vietnam are also handled
adroitly.

168. Martin, Ian Kennedy. Rekill. NY: Putnam, 1977.
     254 pp. 77-7646.
     London: Heinemann, 1977.

NY: Ballantine, 1978. 217 pp.
London: Pan Books, 1978. 174 pp.

Numerous technical mistakes about weapons, military
slang, nomenclature, radio procedure and rock climbing
combine with questionable grammar and unusual
capitalization to suggest that this book may have been
written and edited in some haste. The plot has to do
with a 1968 massacre of Vietnamese civilians and the
vendetta, some eight years later, of a North Vietnamese major against the guilty American officers.
One of the subplots deals with internecine struggles
among different intelligence agencies. Action takes
place also in Albania, where a politiical assassination incidentally destroys a Chinese missile base!
The characters are neither memorable nor credible, but
Martin does describe fast action well, and the revenge
theme is handled strongly throughout.

169. Sadler, Barry. The Moi. Nashville, TN: Aurora
        Publishers, 1977. 214 pp. 75-26255.
        NY: Tom Doherty Associates, Tor, 1983. 314 pp.
        0-523-48051-1. Published as Cry Havoc, a
        slightly rewritten version.

Sadler, a former Green Beret and Vietnam veteran,
certainly knows that the Russian Takarev pistol used
in Vietnam is a semiautomatic, not a revolver. That,
however, is the only mistake in a book replete with
technical information. The story concerns Lim, a
fanatical North Vietnamese major, and Reider, an
American Special Forces sergeant who is his prisoner.
Lim tortures Reider for what seem to be months in an
effort to break his spirit and reduce him to a
"moi"--an animal. Reider resists until he can achieve
what is for him a heroic climax. While revealing much
of Lim's and Reider's thoughts and reflections, Sadler
manages to keep them separate and distinct. The
premise of this story is a bit strained, but it is a
gripping adventure.

170. Tauber, Peter. The Last Best Hope. NY: Harcourt,
        Brace, Jovanovich, 1977. 628 pp. 76-0730.
        NY: Ballantine, 1978. 712 pp.

This huge book is clearly intended to be a statement
about the generation of Americans that reached

maturity during the 1960s. Indeed many of the
characters are recognizable as prosperous, well-
educated, verbose young people who made themselves and
what passed for their ideas apparent in that unfortunate decade. One of them is drafted and sent to
Vietnam. Scenes of the war cover a substantial number
of pages. Willie Bowen, the soldier, is an Army
enlisted man, although his location and military
assignment are neither clear nor consistent. During
one adventure, he survives a battle and hides for a
while in a friendly village. Later, he leads a patrol
to save a general officer whose helicopter has been
shot down. For that achievement, he is awarded the
Congressional Medal of Honor by a newly elected
Richard Nixon.

171. Tran Khan Tuyet. The Little Weaver of Thai-Yen
        Village. Rev. ed. San Francisco: Children's
        Book Press, c1977, 1987. 24 pp. 86-17186.

Beautiful illustrations combine with a simple text in
this children's book. It is the story of a young
Vietnamese girl who is injured in an American bombing.
She is taken to the United States for a successful
operation. From there, she sends her handwoven
textiles back to Vietnam.

172. Williams, T. Jeff. The Glory Hole. London: Corgi,
        1977. 285 pp. 0-552-10499-X.

Williams provides an interesting study of character
degradation in wartime. Jacob Sturm serves as a medic
in an evacuation helicopter based in Quang Tri. Near
the end of his tour Sturm loses his perspective as a
saver of lives and becomes a killer. He is led to
this partly through a growing heroin addiction. Sturm
is surrounded by brutal characters, including a
particularly bloodthirsty Catholic chaplain and a gung
ho aircraft commander. There is the obligatory
romance with a Vietnamese bar girl and a more interesting relationship with an American nurse. By the
end of his tour, Jacob Sturm is in one piece, but it
is a very ragged one.

                              1978

173. Brooke, Joshua. Just a Little Inconvenience. NY:

Dell, 1978.   174 pp.   0-440-15287-9.

The maudlin nature of this story reflects its origins
as a motion picture made for television. Two friends,
Frank and Kenny, grow up together and find themselves
serving as junior officers in the same infantry unit
in Vietnam. In a firefight, Kenny is badly wounded
because of what he believes is the cowardice of his
friend. Much of the story describes Kenny's adjustment to the loss of an arm and a leg and the eventual
reconciliation of the two friends. There is good
material from the perspective of the disabled veteran
attempting to adjust to his circumstances, but the
relationship between the two men is not convincing.

174.   Clark, Ann Nolan. To Stand Against the Wind. NY:
       Viking, 1978.   136 pp.   78-5966.

Em, an eleven-year-old, lives as a refugee in America.
In order to document his family history, he writes a
story of his life in Vietnam. In exhaustive (and
exhausting) detail, this account of rice farming in
the Mekong Delta occupies most of the book.
Characters discuss every event at great length and
recount much Vietnamese history to one another. The
war is far away until an American unit bombs their
village and kills several of Em's family. The
survivors are finally able to emigrate to the United
States. This is children's literature, but only for
patient children.

175.   Corder, E. M. The Deer Hunter. NY: Jove/HBJ, c1978,
       1979.   189 pp.   78-68164.
       NY: Exeter Books, 1979.   189 pp.   79-53098.
       London: Hodder & Stoughton, Coronet, 1979.
       187 pp.

Taken from the well-known motion picture of the same
name, The Deer Hunter describes the lives of a group
of young steelworkers from Pennsylvania who go to war
in Vietnam and suffer capture, mutilation and death.
The motion picture is more a statement about the war
than an accurate depiction of it, and the book follows
the movie completely with a style that reveals its
origin: "She knocked. There was no answer. She
opened the door...." The value of this book is
principally its accurate association with the motion

picture, which is thought by many to be a significant
and talented reaction to the war.

176. Groom, Winston. Better Times Than These. NY: Summit
         Books, 1978. 411 pp. 78-4182.
         NY: Berkley, 1979. 477 pp.
         London: Sphere Books, 1980. 477 pp.

An imagined company of the genuine 7th Infantry
Division leaves for Vietnam in 1966. This is an
unusual beginning for a Vietnam novel in that the
entire unit goes to war as a group. About a quarter
of the book describes activities on the troop ship and
elsewhere prior to the group's arrival in the Ia Drang
Valley. Once there, they engage in much infantry
combat and the usual range of rear area activities.
A platoon commander, Lt. Billy Kahn, is taken out of
action to be court-martialed for complicity in the
rape of two female Vietcong prisoners. While Kahn is
gone, his platoon and others of his company are
overrun, and there are many casualties. To silence
Kahn's complaints about the tactical situation in
which the disaster occurred, he is given an early
discharge. This novel has an interesting subplot
about another officer and his girlfriend at home who
comes under the influence of a professor involved in
the antiwar movement.

177. Karl, S.W. The Last Shall Be First. NY: Manor Books,
         1978. 215 pp. 0-532-15372-3.

The Special Forces are generally thought to have been
the first American troops to serve in Vietnam in any
numbers, and this novel is set among them very early
in the war. Gordon, the hero and virtually the only
significant character, is a draftee who re-enlists in
the Army and joins the Special Forces when Kennedy is
still president. Jump school and other aspects of his
training fill about half the book. Between his first
and second tours in Vietnam, Gordon attends OCS and
receives a commission. Back in Vietnam, he goes on
missions commanded and staffed by South Vietnamese.
When one operation turns into a disaster, Gordon is
blamed, courtmartialed and given a dishonorable
discharge. Then he accepts an offer of employment
with the CIA.

178.   Moore, Robin. Search and Destroy. NY: Condor,
            1978. 316 pp. 78-68007.
        NY: Charter, 1980. 316 pp.

        Marginal for the scope of this bibliography, Search
        and Destroy is included because the first two chapters
        describe a raid into Cambodia during the war by a
        special thousand-man brigade called Wildfire.
        Commanded by Colonel Mike Snyder, the unit penetrates
        twenty miles across the border in a search for the
        elusive headquarters of the VC/NVA. After failing to
        make useful contact with the enemy, the unit is
        disavowed by higher command and must fight its way
        back to Vietnam through ambushes with only the help of
        a renegade fighter pilot who provides air cover.
        Years later, after the war, Snyder and surviving
        Wildfire members both in and out of the service stage
        a complicated robbery of the Houston Astrodome and
        escape to an imaginary South American country.

179.   Nash, Norman Harold. The Last Mission. NY: Vantage,
            1978. 533-03411-6. 141 pp.

        Nash provides a detailed description of a U.S. Air
        Force reconaissance flight out of Thailand. When the
        elderly Lockheed Constellation aircraft fails in
        flight, the crew bails out, and one of them, Sergeant
        John Stern, is captured by the North Vietnamese.
        After a month of relatively mild captivity, he is able
        to escape during an American air strike. Stern walks
        through the jungle until he encounters natives, who
        sell him to friendly South Vietnamese troops. Like
        many subsidized publications, this one could use more
        careful editing. Also, characterization and dialogue
        are rather basic.

180.   O'Brien, Tim. Going After Cacciato. NY: Delacorte/
            Seymour Lawrence, 1978. 77-11723. 338 pp.
            London: Jonathan Cape, 1978. 338 pp.
            NY: Dell, 1979, 1987. 395 pp.
            NY: Delta/Seymour Lawrence, 1979. 338 pp.
            Great Britain: Triad/Granada, 1980.

        This complex novel won a National Book Award in 1978
        and has been very favorably reviewed in major jour-
        nals. Cacciato, an infantryman, walks away from the
        Vietnam battlefield, heading overland for Paris.
        Other members of his platoon pursue him through

Southeast Asia, the Middle East and Europe. Chapters
describing the chase alternate with others that flash
back to realistic infantry action in the war. In
addition to the surface story, the book deals in a
more obscure manner with the effect of war on men and
with human morality.

181. Parker, Gilbert L. Falcons Three. NY: Vantage
        Press, 1978. 154 pp. 553-03585-6.

It is surprising that this modest but adequate novel
could not have found a trade publisher even in 1978.
The story has to do with sergeants who serve in a
Ranger company in 1969. They must contend with a
North Vietnamese unit especially trained to wipe out
American reconaissance units. The author, a retired
Ranger sergeant, knows his characters and their
vocabulary well, and he describes combat with excellent economy of prose. Compared to later exploitative
novels about special operations, this is a welcome,
workmanlike product.

182. Rivers, Gayle and Hudson, James. The Five Fingers.
        Garden City, NY: Doubleday, 1978. 280 pp.
        77-80910.
        NY: Bantam, 1979. 339 pp.
        London: Corgi, 1979, 1985. 316 pp.

The title is the code name for a five-man team of
various nationalities that is infiltrated through Laos
and Vietnam into Southern China in 1969. The first-
person narrative is provided by Warrant Officer
Rivers, who is presumably the author of the same name.
The book is probably "told to" the other author, and
that may account for the awkward phrasing of the
action sequences, e.g., "He was bleeding from every
possible direction." Descriptions of logistics and
equipment throughout are quite detailed, and the
infiltration sequences occupy most of the novel prior
to the chaotic conclusion. At least one of the
authors clearly knows his ground, but the result of
the collaboration is uneven.

183. Sanders, Pamela. Miranda. Boston: Little, Brown,
        1978. 429 pp. 78-18911.

The title of this long and literate novel is the first

name of its heroine, a freelance journalist. The
story moves frequently between the present and the
past, with complicated plots in all times. The
Vietnam sections occur in 1962 and 1963. They appear
to be based on accurate memory of firsthand experience. Moving around in Southeast Asia, Miranda gains
access to American military officers (and to many
other men) by allowing them access to her body. Her
adventures in a mountain Special Forces camp are
supported by careful and detailed cultural background
of the local population. American characters encountered at this early period of the war evince an
aggressive attitude and a belief in eventual victory.

184.   Webb, James. <u>Fields of Fire</u>. Englewood Cliffs, NJ:
        Prentice-Hall, 1978. 344 pp. 78-4046.
        NY: Bantam, 1979. 415 pp.

This painful and realistic account of a Marine
infantry platoon near An Hoa in 1968 is one of the
best novels of the Vietnam War. Webb effectively
relates the experiences, attitudes and relationships
of Marine enlisted men and junior officers. The
dialogue rings true and accurate. The enemies in
numerous small unit actions are both Vietcong and
North Vietnamese regulars. Neither force is elusive;
both are very much in evidence, and the Marines fight
them with competence and professional skill. There
are the usual hostilities between junior enlisted men
and the professional soldiers who command them. Ugly
racial hatred is more apparent in base camp than in
the field. Death, however, is color blind, and by the
end of the book, many of the characters are dead and
others are badly wounded. This is not a pretty story,
but it is an excellent novel.

185.   Werder, Albert D. <u>A Spartan Education</u>. Brooklyn
        Heights, NY: Beekman Publishers, 1978. 251 pp.
        78-7134.

This moving combat novel is set in 1970 among men of a
mechanized infantry company. They fight in the
invasion of Cambodia and later around Tay Ninh City.
Werder evokes the environment of combat well and
writes excellent dialogue. The capable and hardened
young men on the armored personnel carriers do not
enjoy the Vietnam War. They stay stoned when they
can, but they are not incompetent draftees by any

means. Even against a capable enemy on his own
ground, they fight well. Werder's characters are
realized well. The medic, Jameson, is a very heroic
man indeed. This book, like Larry Heinemann's earlier
Close Quarters (166), is a fine story of mechanized
warfare.

1979

186. Avery, Everett. Vietcong Terror Compound. NY: Star
         Distributors, 1979. 180 pp.

      Alice Turney, a nurse at a naval hospital, is captured
      and repeatedly raped by the Vietcong. They take
      special pleasure in debasing her because she is the
      daughter of a U.S. senator. Meanwhile, an enlisted
      Marine has a torrid affair with a beautiful woman
      correspondent. With some effort, the stories are
      brought together.

187. Barfield, H. Eugene. Treachery on the Double. Hicks-
         ville, NY: Exposition Press, 1979. 150 pp.
         0-682-49263-9.

      The literary quality of many Vietnam War novels is not
      particularly high, but this one is almost painful to
      read. Short chapters, a choppy text, superficial
      characters and implausible dialogue combine to
      confuseand bore the reader. Set mostly in Thailand,
      the plot has to do with an attempt by Air Force
      officers and NCOs to stop a drug smuggling operation
      conducted by Chinese and Albanians. Among many low
      points is a lengthy explanation of the supposed
      effects of marijuana that might have been given in a
      grade school classroom sometime in the 1950s. The
      author is clearly a patriotic man who can describe
      Asian and military scenes with some accuracy, but this
      story has neither credibility nor cohesion.

188. Butler, James. Song Vam Sat: River of Death. Reseda,
         CA: Mojave Books, 1979. 115 pp. 0-87881-089-7.

      While it is clear that Butler is not a trained
      novelist, he can certainly tell a good story. The
      main character, Dick Brown, is a career Navy petty
      officer assigned to command a river patrol boat in the
      Mekong Delta in 1968. Brown is a completely human and

sympathetic character, a man who has had both professional and personal setbacks in life. His is a war of
small actions against enemy ambushes from the shore-
line. When he is killed in a disastrous operation
there are not too many people around to miss him.

189. Camper, Frank. The Mission. NY: Manor Books, 1979.
215 pp. 0-532-17243-4.

There is no date for the setting of this story about
an elite team on a secret mission from Vietnam into
Laos. A great many Americans are on hand running the
war. The story is imaginative and competently
plotted. The physical aspects of the review copy are
deplorable, even from a publisher who is not noted for
fine printing. There are numerous misspellings and
other proofreading errors; on some pages, spacing is
so bad it misleads the reader. Clarity of type varies
from pale to smudged, and the bottom edge of the book
is trimmed about ten degrees from true.

190. The Captain's Willing Sex Slaves. NY: Star Distributors, 1979. 180 pp.

The captain of the title is Malone, a Korean War
veteran who has returned to the military because he
likes the brutal life. In what amounts to command of
a Vietnamese rural area, he inflicts various sexual
indignities on whatever women come his way.

191. Cassidy, John. A Station in the Delta. NY: Scribners, 1979. 380 pp. 79-9819.
NY: Ballantine, 1981. 331 pp.

The role of the Central Intelligence Agency was one of
many controversial aspects of the Vietnam War. A
Station in the Delta, written by a former CIA employee, provides an interesting look at how Agency
operations were, or may have been, conducted in
Vietnam. Toby Busch, an experienced agent, takes over
a station in the Mekong Delta and acquires
intelligence that enables him to predict the 1968 Tet
Offensive. However, Busch is unable to move his
information up through channels because of personal
and political problems within the Agency. These
difficulties occupy much of the book, but in the end
Busch emerges as both professionally and personally

heroic. Cassidy makes the point that the Tet Offensive was a military failure for the communists but
that it became a political victory because of misin-
terpretation by the U.S. news media and by civilians
at home.

192.   Certo, Dominic N.   The Valor of Francesco D'Amini.
       NY: Manor Books, 1979.   230 pp.

Certo's competent and interesting story of Marine
infantry deserves better production than in this
paperback. There are numerous spelling and proofreading errors, and the typesetting is so bad that it
distracts attention from the story. There are two
points of view: the first-person narrative of Jason
Davenport and the diary of Francesco D'Amini. Just
before the 1968 Tet Offensive, a Marine platoon works
toward and into a small Vietnamese village. As they
take increasing casualties, the Marines kill one
another in a fight over their treatment of the
villagers. Certo has a powerful intellect and a good
vocabulary. For a first novel, this is a credible
piece of writing.

193.   Derho, John.   The Rocky Road.   San Luis Obispo, CA:
       Man to Man Press, 1979.   202 pp.

Derho provides a central character with the same name
as himself, but he stipulates in a preface that this
is a work of fiction. In fact, it is a mundane story
about a young man coming of age in the 1960s and
1970s. Derho, who is fascinated by Christianity,
basketball and dieting, drops out of Harvard to join
the Army in the late 1960s. As an objector unwilling
to carry weapons, he finds an assignment as a bands-
man. Sent to Vietnam when he has only six months
remaining to serve, Derho stays in rear areas and
provides a good account of a soldier taking a mini-
malist approach to military service. As a veteran,
Derho must contend with throwing off the hated
discipline he learned in the Army. The book trails
off into accounts of half-formed ideas and half-
remembered works of other authors.

194.   French, Robert.   Vietnam: Both Sides.   NY: Manor
       Books, 1979.   220 pp.   0-532-23177-5.

The energetic efforts of Carl Reddin, a football
player, to avoid the draft in 1966 are of no avail.
He is finally captured by the FBI and sent to Vietnam.
There he becomes a renegade and spends three years as
a prisoner of the North Vietnamese. After his release
he becomes an attorney and an FBI agent. None of this
is even marginally realistic, and the very poor
quality of the review copy makes reading difficult.

195. Hasford, Gustav. The Short-Timers. NY: Harper & Row,
        1979.   154 pp.   78-4742.
        Toronto/NY: Bantam, 1980, 1985.   179 pp.

Violence and brutality occur in most Vietnam War
novels, but they predominate utterly in this fastpaced
story of Marine infantrymen set in and around Hue
during what is certainly the 1968 Tet Offensive.
Descriptions of combat are graphic and detailed,
although the extensive use of nicknames and Marine
Corps slang sometimes make the action hard to follow.
The characters are completely brutalized, and death is
everywhere. The narrator, Private Joker, has a fine
eye for detail. The motion picture Full Metal Jacket
is based on this fine novel.

196. Hiler, Craig. Monkey Mountain. NY: Belmont Tower,
        1979.   349 pp.
        NY: Leisure Books, 1983.   349 pp.   0-8439-2065-3.

Near Danang, on Monkey Mountain, the Marines man a
large radar installation. When Corporal Ed Morgan
arrives in 1968, there has been no enemy action
against the site for months, and when he leaves a year
later there has still been virtually none. The war at
Monkey Mountain is between enlisted men, "snuffies,"
and the career officers and NCOs, "lifers." With no
enemy pressure or sense of mission to unite them,
these two groups conflict with each other. There is
some racial violence as well. The lifers invent
useless details and impose military protocol, while
the snuffies goof off, drink, and smoke dope. In one
scene, a Marine captain buys marijuana from an
enlisted man. Morgan is intelligent and competent.
He makes sergeant before the end of his tour, but he
returns to the United States determined to leave the
Marine Corps.

197. James, Allston. Attic Light. Santa Barbara, CA:
          Capra Press, 1979. 96 pp. 78-31541.

      This short book begins in Vietnam when the hero, a
      lieutenant serving as a forward artillery observer, is
      badly wounded in the leg. He comes to growing
      consciousness as he is evacuated through several
      hospitals back to the United States. When the
      lieutenant attempts to resume his former life in an
      unnamed city in the South, he encounters many problems
      adjusting to civilian life. He is alienated from the
      people he loves and from the institutions he under-
      stood before he went to war. After he receives news
      of his best friend's death in Vietnam, he departs for
      Europe.

198. Kim, Samuel. The American POWs. Boston: Branden
          Press, 1979. 273 pp. 77-90036.

      Like its author, the hero of this novel is a Korean-
      American. Much of the book is an unrelenting account
      of deplorable conditions and unspeakable brutality in
      a Vietcong jungle prison camp. With the help of a
      beautiful woman doctor who decides to defect from the
      Vietcong, the hero escapes and returns to an American
      unit after an adventuresome journey through the
      jungle. Both the narration and dialogue are artifi-
      cial and unnecessarily structured. The novel is
      difficult to follow and to believe. Also, there are
      numerous mistakes about weapons and other military
      details.

199. Sadler, Barry. Casca: The Eternal Mercenary. NY:
          Charter, 1979. 246 pp.

      This supernatural story opens in Nha Trang in 1970. A
      wounded Army sergeant in a military hospital begins
      to heal himself of wounds that his doctors believe to
      be fatal. It develops that the sergeant is nothing
      less than an ancient and eternal soldier. As a Roman
      Legionnaire, he thrust his spear into the side of
      Christ on the Cross and was doomed to an everlasting
      life of battle. Most of the action takes place in
      Imperial Rome, and the historical detail is sparse but
      accurate. At the end of the novel, the sergeant and
      all of his records disappear from the hospital in
      Vietnam, and he is seen again fighting in the Israeli
      Army.

1980

200. Alexander, David. When the Buffalo Fight. Richmond,
      Victoria: Hutchinson of Australia, 1980. 236 pp.
      0-09-137280-1.
      NY: Bantam, 1987. 225 pp. 0-553-26448-6. Author
      listed as Lex McAulay on spine.

      The actual deployment of an 800-man Australian
      infantry battalion in 1965/66 provides the basis for
      this unique novel. The Australians are professional,
      long-serving infantrymen. Many have combat experi-
      ence. When they encounter the U.S. Army in Vietnam,
      they are appalled at the Americans' lack of military
      professionalism. What comes from Alexander's attempt
      to create Vietnamese characters is a clear impression
      that the Vietcong are determined and able to win.
      When the Buffalo Fight stands clearly as the Austra-
      lian counterpart of first-rate American novels of
      infantry action.

201. Burke, Martyn. The Laughing War. NY: Doubleday,
      1980. 295 pp. 77-16901.
      NY: Playboy Paperbacks, 1982. 295 pp. 81-84141.

      Barney is a civilian comedian who entertains airborne
      troops around Bien Hoa Airbase in 1967. Audiences of
      enlisted men applaud his ability to draw laughter from
      the tragedy of infantry combat. He is associated with
      a number of highly stylized characters, including a
      fanatical colonel and various lunatic members of the
      International Control Commission. There are no
      quotation marks in this novel with much dialogue, so
      following the story is something of a struggle.
      Ultimately, Barney makes the transition from comedian
      to combatant and takes part in a minor siege just at
      the beginning of the 1968 Tet Offensive.

202. Coleman, Charles. Sergeant Back Again. NY: Harper &
      Row, 1980. 237 pp. 80-7601.

      This intense and serious novel tries too hard to make
      its point. The patients at a military hospital in
      Texas in 1970 must face the prospect of rehabilitation
      or permanent transfer to a mental hospital. Each
      relives his Vietnam experiences. One, Andrew Collins,

served as a surgical technician and mutilated himself
to get out of the war. Collins has also been involved
with an underground GI antiwar organization. Among
the patients who are quite self-conscious about their
mental problems, Collins stands out. He administers a
sort of self-therapy during an illegal leave, but the
ending, like the rest of the book, is confused and
lacking in balance.

203.   De Borchgrave, Arnaud and Moss, Robert. The Spike.
           NY: Crown, 1980. 79-25705.
           NY: Avon, 1981. 458 pp.

Much of this spy thriller is set outside of Vietnam
and after the war, but a substantial segment has to do
with an American reporter on the scene during and
after the Tet Offensive of 1968. Like many other
young members of the antiwar movement, Bob Hockney
confuses his youth, ignorance and physical cowardice
with idealism. His visit to a Vietcong bunker in
Cholon sobers him a little, as does a later experience
with a Marine infantry company that is overrun after a
costly battle. When Hockney goes on to greater
things, he meets another classic character associated
with the war. She is an opportunistic American
actress who has visited Hanoi and given aid and
comfort to the enemy.

204.   Gangemi, Kenneth. The Interceptor Pilot. London:
           Marion Boyars, 1980. 127 pp. 79-56849.

A very potent idea is handled here in an unusual and
unsatisfying style. James Wilson, a Korean War
fighter pilot, is troubled by reports of U.S. bombing
of civilian targets in North Vietnam. Wilson resigns
his reserve commission, leaves his professorship at
the University of Colorado and goes to Russia. There,
he is trained to fly interceptor missions against
American planes over North Vietnam. After some
initial success, Wilson is shot down near Hanoi by a
fighter mission sent from a carrier specifically to
kill him. All of this is told in a literary style so
economical that it is almost barren; it might be notes
for a play or motion picture. Although this may have
some experimental merit, one expects that such prose
is almost as easy to write as it is to read.

205. Johnstone, William W. <u>The Last of the Dog Team</u>. NY:
      Kensington, Zebra, 1980. 345 pp. 0-89083-736-8.

If there is no choice but to read a book about secret
Army killer teams, this one at least has the merit of
unusually good characterization. Anyone who has known
a remorseless killer will recognize Terry Kovacs, a
young man with the right stuff who joins the Army in
the 1950s and serves for about twenty years on the Dog
Team. Terry's travels and adventures, including those
in Vietnam in 1964, are not as plausible as the
character himself. When the U.S. government no longer
finds it fashionable to keep men of his type on the
payroll, Terry winds up as a mercenary in Africa, with
a smile on his face.

206. Kaiko, Takeshi. <u>Into a Black Sun</u>. Translated by
      Cecilia Segawa Seigle. NY: Kodansha Inter-
      national, 1980. 214 pp. 80-50500.

Americans are large, pink and moist in a country of
small, brown, dry Vietnamese. In the eyes of the
narrator of this first-person account, a Japanese
journalist, the war is already lost in 1964. The
Americans are so unsuited to the realities of Asia
that their military cause is doomed, and the South
Vietnamese government is hopelessly corrupt. The
country is at nominal peace most of the time, and the
journalist manages to lead an interesting and essentially civilian life in Saigon. When he visits the
countryside with American advisors and Vietnamese
troops, the descriptions of battle certainly draw
close attention. A competent novel, even in transla-
tion, this represents a singular point of view.

207. Magnuson, Teodore. <u>A Small Gust of Wind</u>. Indianapo-
      lis: Bobbs-Merril, 1980. 403 pp. 80-677.

The American civilian presence in Vietnam during the
war is less well known than the military one. The
characters in this "novel of action and intrigue" are
newsmen, government contract employees and businessmen
who first smuggle gold from Laos into Saigon and later
graduate to moving heroin from Vietnam to the United
States. Their vehicles for this trade are the bodies
of dead American servicemen. Unable to quit while
they are ahead, these amateurs fall afoul of
professional criminals and members of the Vietcong who

soon kill most of them. The story unfolds with a
great deal of dialogue, and that, combined with the
great number of characters, makes it rather hard to
follow. The book is interesting, nonetheless, because
it gives a view of the lives of American civilians in
Saigon during the late 1960s. This is a very different perception of the country from what is usually
received from war novels.

208.   Master Sergeant. NY: Star Distributors, 1980.
            180 pp.

Sergeant Moustaki, a Greek-American serviceman, has
numerous homosexual adventures during training in the
United States. After being sent to Vietnam, Moustaki
is captured by the enemy and held in a jungle camp
where he engages in sex with both inmates and guards.
Eventually, he leads other prisoners in an escape and
is awarded a Congressional Medal of Honor.

209.   McQuinn, Donald E. Targets. NY: Macmillan, 1980.
            499 pp. 79-25493.
            NY: Tor, Tom Doherty, 1983. 512 pp.

Vietnamese characters play a large part in this novel,
which is set in Saigon in 1969. Charles Taylor, a
Marine Corps major near retirement, joins a small
intelligence and security unit that is staffed by
Vietnamese and by Americans from both the Army and the
Marines. The complex plot centers on an attempt to
capture Binh, a gunrunner and black market operator
who supplies American weapons to the Vietcong. The
characters engage in fraud, sabotage, torture and
murder as they pursue Binh and other criminals.
Throughout, there is a sense among them that the war
is already lost. But in the end, Taylor causes Binh
to be captured through the employment of a cruel but
effective ruse. Taylor leaves Vietnam for retirement
in America. There are few scenes of combat in the
field; instead, the book describes much of the
civilian and rear echelon environment in Vietnam.

210.   Moore, Elizabeth Sims. Bend with the Wind. Port
            Washington, NY: Ashley Books, 1980. 281 pp.

It is only 1962 when Marty Fountain, a surgical nurse,
arrives in Vietnam, but there are already many

American military and civilian personnel on hand. She
works in a provincial hospital, near an American
military base. As usual in novels about nurses, Marty
finds a handsome doctor for a love interest, and she
has unlikely adventures with the Vietcong. There are
substantial medical details, and the book conveys a
good sense of life in a hospital in the tropics.

211. Naparsteck, M.J. War Song. NY: Leisure Books, 1980.
206 pp.

The cover blurb calls this "a woeful ballad," and it
is indeed that. Michael Cull, a twenty-year-old
soldier, is assigned as a guard at Phu Nam. He lives
in a hotel in Saigon and rides a bus to work. His
main interest is a love affair with En, a Vietnamese
bargirl, but he breaks off with her after suspecting
that her only interest in him is as a ticket to the
United States. In a Vietcong attack, Cull is slightly
wounded. At the hospital, he takes advantage of being
confused with another, more gravely wounded soldier
and manages an illegal flight to Hawaii. From there,
he deserts, taking a civilian flight home and then
hitching a ride for Canada. He thinks that his
reasons for desertion have nothing to do with patriotism or cowardice. It is simply that the war does
not make sense to him.

212. Saigon Hell Hole. NY: Star Distributors, 1980.
180 pp.

Betty Wriley is an Army nurse in Vietnam in 1968.
Unfortunately, she and some other American women are
captured by the Vietcong. Most of the book is filled
with details of various sexual tortures to which the
women are subjected. After she is rescued, Betty
enjoys an interlude with one of her rescuers before
they are both killed.

213. Slave of the Cong. Star Distributors, 1980. 180 pp.

An American woman reporter, captured by the Vietcong,
is raped and tortured. Back in the United States,
another woman dreams accurately of the reporter's
plight and flies to Vietnam to rescue her. The second
woman is captured, and there is more sex and violence
until both are rescued.

214. Wessler, David. Half a World Away. NY: Vantage,
         1980. 96 pp. 79-63137.

      Wessler describes an infantryman's war at the time of
      the 1968 Tet Offensive. His first-person narrator has
      a good eye for military detail, but there is really
      too little plot here for a novel. It is interesting
      that Vantage would bring out a title like this as late
      as 1980.

                              1981

215. Baker, Richard E. Feast of Epiphany. Tacoma, WA:
         Rapier Press, 1981. 186 pp. 80-85403.

      The dust wrapper offers the information that this book
      should be "learned not understood." That is no doubt
      good advice, because a single careful reading produces
      little or no understanding of the author's plot or
      purposes. The characters are enlisted men in the 4th
      Infantry Division band who serve as infantry around
      Pleiku in what seems to be 1966. There is no sense of
      the general tactical situation, and the men function
      more as a loose gang than as members of an organized
      military unit. There are occasions of crucifixion and
      homosexuality, as well as a bit of combat and a
      lengthy report of a leave in Hong Kong. Difficulty in
      following the book is exacerbated by spelling and
      grammatical errors and by extremely poor reproduction.
      Baker clearly has something to say about the war, but
      he does not say it clearly. The book would have been
      much improved by better editing.

216. Buonanno, C. Beyond the Flag. NY: Tower Books, 1981.
         192 pp. 0-505-51616-0.
         NY: Leisure Books, n.d. 192 pp. 0-8439-2374-1.

      Buonanno's characters deliver some of the best lines
      in any Vietnam novel. The dialogue is tight, capable
      and unpredictable. There are a number of British
      associations in the book. At one point, an Australian
      regular officer acquires command of a joint ARVN-
      Marine patrol and behaves in a manner that surprises
      the Marines. There is action throughout this account
      of the Combined Action Program in Quang Tri Province
      in 1969, but this is much more than a relentless
      combat novel. Poor editing and proofreading are

all the more to be regretted in such an otherwise
satisfying book.

217.   Butler, Robert Olen. The Alleys of Eden. NY: Horizon
           Press, 1981. 256 pp. 81-82842.
           NY: Ballantine, 1983. 246 pp.

This fascinating novel follows an Army deserter and
his Vietnamese girlfriend from the fall of Saigon to
a new life in the United States. The first half of
the book, dealing with the fall of the city and the
evacuation of Americans, is vivid and gripping.
Later, in a small Illinois city, the couple attempts
to establish a new life based on a false identity for
the man. After he foolishly reveals his presence in
the country to his American ex-wife, Army authorities
close in and the book ends as he departs for Canada.

218.   Fleming, Thomas. Officers' Wives. Garden City, NY:
           Doubleday, 1981. 645 pp. 80-1063.
           NY: Warner Books, 1982. 715 pp.

Fleming writes with assurance and familiarity about
military subjects as he describes the lives of four
West Point graduates and their wives from 1950 through
1975. A substantial part of the book is set in Saigon
in 1963 and 1964, and it deals with U.S. Army
officers and their dependents during the overthrow of
the Diem government. There are realistic scenes of
terrorist attacks on American civilians, including one
in which a little girl is killed. The male characters
argue various points of view about the Vietnam War and
convey the impression that many professional soldiers
thought the war was lost as early as the mid-1960s.
The book also describes rather despicable acts against
military wives and children in the U.S. performed by
members of the antiwar movement.

219.   Hathaway, Bo. A World of Hurt. NY: Taplinger,
           1981. 318 pp. 80-18147.
           NY: Avon, 1984. 294 pp.

During the Johnson administration, two men, Madsen and
Sloane, are drafted and meet during Army training.
Although neither of them has much respect for military
values, they volunteer for the Special Forces. After
training, they are sent to a small camp outside of Nha

Trang. They are sympathetic to the Montagnard troops but are contemptuous of the other Vietnamese, who seem little interested in fighting. There is some combat, but no sense that a victory can be achieved. At the end of the book, they are near the end of their Army tours, and both of them are bitter about the experience.

220. Hughes, Frank. _Everyday Heroes_. NY: Leisure Books, 1981. 310 pp.

In contrast to the important role played by carrier based pilots in the war, there is little imaginative writing about them. Accordingly, _Everyday Heroes_ is welcome because it gives a complete view of carrier flight operations in 1966. The _Shangri-La_ is a small, reconditioned, World War II carrier from which Lt. Jim Howard and other pilots in his squadron fly missions against ground targets in North Vietnam and in support of American troops in the south. Aircraft, other equipment and combat flights are all described very fully. Training, family matters and leaves fill about half the book, and some attention is given to the effect of the antiwar movement on pilots' wives. Inaccuracies in spelling, italicization, capitalization, acronyms and printing detract marginally from an adequate novel of Navy pilots at war.

221. Kalb, Bernard and Kalb, Marvin. _The Last Ambassador_. Boston: Little, Brown, 1981. 276 pp. 81-8259. NY: Charter Books, 1984. 276 pp.

The authors bring a wealth of experience in Vietnam to this novel of the fall of Saigon in 1975. Hadden Walker, the last American ambassador to South Vietnam, believes that American honor and policy will best be served by continuing support of the South Vietnamese government. To achieve his ends, he acts contrary to official policy of the United States and, indeed, contrary to the facts. Unfortunately for Walker, the communist military forces are too strong and the ARVN is too weak to change history. In the chaos of the last days of the American embassy, his attempts tonegotiate with the North Vietnamese are futile and he cannot force the hand of the American president. In the end, he is evacuated against his will. A surprise climax adds little to this engrossing story.

222. Linn, Bill. <u>Missing in Action</u>. NY: Avon, 1981.
      220 pp. 80-68427.
      London: Sphere Books, 1983. 220 pp.

In 1973 or 1974, very near the end of the war, Army
Sp4 William Tompkins is captured and taken to a prison
compound in North Vietnam. There, he endures star-
vation, overwork, brutality and torture. There is no
sense that any clandestine network of American
communication or command operates among the prisoners,
and Tompkins is often left alone with his fears.
Eventually, he establishes friendly contact with the
camp commander, an aging graduate of an American
university, and this individual takes Tompkins south
with the final North Vietnamese invasion. After
reaching Saigon, Tompkins escapes and makes his way
aboard one of the last American helicopters leaving
the country. After reaching safety, he has fond
memories of the old man who helped him escape.

223. Naparsteck, M.J. <u>A Hero's Welcome</u>. NY: Leisure
      Books, 1981. 282 pp.

The central character is a Vietnam novelist, Culver
Orbanski. As a young college student, Culver finds
and loses a lady and is subsequently so disheartened
that he flunks out of Columbia. Drafted and sent to
Vietnam as an infantryman, Culver unwisely charges a
sniper on his first patrol and suffers a wound that
causes the loss of his right hand. On the evacuation
helicopter, he is wounded again, losing his right eye.
Culver suffers several lost, alcoholic years as a
veteran before developing his skills as a serious
novelist. Many years after the war, he meets and
seduces the daughter of his now-deceased first love.

224. Nelson, Charles. <u>The Boy Who Picked the Bullets Up</u>.
      NY: Morrow, 1981. 420 pp. 81-9438.
      NY: Avon, 1982. 358 pp.

Kurt Strom is a Navy medic serving with the Marines in
Vietnam in 1966 and 1967. Strom, a homosexual, tells
the story of his service in letters home to several
friends. His work as a medic involves some of the
bloodiest and most realistic action in any Vietnam War
novel. There are also frequent accounts of sexual
activities that suggest that homosexualty was at least
on the scene among American forces in Vietnam. Strom

is wounded twice, and when he returns home he is
addicted to morphine. Nelson is an able writer. This
is a book with a unique point of view.

225. Rollins, Kelly. Fighter Pilots. Boston: Little,
     Brown, 1981. 308 pp. 81-5978.

John Copley begins his career flying P-51s over
Germany in World War II and ends up flying F-105s over
North Vietnam. This account of the career of a
professional Air Force officer includes peacetime
assignments and many colorful pilots. The Vietnam
segments occur in 1966 and 1967 when Copley is
actually based in Thailand. As a lieutenant colonel,
he flies less frequently than lower ranking pilots,
but there are several realistic scenes of air combat.
As in many Air Force novels, aircraft are more fully
realized characters than enlisted airmen.

226. Teed, Jack Hamilton. Gunships #1: The Killing Zone.
     NY: Kensington, Zebra, 1981. 254 pp.
     0-8217-1130-X.

In general, series novels are pretty poor stuff. This
one is peopled with a heroic Special Forces colonel,
corrupt American and Vietnamese officers, a dirty
dozen or so of military criminals turned into an elite
strike team and the inevitable cool black dude. In
what seems to be 1968, the colonel, John Hardin,
survives the crash of a booby trapped helicopter and
successfully resists torture by North Vietnamese in a
Laotian village. The strike team, which had been
sent to kill him, undergoes a change in leadership and
joins him in the village where they withstand attack
for a considerable period by a much larger number of
the enemy. Finally, they are rescued in time for
Hardin to return to Vietnam and murder his nemesis, a
criminal American general officer.

227. Viet Cong Torture Camp. NY: Star Distributors, 1981.
     180 pp.

A group of female American entertainers is captured by
the Vietcong. They suffer detailed sexual and
physical abuse until they are rescued by an American
narcotics agent.

228. Wizard, Brian. <u>Permission to Kill: Viet Nam '68-'69</u>.
      Australia: The Starquill Publisher, c1981, 1985.
      415 pp. 0-949702-01-3.

Despite production and proofreading problems, this is
an engrossing novel of helicopter warfare. Wizard
served as a doorgunner in Tay Ninh Province in 1967
and 1968. In a barely fictionalized account of that
service, he provides a thorough picture of active
combat in support of ground operations. Relationships
among pilots and crew are particularly interesting
because these dangerous young men repect each other's
abilities. Photographs and some songs seem to be
included from the first edition, which may be a
substantially different book. It was not seen for
this bibliography.

                          1982

229. Anderson, Robert A. <u>Cooks and Bakers</u>. NY: Avon, 1982.
      205 pp. 81-66472.

Problems of command and control occupy much of the
attention of the young Marine infantry lieutenant who
is the main character here. The lieutenant has a few
months to learn his job, making mistakes as he goes
along, before he is given charge of a platoon of
noncombatant troops--cooks and bakers--in the 1968
battle for Hue. In the chaotic circumstances of
combat, men die foolishly, and some of the lieutenant's men die or are wounded before he can learn
their names. Nonetheless, Marine discipline asserts
itself, and the lieutenant and his very provisional
platoon play their part in the eventual allied
victory. As in many accounts of this battle, there is
lively speculation about the lack of air and artillery
support. This is an excellent, tightly written
account of what a junior officer actually does in
combat.

230. <u>Bound Captive</u>. NY: Star Distributors, 1982. 180 pp.

A well known homosexual author, Garrett Smalley,
explains to an interviewer how he grew up, discovered
his sexual orientation and enlisted in the Marines in
1965. In Vietnam, he serves first in Danang and later
on operations as a squad leader. He participates in

the rape of some Vietnamese male prisoners and enjoys
other homosexual encounters.

231.   Del Vecchio, John M. The 13th Valley. Toronto/NY:
         Bantam, 1982. 606 pp. 81-70920.
         NY: Bantam, 1983. 666 pp.
         London: Sphere Books, 1983. 606 pp.

       Contrary to what the hyperbole of advertisements and
       reviews would lead one to believe, The 13th Valley is
       not a new dimension of human experience. It is,
       however, an excellent story of Army infantry in combat
       that deserves to stand in the first rank of Vietnam
       War novels, beside, but not above, works by such
       authors as Webb, Heinemann, Hasford, Nelson and
       others. Extensive auxiliary notes explain the basis
       of the story in a real operation by units of the 101st
       Airborne Division in the Khe Ta Laou Valley in 1970.
       There are maps, a glossary and even a chronology of
       Vietnamese history. Huge size allows for immense
       detail that is never boring. Del Vecchio, in this
       first novel, handles characterization and dialogue
       well, and he certainly knows about this particular
       piece of the war in Vietnam.

232.   Doolittle, Jerome. The Bombing Officer. NY: Dutton,
         1982. 225 pp. 82-5136.

       In 1971, the mission of U.S. forces in Laos is to put
       pressure on the Pathet Lao and North Vietnamese Army
       so that, in turn, those forces will be able to exert
       less pressure on the Americans and ARVN in South
       Vietnam. Fred Upson is a member of the U.S. diplo-
       matic staff in Laos whose duty is to coordinate air
       strikes on Laotian territory with the U.S. Air Force.
       Upson becomes disillusioned when he learns of frequent
       U.S. bombing of civilian targets. He releases
       detailed information about these strikes to an
       American newspaperman and plans to quit the diplomatic
       service.

233.   Grey, Anthony. Saigon. Boston/Toronto: Little,
         Brown, 1982. 789 pp. 82-14025.
         London: Weidenfeld & Nicolson, 1982. 789 pp.
         NY: Dell, 1983. 750 pp.

       This attempt to tell the whole story of modern Vietnam

in one huge novel is quite successful. Grey combines
careful historical accuracy with a continuing group of
characters in Vietnam between 1925 and 1975. He
represents the opinions and activities of most
important factions and individuals, and he provides
only slightly fictionaliized accounts of most major
events, including many that occurred before Americans
became involved in the country. Especially notable is
the specificity with which he describes the horrid
human brutality that was a feature of much Vietnamese
history. Grey also knows something about military
operations, relationships and weapons, and his
accuracy in these matters is reassuring. Saigon is
well worth the long, careful reading it requires.

234. Just, Ward. In the City of Fear. NY: Viking, 1982.
        291 pp. 82-70130.

Enough of In the City of Fear is set in Vietnam to
qualify it for inclusion in this bibliography, but it
is essentially a classic novel of Washington insiders.
The characters are soldiers, politicians, bureaucrats,
journalists and spies, and the time appears to be at
the end of the Johnson administration. There are
numerous subplots, and the complicated story moves
fluidly back and forth through time as it describes
political maneuvering around a plan to win the Vietnam
War by technology. The idea, which appears in Just's
earlier Stringer (134), is to plant sensing devices
along enemy infiltration routes. Sam Joyce, an army
colonel with four tours in Vietnam, is wanted by the
President to run the operation, but it is first
necessary to kill an investigation of him for misap-
propriating funds on an earlier tour. Joyce had been
in command of a camp of forty Americans and various
numbers of Vietnamese who ran intelligence gathering
missions on and beyond the borders of Vietnam, and he
had used official funds liberally to entertain his
troops. A great deal about Washington personalities
and their use of power and influence is revealed as
the plans emerge for the new operation.

235. Meyer, Ted. Body Count. Smithtown, NY: Exposition
        Press, 1982. 166 pp.

In 1970, near the Cambodian border, Army infantrymen
are disillusioned by a war that seeks only high body
counts. Some escape by wounding themselves. Three

others--a lieutenant, a sergeant and a young enlisted
man--are initially better motivated and eventually
quite capable. Bitterness sets in when two of them
are wounded and the scene shifts to the VA hospital
system. There the men encounter a bloated, unfeeling
and incompetent bureaucracy that seems to be an
extension of the worst they knew in the Army. After
considerable victimization, the veterans conspire to
introduce poison into the coffee at a large veterans'
hospital. In that way they kill 148 persons and
achieve a notable body count.

236. Pfarrer, Donald. <u>Neverlight</u>. NY: Seaview Books,
          1982. 283 pp. 81-84777.
          NY: Dell, Laurel, 1984. 288 pp.

The use of naval gunfire to support land operations
was a feature of the Vietnam War that is not well
known to most Americans. This novel explains how that
fire was directed and adjusted by Richard Vail, a Navy
lieutenant working with Marine infantry in 1965 and
1966. There are several good scenes about the impact
and effect of naval gunnery directed against enemy
troops. Vail is a potentially interesting person,
with a background as an exploration geologist, but he
is not well crafted as a character. He is still much
of a mystery to the reader when, near the end of the
novel, he is killed in combat. Alternate chapters
describe the life and thoughts of his wife in the
United States as she waits for him and later deals
with his death.

237. Powell, Hollis C. <u>The River Rat</u>. Smithtown, NY:
          Exposition Press, 1982. 218 pp. 82-90279.

Subsidy or "vanity" publishers are often the last
resort of marginal authors, so it is surprising to
find this quite credible piece of fiction under the
imprint of Exposition Press. The story is set in what
may be 1969 and has to do with the men on an Army
landing craft that carries supplies in the Saigon and
Mekong rivers. The central character is the commanding officer, Warrant Officer Herb Poole, a
military problem child who is a competent soldier but
also an insubordinate brawler. There are excellent
scenes of small boat operations and occasional combat,
but the main story has to do with a long-running feud
between Poole and a superior officer. Powell does an

especially good job of conveying the attitude of a man
who has an assured ability with his fists. That does
Poole no good ultimately, but the nature of his end
comes as no surprise to an attentive reader.

238. Powers, Charles. <u>A Matter of Honor</u>. NY: First East
       Coast Theater & Pub., 1982. 154 pp. 0-910829-
       03-9.

Robert Stokes is an eighteen-year-old airborne infantryman when he arrives in Vietnam in 1965. There
is an atmosphere of expectancy in the country as the
American buildup begins. Stokes, unaccountably, is
assigned to a cavalry unit. He is a member of a
special "LORP" squad that fights such enemies as
Vietnamese "zappers" who plant explosives on American
bases. After a year of aimless battles and guard
duty, Stokes returns to the United States on a direct
flight to Ft. Dix, New Jersey. Then he heads toward
home in North Carolina, proud to have done his
patriotic duty. The review copy of this book is
characterized by uneven printing that distracts the
reader.

239. <u>Rear Attack</u>. NY: Star Distributors, 1982. 180 pp.

Sergeant Butch Brannigan, a huge man in his forties,
runs the Blowtorch Brigade, a small infantry unit that
is in frequent combat with the enemy. The time might
be the late 1960s. Military details are preposterous,
but that does not matter because the plot serves only
as filler between lengthy accounts of homosexual rape
and consensual sex. The men take particular pleasure
in victimizing a new second lieutenant.

240. Reisner, Jack. <u>The Last Hope</u>. Honolulu: Cellar Mead,
       1982. 287 pp. 83-061200.

Reisner, an Air Force lieutenant colonel, commanded
the Joint Personnel Recovery Center in Saigon in 1967
and 1968. His novel is based on that experience. The
unit directed all activities to recapture American
prisoners. In fiction, it is quite successful.
Reisner describes not only the operations and missions
that were undertaken, but also the infighting among
various military and civilian services associated with
the Center. There is good material about the theory

and practice of escape and some awkward dialog that
sounds too much like a military manual. The author is
unequivocal about the harm done to prisoners by the
activities of American antiwar personalities.

241. Saigon Memoirs. NY: Star Distributors, 1982.
         180 pp.

Dan Nordheim has a pleasant encounter with another
Army lieutenant on his first night in Saigon. After a
little whiskey and marijuana, they enjoy homosexual
sex. It is Dan's first encounter of many. His job in
communications keeps him well away from the war.

242. Saigon Orphan's Torment. NY: Star Distributors, 1982.

A young Vietnamese girl is forced to submit in detail
to the numerous sexual requirements of American
servicemen. There are some occasional military
events, but not enough to amount to a plot. The girl
survives the war and opens an orphanage.

243. Scofield, Jonathan. Freedom Fighters #15: Junglefire.
         NY: Dell, 1982. 318 pp. 0-440-04163-5.

Apparently, fourteen previous novels in this "Freedom
Fighter" series have chronicled the contributions of
the Hunter family to earlier American wars. In this
one, Captain Jack Hunter serves in Phu Bien, Vietnam,
in 1969 as a helicopter pilot. Hunter is sincere,
thoughtful about the war, brave, loving and competent.
He must contend with an insane, careerist commanding
officer and a Vietnamese couple that seems to be
inspired by Marshall Ky and his wife. Hunter manages
to inflict considerable damage on the legendary
headquarters of the Vietcong in the Parrot's Beak area
and to survive a court martial. After coming through
all that, he finds solace in the arms of a beautiful
nurse.

244. Teed, Jack Hamilton. Gunships #2: Fire Force. NY:
         Kensington, Zebra, 1982. 253 pp.
         London: Star Books, 1982.

Heroic, capable Colonel John Hardin, who was introduced in the first novel in this series, The Killing

Zone (226), is back for more of the same. When he
appears in Fire Force, he beats up a Marine sergeant
in a Saigon bar. The fight takes up most of five
pages in the novel. With Hardin on this new adventure
are members of his killer team, "dregs from the
dirtiest brigs in Nam, none of whom were supposed to
make it back alive." In this lurid, overwritten
story, Hardin's team locates and defeats a group of
Army deserters that has been staging successful
attacks on Special Forces camps.

245. Viet Cong Rape Compound. NY: Star Distributors, 1982.

Readers are asked to believe that "a whole chopper
load of radical lesbian types...on an illegal fact
finding tour" of Vietnam are captured by Vietcong.
The meaningless sexual encounters that follow are
better ignored than read.

246. Viet Cong Victims. NY: Star Distributors, 1982.

Sean, a young liberal journalist, leaves his wife in
the United States in order to cover the Vietnam War.
After arriving, he has many homosexual encounters with
American servicemen. Then he is captured by the
Vietcong and has more. Sean survives everything and
returns to the U.S.

247. Walsh, Patricia L. Forever Sad the Hearts. NY: Avon,
      1982. 385 pp. 81-65070.

American women are underrepresented in Vietnam War
fiction, both as authors and characters. Because so
many nurses were on the scene, it is fitting that this
able and interesting novel is by and about a nurse.
In Da Nang in 1967, Kate Shea works in a civilian
hospital. The human and medical conditions are
appalling. Even when the staff can find the correct
medicines and equipment, patients are returned to a
life so unsanitary and filthy that most die anyway.
Walsh comments on aspects of life and war in Vietnam
that many male authors miss, and she writes dialogue
well. Relentless socializing and sex occupy the
characters' time when they are not attending to
medical duties, and these are not the most successful
topics in the novel.

248.   Winn, David. _Gangland_. NY: Knopf, 1982. 226 pp.
          81-18577.

       Different readers will find the loose disarray of
       settings, characters and fragments of plot in _Gangland_
       either charming or unnecessarily bothersome. The
       story, to the extent one is discernible, has to do
       with Dunkle, a Vietnam veteran, coming to terms with
       college life in Northern California in what seems to
       be 1975. He is surrounded and bewildered by numerous
       characters and comic student groups and social
       organizations. The reader cannot help but share
       Dunkle's confusion. Some of the satire of counter-
       culture institutions is quite on target. A substan-
       tial section in the middle of the book takes Dunkle
       back to Vietnam in what is probably 1969, where he is
       a sergeant in some sort of Army electronic or com-
       munication facility in Long Pig Province. The base
       comes under attack, and there is a helicopter evacua-
       tion. Some characters from the war, including a best
       buddy, a civilian advisor and a colonel, infest
       Dunkle's life later in California, where he turns his
       electronic training to the pirating of cable tele-
       vision signals.

                              1983

249.   Arnold, William. _China Gate_. NY: Villard, 1983.

       Most of this book about American criminals is set in
       Taiwan. The characters are frequently in Vietnam
       because the war represents a great opportunity for
       criminal enterprise. They regularly use U.S. govern-
       ment aircraft to ship narcotics to California. There
       is also an account of a unit of Taiwanese volunteers
       commanded by an American civilian. These old Asian
       crooks take a long view of history, and they see the
       Vietnam War as a major step in America's failed Far
       Eastern policy. Always pragmatic, they are able to
       come to terms with the new communist masters of
       Vietnam and China.

250.   Cain, Jonathan. _Saigon Commandos_. NY: Kensington,
          Zebra, 1983. 462 pp.

       The title is the derogatory term used by field
       soldiers to refer to rear echelon troops. The
       military police in this story accept the term with

pride as they have relentless adventures in Saigon in 1967. Cain is a competent novelist, and he evokes the dangerous, crime ridden environment of the city well. Most of the numerous characters are military police enlisted men, but there are also several Vietnamese, including a prostitute who emasculates the American troops who purchase her favors. For all of its good qualities, the book is little more than a macho police fantasy in which the good guys kill the bad guys with impunity. The military policemen regard themselves as a special breed and share little common humanity with the people they treat so brutally.

251. Cain, Jonathan. _Saigon Commandos #2: Code Zero: Shots Fired!_ NY: Kensington, Zebra, 1983. 285 pp.

These are the continued adventures of Sergeant Mark Stryker and his fellow military policemen in Saigon. Events and characters are continued with no apparent delay from the first book in the series. These fellows are never happier than when racing through Saigon with their lights flashing and sirens screaming. Central to the plot in this episode is an American military policeman who is actually a Russian agent.

252. Caputo, Philip. _DelCorso's Gallery_. NY: Holt, Rinehart and Winston, 1983. 352 pp. 83-156. NY: Dell, 1984. 352 pp.

When Nick DelCorso visits Vietnam in 1975, he is already an old hand, having served there in the 101st Airborne in 1966 and later as a civilian news photographer. Nick photographs the death throes of the ARVN. A year later, he leaves his wife, childrenand a good civilian career to work in Beirut and his luck runs out. Caputo brings his places to life, and he knows about brave, careful men. The comparison of the Vietnam War to the Lebanese civil war will fascinate some readers, as will the journalist's point of view. This is first-rate fiction.

253. Carroll, John. _Token Soldiers_. Boronia, Australia: Wildgrass Books, 1983. 261 pp. 0-908069-09-X.

The members of an Australian infantry platoon around whom this story is built feel that they are token

soldiers in an American war. They do not, however,
fight token battles. In one long patrol that occupies
most of the book, they see a great deal of action and
suffer many casualties. The Australians are not
supported with artillery and aircraft like Americans,
and they are especially short of helicopters. They do
have their share of crazy men and brutal killers.
Indeed, all standard infantry types are present, and
the close combat is utterly ugly.

254. Durand, Loup. The Angkor Massacre. NY: Morrow, 1983.
          476 pp. 82-18818.

The central characters in this long, complex novel are
an American woman and her French-Cambodian husband.
Most events occur in Cambodia between 1970 and 1975,
but a substantial subplot has to do with Americans in
Vietnam. Early in the book, an American deserter is
extracted from a criminal underground in Saigon by
various Corsican, Chinese and Vietnamese operatives
and smuggled to Cambodia. Later he is transported on
a Norwegian freighter to Stockholm, where he begins a
new life in a country that accepts Vietnam deserters
as heroes. Near the end of the book, another character is caught up in the evacuation of the American
embassy in Saigon in 1975.

255. Faherty, Pat. The Fastest Truck in Vietnam. San
          Francisco, CA: Pull/Press, 1983. 150 pp.

Private Piper, a Marine Corps truck driver, earns the
nickname Crash shortly after arriving at a missile
base near Danang in 1968. Since the enemy has no
ground-attack aircraft, there is nothing to do at the
base and it attracts failures and misfits among whom
Crash fits perfectly. There is no sign of either the
Vietcong or North Vietnamese Army, the jungle is not
much of a problem in the relatively urbanized area and
even career NCOs and officers are generally in the
background. All there is for Crash and his buddies to
do is drink, smoke dope, pursue Vietnamese whores and
misuse vehicles. Crash has a great deal of fun doing
all of these things, and he develops something of a
mean streak before he goes home thirteen months later.

256. Heffernan, William. The Corsican. NY: Simon &
          Schuster, 1983. 82-19613. 423 pp.

A frequent theme in this genre is the inability of
Americans, as latecomers, to understand the complex
realities of Vietnam. That idea is expressed better
in The Corsican than in many other books. It is a
very complex tale whose main character is Peter
Bently, an American intelligence officer arriving in
Vietnam in 1966. Bently is the grandson of a Corsican
criminal who has operated a large opium smuggling
enterprise in Southeast Asia since 1946. Bently's
divided loyalties affect his operations among criminals, American military personnel, ARVN personnel,
Vietcong agents and other varied individuals in Saigon
and elsewhere. Official American ideas and activities
are almost childlike andcertainly ineffectual in the
Vietnamese environment of multiple plots and
relationships. No novel of drugs in Vietnam, this one
included, would be complete without some reference to
the use of coffins to transport heroin to the United
States.

257.   Hunt, Greg. _Mission to Darkness_. NY: Dell/Banbury,
        1983. 344 pp. 0-440-05466-4.

Lily Stratton, a pretty young newspaper reporter, is
in and out of South Vietnam in the 1960s. She is
first there in 1963 and observes the coup that ended
the Diem government. She returns to be at Da Nang and
Hue for the 1968 Tet Offensive and finally she comes
back in 1969 for the last time. Lily is able to
obtain restricted information from just about anyone,
and she participates in a startling variety of
adventures. In the last one, she is evacuated under
fire from a remote base near the Laotian border. The
helicopter in which she is a passenger is shot down,
and she is the only survivor. She happens to be found
by a small, long-range patrol commanded by an old
friend and accompanies the unit on its mission to
attack a secret North Vietnamese headquarters. When
that undertaking ends in disaster, she evacuates the
only survivor by raft to the nearest American unit.

258.   Meier, John. _The American Imperialist_. NY: Vantage,
        1983. 109 pp. 82-90432.

Air America, the CIA airline, makes fleeting appear-
ances in Vietnam literature, but this is the only
novel to feature one of its pilots as a main character. Bob Richardson, a civilian pilot, flies military

missions in Vietnam and Laos in the early 1960s.
Richardson is a Korean War veteran and an idealist.
He knows he is killing people for money. In Laos, he
is captured by the Pathet Lao and escapes with the
help of a beautiful nurse. Later, he is killed on a
futile mercy flight. Meier's text has the usual
shortcomings of a subsidy publication.

259. Miller, Kenn. <u>Tiger the Lurp Dog</u>. Boston: Little,
          Brown, 1983. 214 pp. 83-11364.
          NY: Ballantine, 1984. 245 pp.

Lurps are long-range reconaissance patrols put out by
an airborne infantry brigade to monitor enemy movements. They are run by experienced sergeants who lead
capable, gung-ho enlisted men. Everyone is
motivated, serious and realistic as they go about
their terrifying and careful tasks. Miller excellently conveys the spirit and personalities of his
characters, who represent the best and craziest
tradition of the Airborne, and he gives meticulous
detail about their organization, operations and
equipment. Tiger, the Lurp dog, is a Vietnamese mutt
that does not accompany the men on patrols but
nonetheless has a few adventures of his own. This is
a very good war novel.

260. <u>Nam Recruit</u>. NY: Star, 1983. 170 pp.

Set among Marines on an outpost near Khe Sahn, this
novel features nonstop homosexual rape and consensual
sex. There are also flashbacks to similar events when
the characters were in high school. The perfunctory
plot is about an enemy attack. It is interesting that
a market exists for such material so long after the
war.

261. <u>Pilot Torture</u>. NY: Star Distributors, 1983. 170 pp.

See annotation for <u>Viet Cong Prisoner</u> (264).

262. Proffitt, Nicholas. <u>Gardens of Stone</u>. NY: Carroll &
          Graf, 1983. 373 pp. 83-7618.
          NY: Tor, 1984, 1987. 446 pp.

Career NCOs, "lifers," are often objects of contempt

and ridicule in Vietnam novels. In contrast, Proffitt portrays senior sergeants in an honor guard unit at Arlington National Cemetery, the gardens of stone, as sensitive, capable professional soldiers. As they bury the dead from Vietnam during the late 1960s, these hard, honest men react to the military and political events of those times. While the main character is an experienced sergeant, the tragic hero is a young corporal who realizes his ambition to attend Officer Candidate School. He then volunteers for Vietnam, where he is killed. When his body isreturned to Arlington, his old friends bury him. Persons who do not understand why anyone would love the Army might learn something about that from this excellent novel.

263.   Tran Van Dinh. <u>Blue Dragon, White Tiger</u>. Philadel-
       phia: TriAm Press, 1983. 334 pp. 0-914075-00-4.

Like its author, the central character of this fascinating novel is a westernized Vietnamese intellectual. In 1967, Minh leaves a university position in the United States and returns to Vietnam. After initial contacts with the Saigon government and American advisors, Minh joins the National Liberation Front. The account of his life and thoughts as a member of the winning side in the Vietnam War stands in intriguing contrast to American perspectives. Minh is a Buddhist, and his story ends where it began. By 1978 he is disillusioned with communism and manages to return to the United States. <u>Blue Dragon, White Tiger</u> is a significant contribution to Vietnam War literature.

264.   <u>Viet Cong Prisoners</u>. NY: Star Distributors, 1983.
       170 pp. Bound with <u>Combat Buddy</u>.

In a style of publication not often seen, <u>Viet Cong Prisoners</u> is bound with another novel of homosexual sadism, <u>Combat Buddy</u>. The latter novel is set in World War II. In the Vietnam story, a reconaissance patrol of Army troops is captured by the Vietcong. The men are sexually assaulted. Some measure of the style of the book may be taken from the final scene in which the chief captor, Colonel Coc, orders one of the prisoners to have sex with his empty eye socket.

265. Vietcong Rape Raiders. NY: Star Distributors, 1983.
          170 pp.

      Isabel Hill is a nurse at an Army compound near
      Vietnam's borders with Cambodia and Laos. She has a
      good deal of sex with other Americans. Later she is
      captured by the Vietcong and sexually tormented by Po,
      a former exchange student she had known in the U.S.

266. Viet Cong Slave Camp. NY: Star Distributors, 1983.
          170 pp.

      Some attempt is made here to construct a novel in
      order to provide context for abundant explicit sex.
      Heather Michaels is an Australian nurse. She works
      for several months in a hospital in Vietnam, enjoying
      incessant sex with collegues of both sexes. When the
      hospital is captured, Heather and another nurse are
      taken prisoner and forced to perform all manner of
      ugly sexual acts.

267. Vietnamese Pleasure Girls. NY: Star Distributors,
          1983. 170 pp.

      This pornographic novel has marginally more of a plot
      than others from the same publisher. An infantry
      officer observes a massacre and reports it to his
      superiors. They urge him to keep quiet and transfer
      him to Saigon. After five months there, he tells the
      story to a reporter. To fill out the scanty plot,
      there is much graphic sex.

268. Webb, James. A Country Such As This. Garden City,
          NY: Doubleday, 1983. 534 pp. 82-45969.
          NY: Bantam, 1985. 558 pp. 0-553-24734-4.

      Webb established his reputation among Vietnam novel-
      ists in 1978 with Fields of Fire (184). The current
      work is of a much larger scope and deserves con-
      sideration as an historical novel of some merit. The
      subplot set in Vietnam is important here because it is
      the best fictional treatment to date of the lives of
      prisoners in North Vietnam. A career Navy pilot
      endures six years, seven months and eight days in the
      hands of utterly brutal guards who always starve him
      and often torture him. Webb is not shy about de-
      tailing the prisoner-of-war experience graphically,

nor does he fail to mention the effect on the prisoners of an actresses' much-publicized visit to Hanoi.

269. White, Kent Jr. _Prairie Fire_. Canton, OH: Daring
     Books, 1983. 182 pp.
     NY: Critic's Choice Paperback/Lorevan Publishing,
     1987. 243 pp.

Prairie Fire is the code name for Laos, where
Sergeants McShane and Harper lead small teams of Asian
mercenaries on intelligence and assasination missions.
Their weapons, equipment, combat operations and even
such mundane activities as showers, building construction and automobile driving are described in
careful detail, but the personalities and motivations
of these potentially interesting men are left un-
stated. This is very much a sergeants' war. The few
officers appear only briefly, which is just as well,
because they are all dangerous and ignorant fools
whose glory-seeking proposals put the troops into
unnecessary and costly combat. As in so many Vietnman
novels, the 1968 Tet Offensive dominates part of the
action when McShane and the others defend their base
against a determined but unsuccessful communist
attack. In the end, one sergeant is killed on a
fruitless mission, and the other, for reasons unknown
to the reader and probably to himself, volunteers to
return from a safe billet in the United States for a
fourth tour in Vietnam. The ideas and personalities
in this spare and limited novel could certainly
benefit from richer treatment, and as it stands, the
book needs better proofreading and editing and a
higher quality of printing.

270. Woodruff, Paul. _The Personal Success of First-
     Lieutenant Peter Rosillo_. Austin, TX: Pawn
     Review, 1983. 66 pp. 0-932252-07-9.

Despite his Italian name, the title character is tall,
blonde and handsome. Moreover, he has excellent
manners and is admired by all who know him. The
narrator, Lt. Don Howard, thinks, "He gave us an idea
what the Kennedys had been trying to be like." The
two officers encounter each other as they participate
in intelligence-gathering adventures along the
Cambodian border in 1967. Howard likes and respects
Asians, and he has eloquent and profound thoughts
about the effect of the war, win or lose, on the

Vietnamese and Cambodians. Howard also tries to do
his military job well, although he thinks that the
last good American Army officers were those who quit
to join the Confederacy. After an ambush, Howard
finds Rosillo among the wounded enemy, but in the
context of an area and a war where allegiances are
vague, he agrees to cover up the incident. Later, in
1980, Howard confronts Rosillo and learns that from
misplaced liberal idealism the nearly perfect lieutenant had been assisting a group of independent
Cambodian mercenaries.

271. Wright, Stephen. Meditations in Green. NY: Scrib-
          ners, 1983. 342 pp. 83-11666.
          NY: Bantam, 1984. 322 pp. 0-553-24645-3.

From the beginning, when Vietnam is compared to the
foreskin of a phallus hanging from the belly of Asia,
it is clear that Wright is an author of considerable
imagination. His story of the men of the 1069th
Intelligence Group and their search, late in the war,
for the elusive and perhaps nonexistent 5th NVA
Regiment reveals a great deal about a little known
aspect of the American military effort. Characterization and dialogue are especially good. Dope smoking
enlisted men, careerist officers, competent NCOs and
revolutionary blacks are all realized well, as are
circumstances of unwilling soldiers in a war that is
clearly being lost. Indeed, the men who take pride in
their unmilitary attitude pay the price when, near the
end, their camp is devastated by the enemy. Alternate
chapters describing the life of the main character
after the war and other insertions of brief "meditations" about growing opium add little to a competent
novel of incompetent men at war.

                              1984

272. Abused Vietnamese Virgins. NY: Star Distributors,
          1984. 170 pp.

The female characters are Vietnamese rather than
Americans. There are romances with American enlisted
men somewhere in the story, but the Vietnamese girls'
principal role is to be captured and sadistically
raped by the Vietcong. There is actually a "Vietcong
Rape Squad," presumably staffed by volunteers, that
performs the evil deeds.

273. Anderson, Rachel. <u>The War Orphan</u>. Oxford: Oxford
      University Press, 1984. 256 pp. 0-19-271496-1.

Ha, a Vietnamese orphan, comes to live with an
idealistic, liberal English couple and their pre-
adolescent son. Ha appears to be mildly retarded, and
he has difficulty learning to manage himself and
adjusting to the family. His story emerges in
flashbacks that may be his thoughts or those of his
foster brother. It includes village life with attacks
and visits by Vietcong, South Vietnamese and Americans, a stay in a relocation camp next to an American
base, an attempt to return to his village and,
finally, evacuation from Vietnam as an orphan. The
Americans are depicted as mystifying and destructive,
but not cruel or evil. For an English novel, there is
a suprisingly large amount of detail about American
weapons and equipment.

274. Cain, Jonathan. <u>Saigon Commandos #3: Dinky-Dau Death</u>.
      NY: Kensington, Zebra, 1984. 270 pp. 0-8217-
      1377-9.

It is still 1967, and Sergeant Stryker and his men are
blazing on relentlessly. In this adventure, they take
to the field as undercover operatives to investigate a
notorious captain in the First Cavalry Division. This
officer is so hungry for glory that his men have
threatened to kill him. Incidents of "fragging,"
i.e., murdering, unpopular officers were not unknown
in Vietnam. In this episode, alternate chapters are
set back in the military police school at Ft. Gordon,
Georgia, where a recruit who bears the name of a
Vietnam novelist is undergoing training. Cain is less
accurate here than in earlier books about military
procedures and weapons.

275. Cain, Jonathan. <u>Saigon Commandos #4: Cherry-Boy
      Body Bag</u>. NY: Kensington, Zebra, 1984. 270 pp.
      0-8217-1407-4.

There is even less focus to this story than is found
in previous novels in the series. Sergeant Mark
Stryker and numerous other American military policemen
continue to crash and shoot their way around Saigon,
but there is really no central plot. They deal with
nonstop violent events, including brawls, narcotics,
snipers and Vietcong commandos while telling one

another repeatedly how wonderful it is to be a
policeman. An epilogue describes the lives of various
characters ofter the war and gives the false hope that
the series has expired.

276. Cain, Jonathan. Saigon Commandos #5: Boonie Rat
        Body Burning. NY: Kensington, Zebra, 1984.
        270 pp. 0-8217-1441-4.

Lead flies on the streets of Saigon as Sergeant Mark
Stryker and his fellow American military policemen
continue their adventures in 1967. The plot this time
has to do with a mysterious Vietnamese who sets
Americans on fire. There is also a young military
policeman who comes to the city to find his lost twin
brother. As usual, it is the military police against
everyone else. Also as usual, there is a good deal of
explicit sex.

277. Cain, Jonathan. Saigon Commandos #6: Di Di Mau or
        Die. NY: Kensington, Zebra, 1984. 268 pp.
        0-8217-1493-7.

In a preface, Cain expresses gratitude to an individual for assistance in improving this series. Di DiMau
or Die is somewhat different from the previous books,
perhaps because of the advice given. The story has to
do with hijacking of Army payroll convoys near Saigon.
There is a bit less frantic chasing around the city
and a more noticeable main plot. Sergeant Stryker's
personal adventures are, however, simply fantastic.
Some measure of ths may be taken from an incident in
which he is saved from execution during a firefight by
a beautiful Vietnamese woman who keeps a pet tiger.

278. Carn, John. Shaw's Nam. Indianapolis: Benjamin
        Books, 1984. 223 pp. 84-070275.

There is a fascinating account here of the operations
of an Army searchlight unit attached to Marine
infantry. Jimmy Shaw, a black draftee, is assigned to
such operations when he arrives in Vietnam in early
1968. In the field he encounters a substantial amount
of combat. The interaction and cooperation between
the Army and the Marines is uncharacteristically
congenial, and the operation of the jeep- mounted
searchlights is effective against the enemy in the

northern part of the country. In Da Nang and other
rear areas, Shaw and other black soldiers feel
themselves to be the victims of prejudice and racism.
Better editing and proofreading would have eliminated
distracting errors in the text.

279. Carroll, James. _Prince of Peace_. Boston: Little,
Brown, 1984. 531 pp. 84-14336.

Imbedded in this long novel about the Catholic
religion is an interesting account of an American
priest in Vietnam. Miichael Maguire, a Korean War
combat veteran and former POW, visits Vietnam first in
1961 with Cardinal Spellman. He returns in 1965 with
a relief organization. Maguire is horrified by the
war and the huge American role he observes. After
participating in an anti-American demonstration in
Saigon, he is thrown out of the country. Then he
returns to the United States and becomes active in the
antiwar movement.

280. Costello, Michael. _A Long Time from Home_. NY:
Kensington, Zebra, 1984. 270 pp. 0-8217-1391-4.

Harry Pitts, an Army sergeant, extends his tour in
Vietnam long enough to be around Bien Hoa for the 1968
Tet Offensive. In the months prior to that, Pitts and
some friends in an elite infantry platoon search for a
helicopter pilot who had abandoned him on an earlier
operation and caused several men to be killed. In the
course of his search and related adventures, Pitts and
his friends see an unbelievable amount of combat with
the enemy, military police, black market operators and
renegade Vietnamese troops. Their actions and
conversations are expressed in an abbreviated, laconic
style that attempts and fails to pack a great deal of
meaning into very few words.

281. Didion, Joan. _Democracy_. NY: Simon & Schuster, 1984.
234 pp. 84-1216.

Barely within the scope of this bibliography, _Democ-
racy_ is essentially the story of a relationship
between the wife of an American politician and a
covert operative who probably works for either the
U.S. military or the CIA. None of the characters are
attractive, especially the politician's daughter. In

1975, she manages to find her way to the doomed city
of Saigon because she thinks it might be amusing. The
covert operative finds her there and is able to put
her on one of the last planes out, much to the relief
of her mother. There is some valuable information
about how the fall of the city is viewed by different
American politicians and government personnel.

282. Dodge, Ed. <u>Dau: A Novel of Vietnam</u>. NY: Macmillan,
      1984. 243 pp. 83-25599.
      NY: Berkley, 1984. 277 pp. 0-425-07324-6.

Morgan Preston joins the Air Force in 1967 and
subsequently volunteers to go to Vietnam from his duty
station in Guam. Morgan is assigned as a loader on a
cargo plane, so he sees a good deal of the country.
He spends time in two Special Forces camps, one of
which is overrun. A wound allows him to miss the Tet
Offensive of 1968 because he is in a hospital in
Saigon. During his tour, Morgan spends a great deal
of time talking with other men about the rights and
wrongs of the war. He also loses many friends and
acqaintances to wounds and death. Morgan returns from
the war alive, but seriously disturbed. With
assistance from Veterans Administration psychiatric
care, he is eventually able to resume something like a
normal life, but the memory of the war will always be
with him.

283. Edell, Ed. <u>A Special Breed of Men</u>. Guilderland, NY:
      Ranger Associates, 1984. 233 pp. 0-934588-08-2.

In 1966, Sergeant Raymond Heller serves with the
Special Forces in Vietnam. Heller is such a perfect
soldier that experienced commissioned officers, both
American and Vietnamese, listen at length to his
suggestions. They let him, a completely inexperienced
junior sergeant, command a patrol. Until he is
wounded, Heller virtually runs the camp. At an Army
hospital in the U.S., Heller is awarded the Silver
Star and wins the hand of a beautiful nurse. All of
this is told in a text that reads as though it has
been translated into English from another language.
The dialogue, especially, is completely unlike the
speech of soldiers in the 1960s. Four photographs of
bomb damage from the Japanese attack on Pearl Harbor
have no meaning in this novel of Vietnam.

284. Fuller, Jack. <u>Fragments</u>. NY: Morrow, 1984. 211 pp.
        83-13434.
        London: Hodder & Stoughton, Coronet, 1985.
        287 pp.

In one sense, the title refers to the shrapnel that
Bill Morgan, the narrator, carries in his body.
Morgan is a young sergeant in the First Air Cavalry
Division in 1970. He is assigned to a Blue Team, an
elite infantry squad whose real leader is Jim Neumann,
another sergeant on his first tour. Newmann is
obsessed with reconstructing a dispensary in a small
village. In a firefight, he kills four civilians.
The circumstances are ambiguous, and no charges are
brought against Neumann, who is seriously wounded in
the battle. Later, after they are both out of the
Army, Morgan visits Neumann and learns the true story
about the killings.

285. Glick, Allen. <u>Winters Coming, Winters Gone</u>. Austin:
        Eakin, 1984.
        NY: Pinnacle, 1985. 361 pp. 85-6269.
        Toronto/NY: Bantam, 1987. 339 pp.

For a first novel, this is remarkably complex and
successful. It is an excellent account of Marine
infantry in 1966 that takes the main characters,
Schrader and Mingo, through the transition to civilian
life where they are active in the Vietnam Veterans
Against the War. Later, in 1979, they live as friends
in San Antonio. During the war they are in their
teens, but they fight well and have sympathy for the
Vietnamese villagers they are trying to protect. As
they work their way through the antiwar movement, they
also deal with personal problems that originated in
the war. In addition to the great deal of action
here, the main story is one of relationships among
men, and it is a good one.

286. Gold, Jerome. <u>The Negligence of Death</u>. Seattle:
        Black Heron Press, 1984. 179 pp.

Sergeant Ray Dickinson of the Special Forces is
wounded in the hand during his second tour in Vietnam.
In the U.S., he recovers and spends some time with his
former wife before he returns for a third tour. This
appears to be about 1965 or 1966. The first person,
present-tense account of conversations and battles is

choppy. No character, including the narrator, is very
well developed, and most who appear at all die later
in this short book. A belief in the inevitability of
death in battle is so apparent throughout that the end
is no surprise.

287. Groen, Jay and Groen, David. _Huey_. NY: Ballantine,
     1984. 280 pp. 83-91127.

John Vanvorden, the main character in this good novel
of helicopter warfare, arrives in Vietnam in 1970 as a
Warrant Officer First Class and leaves a year later as
a Captain. That unusual increase in rank is due to
his outstanding performance as a combat helicopter
pilot. Assigned initially to an assault helicopter
company at Ban Me Thuot and later to another near Qhi
Nhon, Vanvorden, the "Dutchman," learns quickly and
well how to fly "slicks"--unarmed helicopters used
primarily to ferry troops. Details about the employment of these aircraft abound; the Groens manage to
handle specifics in a manner less boring than the
authors of many novels about aircraft. The Dutchman
earns the repect of other pilots and the troops they
carry and the enmity of careerist officers because of
his devotion to saving men's lives. He is a thoughtful, patriotic man who becomes interested in Buddhism
during a two-week rest and recuperation leave in
Thailand. He and other characters in the book are
aware and resentful of the dangerous and foolish
circumstances that prevail as American involvement in
the war is diminishing, but they do their jobs quite
well.

288. Hawkins, Evelyn. _Vietnam Nurse_. NY: Zebra, 1984.
     384 pp. 0-8217-1459-7.

This is a bit better than the adolescent nurse novels
of Vietnam that share the same title. In 1966 near
Long Binh, Sybil Watkins serves in the 555th Field
Hospital--a place of realistic suffering and death.
Her colleagues are believable characters, including a
cautious commanding officer and an officious senior
NCO. Medical specifics are accurate and bloody, and
some patients die horribly. However, fantasy does
intrude. Sybil's boyfriend is the handsome Green
Beret captain who fills that role in other nurse
novels. In this more realistic version, however, he
helps Sybil achieve her first sexual climax and later

dies in her sight. Military nursing is not as
ill-served by this story as by others.

289. Helm, Eric. The Scorpion Squad #1: Body Count. NY:
          Pinnacle, 1984. 212 pp. 0-523-42290-3.

Despite the flamboyant title and cover art, this first
novel of a series describes a straightforward Special
Forces A team in 1964. After setting up a camp near
the Cambodian border with Vietnamese counterparts, the
team endures several batallion-sized Vietcong attacks.
Without support from higher headquarters, the team
commander, Captain Gerber, executes an ambush across
the border that devastates a large enemy unit. This
brings him difficulties with his commanding officer,
who is suspicious of all Special Forces personnel and
operations. Later, the camp emerges battered but
victorious after another attack. While characterization is trite, battles are described at length and
weapons have detailed nomenclature. This is a case of
the Special Forces versus everyone--their Vietnamese
allies, higher headquarters, the jungle and the enemy.

290. Helm, Eric. Scorpion Squad #2: The Nhu Ky Sting. NY:
          Pinnacle, 1984. 216 pp. 0-523-42291-1.

Captain Mack Gerber of the Special Forces leads the
survivors of his A-team, considerably devastated by
battles in Scorpian Squad #1, on a mission into North
Vietnam. The time appears still to be 1964, and their
objective is to rescue a captured U2 pilot near Son
Tay. This time they are accompanied by a civilianCIA
agent and a token Vietnamese. With European weapons
and equipment, augmented by supposed Japanese Ninja
paraphenalia, the team waltzes through North Vietnamese resistance and achieves its goal. This second
installment in the Scorpian Squad series marks a
notable departure from the realism of the first.

291. Holland, William E. Let a Soldier Die. NY:
          Delacorte, 1984. 324 pp. 84-5914.
          NY: Dell, 1985. 324 pp.
          London: Corgi, 1985. 351 pp.

For helicopter pilots based near Chu Lai, the Tet
Offensive of 1968 is just a temporary intensification
of an already busy war. This novel provides a

thorough view of that war from the pilot's seat of the
machines that came to symbolize it. Bear, Rufe and
the other flyers are similar to infantrymen in other
novels. They are in the Army and in Vietnam only for
the length of their tours. The principal job is to
stay alive and to help other Americans to live. To
them, the self-serving machinations of career officers
are either meaningless or dangerous. Their war
includes the personal tragedy of good friends being
killed and the awful mistakes of firing on friendly
troops. Although they are not the best of soldiers,
they are capable combat pilots, and Holland tells
their story with assured familiarity.

292. Lansing, John. The Black Eagles: Hanoi Hellground.
         NY: Kensington, Zebra, 1984. 330 pp. 0-8217-
         1249-7.

In this first book of a long series, Lansing
establishes the background of his characters and
setting. Early in the war, during the Diem regime,
Captain Robert Falconi assembles an international team
of supersoldiers to perform special missions for the
CIA. Each of the thirteen team members is introduced,
and his or her right to a colorful nickname is
estab-lished. Then, "Falcon," "Malpractice,"
"Junior," "Matador" and the others undertake a mission
into North Vietnam that includes attacking a pagoda/
sex palace, stealing a secret piece of Russian
military eqiupment, shooting down a jet aicraft and
hijacking a train. Along the way, they kill enormous
numbers of the enemy, using weapons and karate
techniques whose specific nomenclature is rendered
lovingly. With their initial mission accomplished,
enough of the Black Eagles are alive and apparently
greatly pleased with themselves.

293. Lansing, John. The Black Eagles #2: Mekong Massacre.
         NY: Kensington, Zebra, 1984. 235 pp. 0-8217-
         1244-2.

It is still 1964 when the Black Eagles take on their
second mission for the CIA. Captain Falconi and his
team engage the services of a Navy SEAL doctor and a
former French legionnaire to rescue American prisoners
from North Vietnam. After the prisoners, especially
an Air Force pilot, have been tortured in grisly
detail, "Falcon" and his Black Eagles descend on the

camp, release them and capture the North Vietnamese
camp commander and his North Korean advisor. A
planned helicopter extraction fails, and the team
stages a fighting retreat until they are finally met
by an Australian SAS force sent to assist. Like its
predecessor, Black Eagles, this adventure story is
lurid, over-written and quite casual about danger and
death.

294. Lansing, John. The Black Eagles #3: Nightmare in
      Laos. NY: Kensington, Zebra, 1984. 224 pp.
      0-8217-1341-8.

The Black Eagles now embark on their third mission.
Among new replacements on this international team is
an officious master sergeant, who, in the course of
the book, learns that his regular Army ways are not
acceptable in a special warfare situation. Following
the standard formula for this series, the team has a
dangerous mission behind enemy lines. This time they
destroy a Russian nuclear reactor in Laos, arriving
and leaving by glider! Weapons are described in
customary loving detail, notably the M-79 grenade
launcher that the team has just acquired. By now, the
North Vietnamese and their Russian advisors have
noticed the Black Eagles and begin to acquire intelligence about them.

295. Lansing, John. The Black Eagles #4: Pungi Patrol.
      NY: Kensington, Zebra, 1984. 236 pp.

Robert Falconi, commanding officer of the Black
Eagles, is newly promoted to major, but the time seems
clearly still to be early in the war, probably 1964.
This adventure takes the international team of special
warfare experts in pursuit of a group of East Germans
who, disguised as American soldiers, are commiting
atrocities. The team must also contend with increased
efforts by the enemy to use traitors to discover
information about the Black Eagles. As usual, bodies
fall in all directions, and at least six team members
are among them. This series combines competent
information about weapons, karate techniques, etc.,
with unrealistic descriptions of men in combat.

296. Lansing, John. Black Eagles #5: Saigon Slaughter.
      NY: Kensington, Zebra, 1984. 235 pp. 0-8217-

1476-7.

It is early 1965, and the ranks of the Black Eagles
are considerably depleted by casualties during their
first four missions. Moreover, Major Falconi,
"Falcon," and his team of superwarriors are still
pursued by North Vietnamese intelligence officers who
have managed to place a traitor among the team's new
recruits. The Black Eagles remain in Saigon for this
story, taking on a Chinese black market operator who
is also a North Vietnamese spy. Among their enemies
is a renegade Japanese sumo wrestler, and Lansing uses
this character to give accurate information about that
art. The body count, as usual, is very high.

297. McMath, Phillip H. Native Ground. Little Rock, AK:
        August House, c1984, 1985. 167 pp. 84-20527.

A revealing look at Marine tanks in combat contrasts
with the civilized life of Saigon and a young lieutenant's youth in Arkansas prior to the war in this
short but complicated novel. Chapters and passages
describing a tank and infantry patrol alternate with
descriptions of other times and places. Lieutenant
Christopher Shaw and his men fight the war with some
enthusiasm, but they have the wrong weapons in the
wrong country and pay the price. The author served in
Vietnam in 1969 and 1970. He is a lawyer, not a
professional writer, and might have been advised to
adopt a simpler story form.

298. Nik-Uhernik. War Dogs. NY: Kensington, Zebra,
        1984. 445 pp. 0-8217-1474-0.

In a prefatory statement, the author expresses his
gratitude to individuals at Soldier of Fortune
magazine. Persons familiar with that publication will
recognize the very vivid style of writing and emphasis
on the weapons and tactics of special warfare. The
first half of the book describes the backgrounds,
selection, and training of the War Dogs--an elite
military team of assassins. Very little of this is
believable at all, and when the hardened crew arrives
in Vietnam in 1963, their activities become even less
plausible. After several feats of derring-do, the
team participates in the assassination of President
Diem. Nik-Uhernik has some skill as a writer, and he
obviously knows Vietnam well, but it is difficult to

take this macho adventure story seriously in the
context of better Vietnam War novels.

299. Orgy in Saigon. NY: Star Distributors, 1984. 170 pp.

Even in the context of similar books from the same
publisher, Orgy in Saigon has a very superficial plot.
Almost all of the book describes sex among soldiers in
Saigon and elsewhere in Vietnam.

300. Parque, Richard. Sweet Vietnam. NY: Kensington,
      Zebra, 1984. 300 pp. 0-8217-1423-6.

The Air Force is underrepresented in Vietnam fiction,
so this effort by Parque is welcome because it is set
among pilots of F4 Phantom jets. Major Vic Benedetti
becomes the first U.S. ace of the war after five Mig
kills, but finally is shot down and killed himself by
a superior North Vietnamese pilot. Most of the
conversations among the pilots are in the form of
radio transmissions, e.g., "Bullseye sixty, Cobra
leader," that mean little to a general reader. Even
less convincing is Benedetti's idyllic romance with a
Vietnamese woman and his associated love affair with
the Vietnamese countryside and way of life.

301. Pendleton, Don. Mack Bolan: Skysweeper. Toronto:
      Worldwide Library, 1984. 184 pp. 0-373-61069-6.

These superhero series are neither interesting nor
pleasant to read, especially in the context of serious
books about war. In most cases, the superhero is a
Vietnam veteran. Here, another character, an engineer
working on an amazing new weapon, is a former POW who
has been brainwashed. Two pertinent chapters describe
what this individual goes through after he is shot
down and imprisoned in North Vietnam. The Vietnamese
are cruel and inhuman, but the sophisticated brain-
washing is done by a Russian specialist. Later, after
the war, the hero is drawn into impossible adventures.

302. POW in Chains. NY: Star Distributors, 1984. 170 pp.

Vietcong captors torture and rape American prisoners.
Later, the men escape and engage in frequent sex among

themselves and with others. They also remember many
homosexual encounters from their earlier lives.

303.   Reeves, James R. Mekong! NY: Ballantine, 1984.
          309 pp. 83-91241.

According to notes on the back of this paperback, the
story is based on a true account of events told to the
author by a former Navy SEAL. Memory and retelling
are both great improvers, and the characters come
across as a bit larger than life. They are all
members of the Navy's most elite unit, fighting a
very irregular war in and around the Mekong Delta in
what seems to be 1970. In the small boat Navy,
command authority is present and effective, but
military formality is completely absent. The SEALs
win most of their battles at considerable cost to
themselves, but they are aware that the war is being
lost both in Vietnam and at home. Criticism of war
protesters in general and of a particular actress is
present here as it is in many Vietnam novels.

304.   Riggan, Rob. Free Fire Zone. NY: Norton, 1984.
          426 pp. 83-42537.
          NY: Fawcett Crest, 1985.   354 pp.

Jon O'Neill works in a medical casualty company where
men wounded in combat receive immediate care before
those still living are sent on to more sophisticated
facilities. The environment of the post, with its
surrounding Vietnamese shantytown, is evoked accurately. The threat to O'Neill and his fellow enlisted
men comes not directly from the enemy but instead from
"lifer" NCOs and officers who insist on correct
military appearance and other formalities. The
conflict between draftees and career soldiers is
really more central to the story than the broader
military situation. Two of O'Neill's buddies do not
play the game well enough and are sent to the dreaded
LBJ--Long Binh Jail. O'Neill manages to survive, and
after his Vietnam sevice he enters into a relationship
with a woman in the United States.

305.   Sadler, Barry. Phu Nham. NY: Tor, Tom Doherty,
          1984. 285 pp. 0-812-58825-8.

Phu Nam is the name the Vietnamese have given to the

American sniper, Jim Rossen. With twelve years in the
Army, service in Korea, and sixty-four confirmed
kills, Rossen is at the top of his profession. Most
of this imaginative story describes Rossen working in
the jungle, carefully killing Vietnamese. He talks at
some length with an Army psychiatrist, and each man
comes to understand the other better. In the end,
Rossen is drawn into an unbelievable duel with a North
Vietnamese sniper.

306. Teed, Jack Hamilton. Gunships #3: Cobra Kill. NY:
     Kensington, Zebra, 1984. 252 pp. 0-8217-1462-7.

Colonel John Hardin, still alive and thriving in
Vietnam after his unbelievable adventures in the first
two Gunships novels, survives a helicopter crash and
observes a North Vietnamese force removing something
from another downed American aircraft. Hardin
assembles his band of criminal warriors and returns to
the site to investigate. When not fighting with other
Americans or their allies, this hardy crew slaughters
numerous North Vietnamese in extended firefights and
hand-to-hand combat. Somewhere in the jungle, they
find and destroy a gang of Corsican and American drug
smugglers.

307. Teen Sex Slaves of Saigon. NY: Star Distributors,
     1984. 170 pp.

In 1967 in Saigon, the C.I.A. runs a bordello for
general intelligence purposes. In the perfunctory
plot that ties sex scenes together, the dreaded Viet
Cong Rape Squad gets control of some of the whores.
Ugly sex follows, indeed it continues to the last page
of the book.

308. Vaughan, Robert. The Quick and the Dead. NY: Dell/
     James A. Bryans, 1984. 316 pp. 0-440-07203-4.

Vaughan is an experienced novelist and a Vietnam
veteran. While The Quick and the Dead has the scenes
of infantry combat characteristic of many Vietnam War
novels, it is a more ambitious and successful literary
product than most. The main character, Jake Culpepper, rises from major to major general between 1963
and 1973. He serves several times in Vietnam and
encounters careerist officers, Vietcong, a French

planter, a nurse and other representative characters.
One of his sons serves too and is killed in an
infantry fight. At home Culpepper contends with
military and civilian politics, emerging always as a
sympathetic and moral individual. Numerous sex scenes
do not help the story.

309. Windisch, Charles. Footsteps of a Hero. NY:
          Dorrance, 1984. 129 pp. 0-8059-2907-X.

It is possible that this effective and austere novel
may be missed by many reviewers. It is short, with
few characters and restrained action sequences.
Kohlhouse, a Marine corporal, fights his war in and
around Chu Lai and Phu Bai in the late 1960s. The
reader does not come to know him well, but there is
the impression that, at nineteen, he does not know
himself well. Kohlhouse and his fellow Marines fight
reluctantly but well in a war they do not understand.
They are less profane than Marines in other novels.
Racial friction and hatred between enlisted men and
career Marines is also underplayed. In all, Windisch
manages to convey the experience of combat with great
literary control.

310. Wright, Glover. The Hound of Heaven. NY: Arbor
          House, c1984, 1986. 315 pp. 85-15797.

The portion of this novel set in Vietnam ends at page
37, but it is fascinating and essential to the rest of
the story. In 1967, a special operations unit
observes the torture and crucifixion of a French
priest by the Vietcong. The unit commander rescues
the priest and arranges his evacuation by aircraft in
a very costly operation. As a result, the commander
endures substantial sanctions by the military. Years
later, at a time just in the future, he himself is a
priest, and he meets the man he saved in very unusual
circumstances that result from complicated and amazing
Vatican politics.

                              1985

311. Bodey, Donald. F.N.G. NY: Viking, 1985. 272 pp.
          85-10629.
          NY: Ballantine, 1987. 322 pp. 0-345-53945-2.

Among many accounts of infantry combat in Vietnam, this one is notable bacause of its completely personal perspective. In 1969, Gabe Sauers arrives in the Central Highlands as a draftee--F.N.G. does not stand for "Fragrant New Guy." He learns his trade on landing zones and in the bush. As more experienced soldiers return to the U.S., Sauers is promoted to sergeant and made an infantry squad leader. Throughout, his life is recounted in complete, personal detail. The enemies, as is often the case in these novels, are primarily the natural environment of the country and career officers. When Sauers finally leaves Vietnam, it is after suffering combat fatigue. Better than most others, this novel points out the effect of the U.S. military's policy of brief combat tours. Sauers and his friends have no interest at all in victory; they want only to be alive at the end of their tours.

312. Butler, Robert Olen. On Distant Ground. NY: Knopf, 1985. 245 pp. 84-48517.
      NY: Ballantine, 1986. 263 pp.

David Fleming, an Army captain, is court-martialed in 1975 for freeing a dangerous enemy prisoner in Vietnam. Fleming is a character from Butler's earlier Alleys of Eden (217), a novel also set, in part, in Saigon during the last days. After being found guilty and receiving a dishonorable discharge from the Army, Fleming returns to Saigon, just at the time of the fall of the city, with a false passport and other documents supplied by the CIA. His purpose is to find a son he had fathered four years before. The CIA wants him to contact agents posing as deserters. The city, during and after the fall, is chaotic, but Fleming eventually obtains assistance from the man he released from prison. In the end, he is able to leave Vietnam with his boy.

313. Cain, Jonathan. Saigon Commandos #7: Sac Mau Victor Charlie. NY: Kensington, Zebra, 1985. 285 pp.
      0-8217-1574-7.

Media meets life in this seventh episode in the adventures of Sergeant Mark Stryker and his Saigon military policemen. They must provide security for an American motion picture being shot in Saigon. It is still 1967 (or perhaps 1968) and the policemen are

going strong, crashing through the city with lights
shining and sirens wailing. Stryker, as always, has
more sexual opportunities than he can handle. Secondary characters die like flies, but everyone is so
full of joy at just being there that they cannot fully
express it.

314. Cain, Jonathan. Saigon Commandos #8: You Die, Du Ma!
          Kensington, Zebra, 1985. 318 pp. 0-8217-1629-8.

Cain's pace of writing must be as incessant and
frantic as his characters' activities. The fantasy
never stops, nor does the action for "Stryker and his
war cops." Number 8 is standard fare for the series,
with the Saigon military police in love with themselves and their horrid jobs. As usual, a thin plot
provides the basis for nonstop action. This time, a
Vietcong is attacking the wives and children of the
military policemen.

315. Cain, Jonathan. Saigon Commandos #9: Mad Minute. NY:
          Kensington, Zebra, 1985. 268 pp. 0-8217-1698-0.

Sergeant Mark Stryker and his fellow military policemen continue their exciting and dangerous jobsin
Saigon in 1967. As their jeeps career wildly from one
gory gunfight to another, Stryker must contend with a
deserter who turns sniper and an unrelated attempt to
frame him for the murder of a Vietnamese woman. An
important secondary character is a Chicano enlisted
man who survives a year in Saigon only to come to
grief when he returns to Colorado.

316. Charyn, Jerome. War Cries Over Avenue C. NY: Donald
          I. Fine, 1985. 359 pp. 84-073516.
          NY: Penguin, 1986. 359 pp.

If this novel has a central character, it is Saigon
Sarah, who serves as a sort of Jewish mother for a
group of strange characters who inhabit Avenues A, B,
C and D in Manhattan. Most of them appear to have
connections with Vietnam, and a good part of the book
is set there. Sarah serves as a nurse in a weird
field hospital that is used as a sort of rest home for
irregular fighters from all sides in the war. Her
boyfriend, Howie, spends a good deal of time in a

Montagnard village where he is involved in the opium
trade. There is a visit to Ho Chi Minh City after the
war. A great deal of action occurs in New York City.

317. DeMille, Nelson. <u>Word of Honor</u>. NY: Warner Books,
      1985. 518 pp. 85-40005.

Throughout the 1970s, there were rumors in military
and ex-military circles that legal charges might be
brought against individuals for actions during the
war. Here, the main character, Ben Tyson, is forced
back into the Army in the 1980s and court-martialed
for a supposed massacre of civilians in the Battle of
Hue during the Tet Offensive. The events in Vietnam
are revealed fully in flashbacks, quotations from an
historical account that figures in the novel and legal
testimony. The futility and stupidity of a court in
peacetime trying a man for activity in a war nearly
two decades old is manifest. Two sentences say it
all: "I'm glad war has rules. Can you imagine how
dangerous it would be without them?" Tyson is one of
the most complete and mature characters in Vietnam
fiction, and his wife, a former protester, is one of
the most disgusting. Characterization is one of the
many fascinating and competent aspects of this excellent novel.

318. Dye, Dale A. <u>Run Between the Raindrops</u>. NY: Avon,
      1985. 327 pp. 85-90668.

The most notable urban battle of the Vietnam War was
in Hue during January and February of 1968. This
account of two Marine combat correspondents emerges
from the pen of an author who served there in that
capacity. It is a close and accurate story of Marine
infantry in an unusual situation. Eventually pressed
into service as infantrymen, both correspondents
survive while most of the men around them are wounded
or killed. Dye is incensed at the political dimension
of the battle. Heavy artillery is forbidden in order
to preserve the Hue Citadel, and the ARVN is given
credit for a victory achieved at great cost by the
Marines. Present tense narration and phrases punc-
tuated as sentences ably convey the immediacy of
battle.

319. Edwards, Ellis. <u>Operation Golden Buddha</u>. Boulder,

CO: Paladin Press. 258 pp. 0-87364-342-9.

Just as the cities of Saigon and Phnom Penh are about
to fall to communists, three old Special Forces
buddies return to Southeast Asia to plan a major
crime. They move through the doomed streets of Saigon
looking up old American and Vietnamese friends and
promising them various things--often a way out of the
country--to assist in the plot. After encounters with
the Vietcong, North Vietnamese troops and the obligatory Eurasian beauties, the men are successful in
their scheme to rob a Cambodian temple of a large gold
statue of the Buddha. While the adventure may be a
little farfetched, the settings and characterization
are convincing.

320.   Flowers, A.R. De Mojo Blues. NY: Dutton, 1985.
            216 pp. 85-13019.
       NY: Ballantine, 1987. 242 pp. 0-345-33995-9.

The solidarity of black soldiers in Vietnam and of
black veterans after the war is an important theme   in
this book. Most of the action takes place in the
1970s and 1980s as three black veterans adjust to
civilian life. The central character, Tucept
High-John, undergoes "hoodoo" training, a form of
witchcraft, and finally draws the other two into his
thinking. Extensive flashbacks to Vietnam describe
conditions among black soldiers late in the war and
tell the story of the murder of an unpopular officer.
Flowers' characters uniformly believe that there is
little, if any, value in white people.

321.   Frankland, Mark. The Mother-of-Pearl Men. London:
            John Murray, 1985. 188 pp. 0-7195-4221-9.

The setting here is Vietnam, especially Saigon, of the
late 1960s or early 1970s, but it is a very different
place than was known to most Americans. Michael
Bishop, an employee of a British bank, moves through a
world of civilians and politicians where the Americans
and the war are only in the background. Bishop is
involved with a British intelligence officer in a plot
to assist an English-educated Vietnamese to defect
from the Vietcong and escape to Europe. As the
amatuerish secret agent bumbles toward inevitable
failure, he encounters a variety of Vietnamese
individuals and groups that the Americans, who are far

away in the field, do not know exist. The only common
idea held by everyone in the book is that the American
cause is already hopelessly lost.

322. Glasser, Ronald J. Another War, Another Peace. NY:
      Summit Books, 1985. 247 pp. 85-2646.

David, a young American doctor, arrives in Vietnam in
1968 and adjusts slowly and reluctantly to the military and the war. Serving in civilian medical assistance programs, David comes to respect and like the
young, experienced corporal who serves as his driver.
The corporal shows interest in learning basic medicine
from the doctor and he extends his tour to continue
his informal education. When the corporal is killed
in an ambush, David is transfered to another hospital.
Then he is almost immediately wounded in the 1968 Tet
Offensive. David is evacuated to Camp Zama, Japan,
where he demonstrates a well-known truth that doctors
make bad patients.

323. Griffin, W.E.B. Brotherhood of War, Book V: The
      Berets. NY: Jove, 1985. 408 pp.

This is the fifth book in a series whose earlier
numbers deal with the American military prior to
Vietnam. As the title suggests, The Berets is primarily about the Special Forces. The characters are
officers who have come to special warfare from other
specialties and are anxious to try their skills in the
new war in Vietnam. In 1962, a few of them visit
Vietnam briefly to establish base camps and conduct
preliminary operations against the Vietcong. These
are highly motivated professional soldiers, many with
experiences in World War II and Korea, and they have
access to the most up-to-date weapons and equipment.
In these very early days, they achieve some successes.

324. Helm, Eric. The Scorpion Squad #3: Chopper Command.
      NY: Pinnacle Books, 1985. 217 pp. 0-523-
      42434-5.

After their excursion into North Vietnam in Scorpion
Squad #2 (290), Captain Mack Gerber and his hardy crew
are back at their camp in the "Mekong River Region" of
South Vietnam. No dates are given, but internal
evidence suggests that it is still 1964 or 1965. This

time they rescue a beautiful Vietnamese girl who is
being tortured by the enemy and capture a large number
of prisoners. Weapons and battles are once again
described with excruciating and boring specificity,
and the ARVN is cursed on almost every page. At the
end of the book, the reader is promised that a sequel
is due.

325. Helm, Eric. The Scorpion Squad #4: River Raid. NY:
          Pinnacle Books, 1985. 211 pp. 0-523-42293-8.

The war is clearly affecting Captain Mack Gerber. The
effect increases thoughout the book. He begins by
drinking and cursing more than in the three previous
Scorpion Squad books. He is also having trouble with
his girlfriend, a beautiul American nurse. The
members of his A-team also feel the pressure of the
war. They argue more frequently among themselves and
with Captain Gerber. They have also picked up a new
communications sergeant who appears to be a vampire.
Beset by Vietcong in sampans, Gerber's men use a
stolen waterskiing boat to invent mobile riverine
warfare. The U.S. Navy, always eager to learn from
soldiers, adopts the concept and places vessels and
men under Gerber's command for a final, tragic battle.

326. Heywood, Joe T. Taxi Dancer. NY: Berkely, 1985.
          315 pp. 0-425-07966-X.

Captain Byron South is the first ace of the Vietnam
War and a winner of the Congressional Medal of Honor.
In 1966, he flies F105s from a base in Thailand.
South's outspoken and irreverent ways irritate Colonel
Wainright, his careerist wing commander. Wainright
sends South on a dangerous solo mission. He is shot
down and spends six horrible years in a North Vietnamese prison while the colonel's career prospers. As
usual in Air Force novels, the aircraft and their
mechanical components and properties recieve detailed
description. Development of the human characters is
also quite full.

327. Lansing, John. The Black Eagles #6: AK-47 Firefight.
          NY: Kensington, Zebra, 1985. 222 pp. 0-8217-
          1542-9.

In this sixth book, the Black Eagles follow CIA orders

to blow up a secret Vietcong supply base in the A Shau
Valley. It is early 1965, and the international
commandos are beginning to find fault with their M-16
rifles, so they rearm, through irregular channels,
with a variety of older, larger caliber weapons. Once
again they are successful in carrying out their
mission, especially after one member of the team
tortures a captured enemy soldier to learn the exact
location of the base. As in previous adventures,
Major Falconi and his men are completely contemptuous
of security precautions and death.

328. Lansing, John. <u>The Black Eagles #7: Beyond the DMZ</u>.
      NY: Kensington, Zebra, 1985. 238 pp. 0-8217-
      1610-7.

Major Robert Falconi and his Black Eagle commando team
are still operating after six previous adventures in
1964 and 1965. This time they are sent into the
mountains near the Laotian border to lead a tribe of
Chinese mercenaries against the Vietcong. When these
two belicose groups combine, they wreak costly havoc
on their enemies, who now include a team of Czech
helicopter pilots and a specially trained NVA killer
unit. To supply their new allies with heavy weapons,
Falconi and some colleagues burglarize a North Vietnamese supply depot. As usual, the Black Eagles are
victorious in all they do.

329. Lansing, John. <u>The Black Eagles #8: Boo Coo Death</u>.
      NY: Kensington, Zebra, 1985. 238 pp. 0-8217-
      1677-8.

The formula for novels in this series is by now so
practiced as to be trite. There is the customary
biography of Major Falconi, the exhaustive detail
about weapons, the usual colorful crew and the worn
North Vietnamese and Russian adversaries. The plot in
this one includes a tiger hunt and the rescue of a
female operative from enemy hands.

330. <u>Mercenary Stud Squad</u>. NY: Star Distributors, 1985.
      170 pp.

A wealthy homosexual businessman hires a mercenary
group to release his son from captivity in Vietnam.
The son is in the hands of a private Oriental army

which also captures some of the would-be rescuers.
There is abundant torture, homosexual rape and some
technical modifications to sex that do not bear
repeating.

331. Nik-Uhernik. War Dogs #2: M-16 Jury. NY: Kensington,
      Zebra, 1985. 268 pp. 0-8217-1539-9.

In a preface, the author asserts that a character in
this novel is entirely fictitious. She is June Wanda,
a leftist American entertainer who visits Hanoi and
makes life even more miserable for POWs who suffer
unspeakable torture. June Wanda meets her match when
she is captured and interrogated by the War Dogs--an
utterly implausible band of super U.S. Army warriors
As in the earlier book, there is just too much action
to be taken seriously. Indeed, the central thread of
the story is lost amidst constant firefights, car
crashes and heroic deeds.

332. Parque, Richard. Hellbound. NY: Kensington, Zebra,
      1985. 364 pp. 0-8217-1591-7.

Like Parque's earlier novel, Sweet Vietnam (300),
this, too, is about a romance between an American
Phantom pilot and a Vietnamese woman. Here, the
woman, Xinh, is a secret Vietcong agent whose love for
the pilot, Steve Randall, overcomes her political
loyalty. When Steve is shot down and captured in
Cambodia, Xinh and her sister become a two-woman army
to rescue him, dying in the successful undertaking.
Parque obviously has direct access to Vietnamese
sources, but his characters are simply too good, loyal
and loving to be interesting, much less convincing.

333. Pendleton, Don. Mack Bolan: Dirty War. Don Mills,
      Ontario: Worldwide Library, 1985. 376 pp.
      0-373-61404-7.

There is no denying the immense popularity of the
Executioner series featuring the superhero, Mack
Bolan. One may, however, be amazed that adolescent
stories achieve such wide readership. In this novel,
Bolan and his colleagues, each of whom has a suitably
characteristic and bellicose nickname, tear through
the ranks of the Vietcong and the North Vietnamese
Army. From these characterizations, it is clear that

the foolish and incompetent Vietnamese will lose the
war to the Americans, who are their moral and military
superiors. If Vietnam War literature had a television
equivalent, this would be a daytime soap opera.

334. Rich, Curt. The Advisors. NY: Kensington, Zebra,
1985. 460 pp. 0-8217-1692-1.

With The Advisors, Curt Rich joins the short list of
really excellent Vietnam novelists. Zebra is to be
congratulated on this book. Not only is this a
realistic and moving account of infantry combat, but
it is also a detailed picture of South Vietnamese
units at war in 1969 and 1970. The hero, Captain
Harris, has more than his share of bad luck; he is
terrified most of the time; his superior officers do
not like him; and the Vietnamese do not especially
want his advice. His wife's letters are full of
feminist and antiwar ideas that have no meaning to
him. At the end, he is captured briefly, but he
manages to escape and complete his tour in one battered piece.

335. Rinaldi, Nicholas. Bridge Fall Down. NY: St.
Martin's, c1985, 1986. 278 pp. 0-312-90085-6.

This may well be a Vietnam novel. It has to do with a
team of saboteurs moving through the jungle to blow up
an enemy bridge. It is a highly improbable group, led
by a general and including two women. They have
various adventures, including combat with the enemy,
before they achieve their objective. There is as much
internal evidence against the locale being specifically Vietnam as there is in favor of it, and the
novel is deliberately ambiguous.

336. Sadler, Barry. Casca: The Phoenix. NY: Charter
Books, 1985. 187 pp. 0-441-09329-9.

Casca, the "eternal mercenary," cannot die. He goes
on from war to war throughout history. He appeared in
Vietnam in the first novel of this series, Casca: The
Eternal Mercenary (199). Now in the fourteenth, he is
back again, manifested as Casey Romain, a Special
Forces sergeant. The action of ambushes, firefights
and duels to the death has little real meaning. In
one episode, for example. Casca and his Asian mer-

cenariies enter a North Vietnamese Army barracks and
kill twenty-two sleeping soldiers silently with
knives. As a supernatural character, Casca has no
need to be believable and he is not.

337. Scott, Leonard B. Charley Mike. NY: Ballantine,
      1985. 438 pp. 84-91669.

This sentimental but moving account of the 75th
Airborne Rangers is set before and during the invasion
of Cambodia. In their role as scouts and trail
watchers, the Rangers are an elite unit. The enlisted
men and officers respect one another, and there is
little of the hostility between draftees and career
soldiers that appears in other novels. Combat is
described with a chilling realism that emerges from
firsthand experience. The author fought in Vietnam
with a unit very similar to the one in his novel, and
he is still a serving officer. If the characters are
a bit larger than life, the extra size can be put down
to the author's justified enthusiasm for the special
craziness of the airborne infantry. Unfortunately,
the review copy is a notably poor example of modern
book manufacture. The cover fell off during the first
reading.

338. Stone, Scott C.S. Song of the Wolf. NY: Arbor House,
      1985. 377 pp. 84-24168.
      NY: Signet, 1987. 383 pp.

In John Dane, the hero of this novel, Stone has
crafted a fascinating character. Dane is a half-
Cherokee mercenary who is very good at his work. His
first association with Asia is as a Marine during the
Korean War. Later, he studies in Hong Kong and takes
on mercenary work throughout Southeast Asia. In the
mid-1960s, Dane is a nominal colonel in the U.S. Army
working with riverine forces in the Mekong Delta.
Even that early, the eventual loss of the war is a
foregone conclusion to Dane and the other professionals. The grand American strategy is utterly wrong
for Asia, but there is still money to be made. Dane
eventually runs out of luck in Cambodia trying to
evacuate his girlfriend and a group of refugees from
the hands of the Vietnamese.

339. Topol, B.H. A Fistful of Ego. NY: Critic's Choice/

Lorevan, c1985, 1987.   1-55547-167-6.   260 pp.

In this story about a president facing nuclear war in
the 1990s, several chapters recount his experiences in
Vietnam. As a young lieutenant recently graduated
from West Point, Robert Jennings served as an intelligence officer in Saigon. He encountered a Buddhist
monk who provided him with a measure of enlightenment.
Jennings then informed General William Westmoreland
and a group of other senior officers of his conclusion
that the U.S. should withdraw from Vietnam. He was
immediately sent into combat. There followed an
unlikely battle during which Jennings displayed
uncharacteristic heroism. He was subsequently awarded
a Congressional Medal of Honor and began his political
career.

340.   Wandke, Richard D.   <u>Vietnam Remembered</u>.   NY: Vantage,
         1985.   66 pp.   83-90866.

The title is probably more accurate than the author
knows, for this marginal work is much more a combat
memoir than a novel. The hero, whose career is
certainly modeled closely on the author's, serves
several tours in Vietnam as an advisor, troop commander and staff officer. The huge paragraphs, almost
without characterization and dialogue, describe the
war in relentlessly patriotic and positive terms.
Wandke tells some interesting stories, and his point
of view is valid, but he would have done better to
select a form of publication offering more professional editing and proofreading.

341.   Weinberg, Larry.   <u>War Zone</u>.   Toronto/New York: Bantam,
         1985.   163 pp.   0-553-23612-1.

The Vietnam War hardly seems to be a suitable topic
for adolescent literature, but Weinberg manages it
with good taste and some measure of literary skill.
In 1967, two young men from classic, feuding southern
families go to war together.   One is sworn to kill
the other, but combat conditions quickly teach them
something about the scale of human hurt. When one is
killed and the other wounded, the survivor returns
home and declines to participate in the continuing
family feud. Characterization is adequate, particularly in the instance of a young antiwar woman whose
ideas and statements are typical of the people she

represents.

1986

342. Anderson, Robert A. Service for the Dead. NY: Arbor
      House, 1986. 274 pp. 86-10856.
      NY: Avon, 1987. 274 pp.

      Following his capable 1982 novel, Cooks and Bakers
      (229), Anderson provides another realistic account of
      Marine infantry at war in the late 1960s. Mike
      Allison survives a few months in Vietnam before he is
      wounded and returned to the United States. Allison is
      in the field most of the time and frequently in
      combat. His experiences emerge in lengthy flashbacks
      that compose most of the book. These contrast
      effectively with his later experiences in hospitals
      and with his parents after he returns to this country.
      There is a bit more soul searching about the meaning
      of the war than is usual for a combat novel, but the
      dialogue is always believable.

343. Boyne, Walter J. and Steven L. Thompson. The Wild
      Blue. NY: Crown, 1986. 626 pp. 86-2636.
      NY: Ivy, 1987. 628 pp.

      Aptly subtitled "The Novel of the U.S. Air Force,"
      this huge book begins in 1947 and ends sometime in the
      immediate future. By following the careers of several
      pilots through training, peacetime assignments, Korea
      and Vietnam, the authors provide a fictional account
      of the development of the Air Force from a branch of
      the Army to the military arm for space flight. There
      is a fine sense of history and good skill at
      characterization and dialogue. Happily, for the
      nonpilot, specifics of the many aircraft in the story
      are explained simply and fully. About a third of the
      story is set in Vietnam and and Thailand during the
      war, including a section about pilots captured and
      tortured by the North Vietnamese. Although both
      authors clearly love the Air Force in which they
      serve, they are not blind to its shortcomings.

344. Cain, Jonathan. Saigon Commandos #10: Tortures of
      Tet. NY: Kensington, Zebra, 1986. 272 pp.
      0-8217-1772-3.

Bullets fly and tires scream as Sgt. Stryker and his
Saigon military police defend the city during the 1968
Tet Offensive. Books in this series differ from one
another only in details. This one features some nasty
sex. As usual, some characters continue from earlier
installments and other new personalities are
introduced. There is no questioning Cain's devotion
to the men he characterizes.

345. Cain, Jonathan. <u>Saigon Commandos #11: Hollowpoint
      Hell</u>. NY: Kensington, Zebra, 1986. 252 pp.
      0-8217-1848-7.

In five days of the famous 1968 Tet Offensive,
Sergeant Stryker and the other Saigon military
policemen fight continuous battles in the role of
urban infantry. This series is notable for almost
nonstop action; there is so much of it that all
perspective is lost. Subplots describe an American
MP accused of shooting an unpopular officer and a
Saigon policeman involved in events that lead to a
famous shooting. There really is not a story here,
however, just a group of combat segments as uncon-
nected to each other as they are to the title.

346. Cain, Jonathan. <u>Saigon Commandos #12: Suicide Squad</u>.
      NY: Kensington, Zebra, 1986. 271 pp.
      0-8217-1897-5.

The Saigon military policeman fight their way through
the latter part of the 1968 Tet Offensive with even
more than their usual spirit. Racism and revenge
combine with continuous action in an utterly unbelievable novel. One subplot, for example, has Sgt. Mark
Stryker's sister surviving for three weeks in the
sewers of Saigon, eating berries. She manages to
escape twice from Vietcong capture and avoid being
eaten by two panthers. Above ground, the MPs drive
jeeps fast and shoot at everything that moves. The
more hardy souls among them love the heat of battle.
During the quiet times, these heroes bowl a few lines,
using enemy heads for balls.

347. Coonts, Stephen. <u>Flight of the Intruder</u>. Annapolis,
      MD: Naval Institute Press, 1986. 329 pp.
      86-16440.
      NY: Pocket Books, 1987. 437 pp.

Disobedience of orders by a Navy flyer forms the
central theme of this interesting novel. Jake Grafton
flies A-6 Intruders from a carrier on Yankee Station
off the coast of Vietnam in 1972. Tired of risking
his life and seeing friends die in pursuit of such
worthless targets as "suspected truck parks," Grafton
and his navigator make a bombing run on administrative
buildings in Hanoi. When caught, they are nearly
court-martialed, but a forthcoming change in American
policy saves them. In addition to a convincing
portrait of pilots at war, Coonts provides a close
look at carrier operations.

348.   Cragg, Dan. The Soldier's Prize. NY: Ballantine,
       1986.   326 pp.   86-90948.

Senior sergeants, the often-hated "lifers" of the
Vietnam era, appear here as sympathetic main characters. The author is a retired sergeant major. In and
around Saigon during the 1968 Tet Offensive, these old
Army hands fight with a much different attitude than
the privates in the field. Subplots have to do with a
black-led heroin ring and the inevitable romances
between American soldiers and Vietnamese women.
Better than many Vietnam novels, The Soldier's Prize
conveys a sense of the Army as a durable social
institution.

349.   Cross, David. Chant. NY: Jove, 1986.   231 pp.
       0-515- 08441-7.

Enough chapters are set in Vietnam in 1971 to cause
this potboiler to belong among Vietnam War novels.
The main character, John Sinclair, is a supersoldier
employed by the CIA to lead Hmong tribesmen. After
the war, he takes on a rural Washington State businessman who victimizes Hmong refugees. In the long
fight, Sinclair fights his old martial arts instructor
and demonstrates proficiency with numerous weapons and
techniques. Many people know as little as Cross about
the Oriental martial arts, but they, fortunately, do
not reveal their ignorance in novels. This one is
not worth reading.

350.   Dickason, Christie. The Dragon Riders. Great
       Britain: Century Hutchinson, 1986.
       Great Britain: Coronet Books, Hodder & Stoughton,

1987. 724 pp. 0-340-41219-4.
NY: Villard, 1987. 0-394-55943-6. Published as
Indochine.

When Americans begin arriving in Vietnam in the late
1950s, they are just the latest and eventually the
most numerous of foreign devils to be outsmarted and
victimized by the Vietnamese in this huge novel. The
central character, a Eurasian named Nina, inherits
from her father the resources and inclination to
conduct criminal enterprises, especially opium
trading. She is not a convincing character, but the
author does a much better job with the environment and
attitudes in the country. The criminal element sees
itself as partly patriotic, using drugs to corrupt
American civilians and soldiers, as well as various
Vietnamese groups on the scene. As in some other
books with a long historical perspective, it is clear
that the American cause is lost from the beginning
because Americans have no understanding of the social
and religious realities of Vietnamese life.

351. Dye, Dale. Platoon. Based on a screenplay by Oliver
      Stone. NY: Charter, 1986. 247 pp.
      0-441-67069-5.

In the hands of Dye, an ex-Marine, Oliver Stone's
screenplay receives acceptable novelization. Dye
served as a technical advisor for the motion picture.
The straightforward story about Chris Taylor's
introduction to war in an infantry platoon is a less
dramatic book than a motion picture, although the
novel follows the plot closely. Much of the story is
set in the bush in late 1967 and early 1968 where men
do awful things to survive and obtain revenge in
combat. Their enemies are not always North Vietnamese.

352. Fleming, Stephen. The Exile of Sergeant Nen. Chapel
      Hill, NC: Algonquin Books, 1986. 186 pp.
      86-3471.

Nen, a Vietnamese refugee, lives near Washington, D.C.
and works as a headwaiter in his family's restaurant.
His memories, however, frequently take him back to
Vietnam where he served as a paratroop sergeant for
over twenty years. Nen remembers battles with the
Vietminh when he was in the French Army and his

subsequent capture. He was also present at the fall
of Saigon and forced his way onto a plane to leave the
country. He remembers especially an incident in the
countryside when he forced a police colonel to
interrupt the torture and rape of a peasant woman.
Later, the colonel, who has also escaped to the United
States, attempts to make trouble for Nen, but the old
sergeant is simply too tough for him.

353.   Gilkerson, Seth. The Bastard War. Great Neck, NY:
       Todd & Honeywell, 1986. 175 pp. 0-89962-478-2.

Enough of this awkward novel about a Vietnam veteran
is set in Vietnam to warrant inclusion here. The long
flashback has to do with a heroic woman resistance
fighter, Miss M, who rescues an American from captivity and later performs other good works during the
evacuation of Saigon. There is no indication that
Gilkerson has any direct experience of the war. A
preface by his daughter does little to help an
unbelievable plot and stylized characters.

354.   Gillis, Gerald L. Bent, But Not Broken. Orangeburg,
       SC: Sandlapper Publishing, 1986. 412 pp.
       85-19657.

As the title implies, Mike Billingsley survives the
Vietnam War. The novel takes him through Marine
Officers' Basic School, into intense infantry combat
in 1969 and 1970 and finally back to the United States
with three wounds and a Silver Star. Billingsley has
a good woman who waits for him, considerable skill as
a platoon leader and the respect of his men. In
Vietnam, he is either in combat or in the hospital.
Back in this country, he is especially tolerant of
antiwar activists who insult him. As the book ends,
he decides to leave the Marine Corps and enter law
school.

355.   Griffin, W.E.B. Brotherhood of War, Book VI: The
       Generals. NY: Jove, 1986. 378 pp. 0-515-
       08455-7.

Featuring characters continued from earlier novels in
this series, this is an account of how the Son Toy
Raid might have been. Here, a large team of Special
Forces raids a prison camp near Hanoi in 1969 and

successfully rescues a number of prisoners. Prior to
that, the officers who are to lead the raid play
various types of military politics and talk over old
times, mostly telling one another what brave, memorable characters they are.

356. Groom, Winston. <u>Forrest Gump</u>. Garden City, NY:
        Doubleday, 1986. 228 pp. 85-13000.
        NY: Berkley, 1988. 241 pp.

Forrest Gump, a huge young man from Alabama, has an
I.Q. of 70, but is blessed with a fine, observant eye.
In high school, and later in college under Bear
Bryant, he is allowed to play football until he flunks
out. Drafted into the Army in time for the 1968 Tet
Offensive, he lands immediately in combat and manages
to earn the Congressional Medal of Honor. Gump is
later sent on a pingpong tour of Red China before the
Army finally gives up on him and releases him early.
Gump goes on to have fascinating and very funny
adventures, but from the point of view of Vietnam
fiction, his notable quality is that he sees clearly
the sheer idiocy of the war.

357. Hardesty, Steven. <u>Ghost Soldiers</u>. NY: Walker, 1986.
        206 pp. 86-1320.

Hardesty's Vietnam is an unusual place. The vocabulary and slang of his infantrymen are different from
the language used by other Americans in the war. The
location is in the Central Highlands, sometime in the
1970s. An infantry company, sent to rescue the crew
of a downed helicopter, is destroyed by the Vietcong.
As two survivors wander through the jungle, they are
joined by recently killed comrades, returned somehow
to life. The rejuvenated company fights excellently
against the enemy and confuses American commanders
with radio messages from a unit thought to have been
destroyed. In the end they are visited again in
death. There are elements of a good infantry novel
in this tale of the supernatural.

358. Heinemann, Larry. <u>Paco's Story</u>. NY: Farrar Straus
        Giroux, 1986. 209 pp. 86-19527.
        NY: Penguin, 1987. 209 pp.

Paco's Story is narrated by dead men, an entire unit
destroyed in Vietnam. The one exception is Paco, who
lies wounded for a day and a half. Paco works his way
through the military and VA hospital system and finds
himself washing dishes in a smalltown diner. He walks
with a limp and carries a cane. Paco has a little
trouble communicating. He drinks too much, misses an
opportunity for a romance and sleeps badly. Eventually, he leaves town. Heinemann is a serious literary
talent and a major figure among Vietnam War novelists.
Paco's Story confirms his stature; it won the 1987
National Book Award. Chapters of this book appear as
short stories elsewhere in this bibliography.

359.   Helm, Eric. Vietnam: Ground Zero. Toronto/NY:
          Worldwide, Gold Eagle, 1986. 220 pp.
          0-373-62701-7.

A typical disclaimer at the beginning of this book
assures the reader that it is entirely fictional and
bears no resemblance to any real events. That is just
as well. The story is set in the mid-1960s, at the
beginning of the Phoenix assassination program.
Special Forces personnel cross the Cambodian border
and kill a Chinese officer. A careerist general
learns of the operation and brings charges against two
men. Their commanding officer crosses the border
again, in the company of a woman reporter, and
captures prisoners whose presence in Cambodia thwarts
the general's plans. Not quite a potboiler, this
novel has an interesting premise that would have been
better developed with more realistic treatment.

360.   Helm, Eric. Vietnam: Ground Zero--P.O.W. Toronto/NY:
          Worldwide Library, Gold Eagle, 1986. 1986.
          219 pp. 0-373-62702-5.

In a much better book than the first one in this
series, the two Vietnam veterans who write as Eric
Helm describe the fall of a Special Forces camp and
the subsequent capture and torture of three American
survivors. The story is based on a true account of
American prisoners executed by the Vietcong in 1965.
Eventually, in the novel, one escapes and leads a
successful rescue effort. Captain Matt Gerber,
continuing from the earlier book, is very much on the
scene, although not as one of the prisoners.

361. Helm, Eric. _Vietnam: Ground Zero--Unconfirmed Kill_.
     Toronto/NY: Worldwide Library, Gold Eagle, 1986.
     221 pp. 0-373-62703-3.

In the early 1960s, Captain Matt Gerber and his
Spedial Forces team extened their tours for six months
in order to track down their nemesis, a mysterious
Chinese officer. After leading green American troops
in a successful assault on an enemy base, Gerber joins
his men in Hong Kong. There they have another
encounter with their Chinese opponent. As usual in
this series, a beautiful American newspaperwoman
provides romantic interest and serves as damsel in
distress.

362. Hunter, R. Lanny and Hunter, Victor L. _Living Dogs
     and Dead Lions_. NY: Viking, 1986. 260 pp.
     84-40564. NY: Penguin, 1987. 278 pp.

Twelve years after a costly battle for a Special
Forces camp in 1967, Joshua Scott, one of three
American survivors, seeks out the widow of his former
commanding officer, who died in the battle. As Joshua
and the widow come to know each other, the story of
the battle emerges in detached flashbacks. Con-
fronting trouble and violence together on a farm in
rural Kansas, they become friends and fall in love.
These are two persons of character, whose story is
told with realistic action and natural dialogue. The
violence in 1979 is overdone, and a brutal surprise
near the end is not effective. At least one of the
authors knows well how to describe fear.

363. La Fountaine, George. _The Long Walk_. NY: Putnam,
     1986. 256 pp. 85-30085.

Frank Turco, a Special Forces enlisted man, is
captured in 1965 and not released until ten years
later. Turco endures a terrible, lonely captivity
and much torture. After his release, he cannot
accept that he is back in America. He thinks the
Veterans' Administration hospital is a Vietnamese
trick. After three years as a psychiatric patient,
Turco is rescued by a Navaho doctor who knew him in
Vietnam. On the Navaho reservation, Turco gradually
returns to reality. Eventually, he enjoys a reunion
with other Special Forces veterans.

364. Lansing, John. Black Eagles #9: Bad Scene at Bong
        Son. NY: Kensington, Zebra, 1986. 269 pp.
        0-8217-1793-6.

      Lansing's style has grown to be more realistic and
      consequently more plausible since the first Black
      Eagles novel was published in 1983. Major Falconi
      still commands his special team. The time seems to be
      1967 or 1968 and the Black Eagles are engaged in a
      routine village pacification program with units of the
      7th Cavalry. They stumble onto a North Vietnamese
      regiment and finally defeat it in a long and costly
      fight. There are numerous secondary characters, all
      of whom are introduced with entire life stories.

365. Lansing, John. Black Eagles #10: Cambodia Kill-Zone.
        NY: Kensington, Zebra, 1986. 224 pp.
        0-8217-1953-X.

      For the benefit of those who have not read the nine
      previous books in this series, the author uses part of
      the first chapter to recount the fantastic history of
      Major Falconi and the Black Eagles. This time they
      take on unusual opponents. It seems that the North
      Vietnamese and their Russian KGB masters have im-
      ported, of all things, a team of fanatical Algerian
      commandos to kidnap Falconi. In a desperate jungle
      battle, the Black Eagles defeat the Algerians and the
      Vietnamese allies, and another international communist
      plot is thwarted.

366. Martin, Ron. To Be Free! NY: Vanguard Press, 1986.
        250 pp. 86-9052.
        Montreal: Book Center, 1986.
        NY: Pocket Books, 1987. 221 pp.

      Jack Ramsey is a Marine sergeant on his second tour in
      Vietnam in 1968. Ramsey is captured, and he endures
      months of starvation and torture in North Vietnam.
      While he and other prisoners resist, some men
      cooperate with their captors. Under great strain,
      Ramsey remembers a visit to the United States where he
      was insulted by antiwar activists and rejected by his
      girlfriend. Finally, Ramsey escapes and makes his way
      to the sea, where he is found by an American ship.
      After the war, he is able to adjust successfully to
      civilian life.

367. Maurer, David A. <u>The Dying Place</u>. NY: Dell, 1986.
253 pp. 0-440-12183-3.

A good deal is heard, but relatively little is said,
about the cross border operations conducted in Laos
and elsewhere by the Special Forces. This realistic
and capable novel describes both the secret activities
and the men who led them. In 1969, Sergeant Sam
Walden commands a mixed team of Vietnamese and Chinese
mercenaries from a base in Da Nang to the Ho Chi Minh
Trail in Laos, where they observe enemy troops, take
photographs, tap telephone lines and accomplish other
dangerous tasks. In Walden, Maurer creates one of the
most interesting and well-realized characters in Vietnam fiction.

368. Merkin, Robert. <u>Zombie Jamboree</u>. NY: Morrow, 1986.
335 pp. 86-745.

Heiser and Becker are enlisted men at Ft. Benning in
1970. They are not airborne, but part of the permanent garrison. They spend most of their time
avoiding duty and discussing how much they hate the
Army. Many of their colleagues are blacks who hate
the Army even more. When they are sent separately to
Vietnam, Heiser is involved in the assassination of an
officer and receives a general discharge. Becker is
posted to a meteorological unit where he works with
sophisticated weather balloons. He survives his tour
and is then sent to Ft. Sam Houston for the brief
remainder of his Army service. Many soldiers hated
the war and the military, but everything here is so
overdone that the critical effect is diluted.

369. Mullin, Chris. <u>The Last Man Out of Saigon</u>. London:
Victor Gollancz, 1986. 216 pp. 0-575-03872-1.

MacShane, a CIA agent with experience in South
America, is sent to Saigon a few days before the North
Vietnamese victory. His mission is to create a
network of agents. MacShane makes a few amatuerish
attempts to enlist spies, but the Vietnamese catch him
easily within a few weeks. He is taken to North
Vietnam where he reveals his entire CIA history in
response to very gentle pressure. After a few month's
work on an agricultural cooperative near Haiphong,
MacShane is released. The Vietnamese are portrayed in

a generally favorable light in this essentially simple
book, and the CIA appears as a corrupt agent of evil.

370.   Parque, Richard. Firefight. NY: Kensington, Zebra,
       1986. 365 pp. 0-8217-1876-2.

       This unrealistic adventure tale has to do with an
       almost superhuman Vietnam veteran who is lured back to
       that country by the CIA just as Saigon is about to
       fall. He is launched into the northern part of the
       country on a mission that leads to the rescue of some
       American prisoners. He also manages to bring out his
       Vietnamese wife who he has not seen for seven years.
       Scenes of panic during the death of South Vietnam are
       well written. Frequent bar and street fights, always
       won by characters with such colorful names as
       "Montana" and "Mustang," are not. Parque, a competent
       novelist, is capable of much better than this.

371.   Proffitt, Nicholas. The Embassy House. Toronto/NY:
       Bantam, 1986. 399 pp. 85-48234.

       Jake Gulliver is an old Vietnam hand. He has been
       there for seven years, running special operations and
       performing an occasional assassination. In 1970, he
       finds himself in the Mekong Delta, participating in
       the famous Phoenix Program under CIA auspices. The
       mix of characters, plots and confused loyalties is
       fascinating and it represents a part of the war that
       did not appear on television. This is more a novel
       about spies than about soldiers, and Jake is almost
       more Vietnamese than American. Proffitt asks much of
       his readers' credulity when he introduces a beautiful
       American woman in the role of CIA agent and equips
       Jake with both profound skill as a killer and an
       idealistic moral code.

372.   Tate, Donald. Bravo Burning. NY: Scribners, 1986.
       214 pp. 85-29481.

       The difference of perception and attitudes between the
       senior officers who plan battles and the enlisted men
       who fight them figures in many Vietnam novels. Here
       it is the central theme. Colonel Gurgles has gran-
       diose ideas about his infantry battalion in 1967, but
       he views battles from his helicopter. Michael Ripp

and the other soldiers do their frightening and
dangerous work on the ground. Their view is often
farcical. A sense of humor and the use of marijuana
help only a little as they suffer the deaths of their
friends and the unfaithfulness of their wives at home.
On Hill 711 in the Central Highlands, the battalion
suffers 60% casualties and Corporal Ripp survives, not
intact, but a hero.

373. Teed, Jack Hamilton. Gunships #4: Sky Fire. NY:
      Zebra, 1986. 251 pp. 0-8217-1879-7.

By late 1970, Colonel John Hardin is convinced that
the war is lost. Even so, he and his small band of
supersoldiers continue to fight on. In this fantastic
adventure, the characters include factions of the
North Vietnamese government, KGB agents, Mafia
criminals and the inevitably corrupt CIA. With the
brilliant foresight and consumate military skill that
they show in earlier novels, Hardin and his crew
manage to foil a North Vietnamese plan to introduce
poison into the war. They destroy the substance in a
huge fire that provides the title for this episode.

374. Thacker, Jada. Finally, the Pawn. NY: Avon, 1986.
      298 pp. 85-90674.

The first half of this book explores the relationship
between a new second lieutenant and an experienced,
but young, sergeant. They are infantrymen, fighting
in the jungle late in the war. The difficulties of
the natural environment are given exceptional emphasis. After the lieutenant is killed, the sergeant
rotates to the U.S. and deserts rather than complete
his remaining time in the Army. He locates the
officer's sister and, through her, becomes acquainted
with antiwar students in the San Francisco area.
These "screamers," as they are called in the book, are
notable for the superficiality of their characters and
ideas. Through the metaphor of chess and with the
guidance of an older vetern, the former sergeant comes
to terms with his combat experience.

375. Whittington, Ruben Benjamin. Moonspinners, Viet Nam
      '65-'66. NY: Vantage, 1986. 87 pp. 85-90277.

The Moonspinners are airmen trained to fight as

infantry. Their primary mission is to defend U.S.
airbases against ground attacks. They also serve on
operations with American, South Vietnamese, Australian
and Korean units. A black airman with the same name
as the author spends his year in Vietnam in the
Moonspinners. He endures racism, combat and the loss
of friends. It is not surprising that this short work
found only a subsidy publisher.

376. Wise, Leonard. Doc's Legacy. NY: Richardson &
      Steirman, [1986]. 384 pp. 0-931933-16-1.

Doc Ella is an Iowa pig farmer and a world-class poker
player. His experiences in Vietnam emerge in conversations, memories and flashbacks. Doc earned a Silver
Star at Khe Sanh and later won a big poker game in
Saigon. When an aircraft carrying him crashed, he was
taken prisoner and suffered years of brutality in
North Vietnam. After killing the camp commandant, he
was tried and incarcerated in a Vietnamese civilian
prison. Back in Iowa, Doc's hard life is haunted by
his memories, but he is a tough, capable man and he
survives.

377. Zeybel, Henry. The First Ace. NY: Pocket Books,
      1986. 314 pp. 0-671-62868-2.

Often in novels of combat flying, the emphasis on
aircraft characteristics is so technical that it
escapes the understanding of nonflying readers.
Zeybel makes things comprehensible. Lt. Colonel Cy
Allen flies F-4 Phantoms out of Thailand in 1967. At
one point he mentions that he has never met a Vietnamese. His goal is to shoot down five enemy aircraft
and become the first ace of the Vietnam War. The
story describes much fighter combat and other aspects
of the lives of pilots and navigators. Action,
characterization and dialogue are all competent and
the occasional speculation about the nature of warfare
is interesting. This is a fine Air Force novel.

378. Zlotnik, Donald. Eagles Cry Blood. NY: Kensington,
      Zebra, 1986. 494 pp. 0-8217-1742-1.

Zlotnik thinks an assault rifle is a submachine gun,
and there are a few other lapses in this otherwise
able novel of a Special Forces lieutenant during what

seems to be 1968.   There is a background of drug
dealing, racial tension and threats against unpopular
officers.   Paul Bourne, on his second Vietnam tour, is
a genuine hero, but a longstanding feud with his
commanding officer threatens his career.   Often on
operations and in combat, Bourne is a gifted soldier.
At the climax of the story, he risks his life to
destroy a major enemy ammunition and supply dump, and
his battle with his superior ends in a sort of
victory.

1987

379.   Anderson, Kent.   <u>Sympathy for the Devil</u>.   Garden City,
        NY: Doubleday, 1987.   350 pp.   87-630.

In the early days of the first Nixon administration,
Hanson and other Special Forces sergeants perform
clandestine missions in the northern part of South
Vietnam.   The uniquue status of the Special Forces is
clear.   These professionals have little use for the
cowardly Vietnamese and incompetent American soldiers
who are their allies.   Hanson tried to live in the
United States after his first tour, but he could not
adjust and so returned to the war.   The sergeants and
their Montagnard troops fight with care and competence, secure in their own professionalism.   They
are contemptuous of the political goals of the war.
In the end, however, the military incompetence they
cannot avoid devastes them.

380.   Baker, Kenneth Waymon.   <u>Alone in the Valley</u>.   Pompano
        Beach, FL: Exposition Press of Florida, 1987.
        296 pp.   87-090898.

While the story of Daniel Perdue's year in the
infantry is not particularly original or moving, it is
surprising that this respectable and realistic novel
did not find a national publisher.   This is a better
book than most of the paperback potboilers that have
appeared in the recent years.   The story is simple
enough.   Perdue arrives in Vietnam in November 1965,
spends a year with the First Cavalry Division in the
Central Highlands, and goes home alive a year later.
Baker is good at describing combat, and his characters
are solid and convincing.

381. Barrus, Tim. _Anywhere, Anywhere_. Stamford, CT:
         Knights Press, 1987. 239 pp. 86-27374.

      The topic of homosexuality among American forces in
      Vietnam receives awkward and uneven treatment here.
      The account of two former Marines, one in a wheel-
      chair, living in the gay community in New York City
      includes substantial flashbacks to Vietnam. They
      served in the Khe Sanh and Hue, devoting themselves to
      erotic activities, Vietnamese orphans and the hatred
      of a particular officer. Lyrics from popular songs,
      especially those by Elvis Presley, are scattered
      through the text in bold capitals but with little
      apparent connection to the narrative. The sincerity
      and love evoked by this novel are uunquestionable, but
      the form of their expression is uneven.

382. Bunch, Chris and Cole, Allan. _A Reckoning of Kings:_
         A Novel of the Tet Offensive. NY: Atheneum,
         1987. 449 pp. 85-48147.
         NY: Ballantine, 1988. 493 pp.

      By the time an American division and a North Viet-
      namese division contest for a provincial capital
      during Tet of 1968, the reader is well acquainted with
      their respective personnel. The soldiers include
      everyone from private to general on both sides. This
      is a more original and imaginative work than many
      other good novels of the infantryman's war. A single
      example is the interesting account of radio communi-
      cations in a North Vietnamese unit. Much of the
      Battle of Hue is here, slightly disguised. That
      provides the plot for a very readable piece of
      fiction.

383. Chapel, Ernie. _Dateline: Phu Loi_. Toronto/NY:
         PaperJacks, 1987. 195 pp. 0-7701-0644-7.

      Ernie Chapel, the name of the main character in this
      superficial novel, is probably a _nom de plume_. Chapel
      is a reporter in Vietnam in 1968. What there is of a
      plot describes his experiences with an attack heli-
      copter company in combat and at rest. When one pilot
      is courtmartialed for accidentally killing South
      Vietnamese troops, Chapel is able to contribute to his
      successful defense. Grattuitous sex scenes are
      especially badly written, but there is some unusual
      and pointed criticism of television journalists.

384. Durham, Harold. _Strawman_. NY: Zebra, 1987. 364 pp.
     0-8217-2165-8.

Much of this complex novel is successful. In 1968,
Michael Kelly is an Air Force captain grounded from
flying jets because of an unjust accusation of
cowardice. As a forward air controller in a light
aircraft, he sees much of the war at close range and
encounters a great deal of danger--too much in the
end. Kelly must contend with a superior officer who
hates him. He also has a romance with a beautiful
woman journalist who has romances with many other men.
While the descriptions of combat flying are excellent,
the characters and their motives are not always
convincing.

385. Eickhoff, Randy Lee. _A Hand to Execute_. NY: Walker,
     1987. 224 pp. 86-32527.

Con Edwards is the Saigon bureau chief for a pres-
tigious American newspaper. When his ambitious
assistant is tortured and killed at about the time of
the 1968 Tet Offensive, Edwards undertakes a dangerous
search through the Saigon underworld to find his
killers. There is a great deal of background about
crime and corruption in South Vietnam as well as more
heroic action than might be expected from a
middle-aged reporter. Among the more successful
secondary characters is a lethal Vietnameses police
official. In the end, Edwards solves the mystery and
exposes a major black-market operation.

386. Ely, Scott. _Starlight_. NY: Weidenfeld & Nicolson,
     1987. 195 pp. 86-19058.

The starlight scope, a night vision device, was a
notable innovation in the Vietnam War. The scope used
by Tom Light, a legendary sniper, can also view the
future. Light works out of a firebase commanded by a
mad major and garrisoned by a variety of weird
soldiers. There is also a monkey trained to attack
the enemy with hand grenades. Light is unpopular, but
he can raise the dead. His only friend is a terrified
radio operator, whom Light promises to keep alive.
Light keeps his promise, even after the rest of the
unit is destroyed on a futile raid into Laos.

387. Ferrandino, Joseph. Firefight. NY: Soho, 1987. 196
      pp. 87-13052.

      Amaro, an infantryman in the 101st Airborne, is a
      relatively old soldier. Reduced from the rank of
      sergeant, he brings a bad attitude to his new unit.
      Here, more than in other novels, there is conflict
      between career NCOs and dope smoking enlisted men. So
      many soldiers are killed or wounded that there is no
      sense of unit cohesion. Each man seems to fight for
      himself or for one or two friends. Amaro's particular
      struggle is with a hated first sergeant, and, at the
      end of the story, it appears that Amaro might win.

388. Hawkins, Jack. Chopper 1 #1: Blood Trails. NY: Ivy
      Books, 1987. 361 pp. 86-82545.

      A note in the back of the book announces that Hawkins
      has written sixteen other Vietnam "adventure" novels
      under different pseudonyms. Indeed the hot lead and
      roaring engines here are reminiscent of at least one
      other series. The plot has to do with the First Air
      Cavalry in the Ia Drang Valley in 1965 and 1966. It
      is wildly improbable; the prose is florid; and
      colorfully nicknamed characters toss casual one-liners
      back and forth. If writing these books is nearly as
      tiring as reading them, the author must be quite
      fatigued.

389. Hawkins, Jack. Chopper 1 #2: Tunnel Warriors. NY:
      Ivy Books, 1987. 337 pp. 86-82550.

      Trent Brody, a Specialist Fourth Class in the First
      Air Cavalry, fights a fantastic war of adventure in
      Vietnam. Free of anything remotely like a military
      command structure or ordinary duties, Brody and a band
      of soldiers with colorful nicknames use military
      helicopters as private taxis to battles they find
      interesting. Sometime in late 1965, Brody warms up by
      searching a Vietcong tunnel complex, then he assists
      in the rescue of a besieged Special Forces camp.
      After surviving all of that, as well as some sexual
      torture by female Vietcong, Brody is probably ready
      for at least one more of these novels.

390. Hawkins, Jack. Chopper 1 #3: Jungle Sweep . NY: Ivy
      Books, 1987. 343 pp. 86-91842.

The bold troopers of the First Air Cavalry are back
again, fighting a war that exists only in the author's
imagination. The time is apparently 1966. Corporal
Brody is in Saigon, pursuing an involved affair with a
Vietnamese prostitute. Two of his friends are on
leave in Bangkok, playing at being military policemen.
Other troopers, at work in the regular Vietnam war,
perform heroic acts and endure sexual torture at the
hands of beautiful Vietcong women. For shallow
characters and improbable dialogue, this series is
matched only by the Saigon Commandos. The authors of
both are almost certainly the same person.

391. Hawkins, Jack. Chopper 1 #4: Red River. NY: Ivy
     Books, 1987. 339 pp. 87-90790.

In this relentless adventure, Treat Brody and his
fellow members of the First Air Cavalry Division are
in the Mekong Delta in late 1966. As in other books,
the scenes of combat are virtually interchangable, and
there are numerous subplots. Here there is a sergeant
who believes he is the reincarnation of an ancient
Vietnamese hero; a beautiful, half-naked Australian
woman; another love affair between a soldier and a
Vietnamese woman; a secret CIA helicopter; and a
female Vietcong determined to kill Brody. As usual,
the story is laden with nicknames and slang, and the
soldiers have time to exchange wisecracks in the midst
of combat.

392. Hawkins, Jack. Chopper 1 #5: Renegade MIAs. NY: Ivy
     Books, 1987. 341 pp. 87-90909.

This fifth book in the series shares several unfortunate characteristics with its predecessors. It is
lurid, overwritten and disjointed. The central
character is still Sergeant Treat Brody, and the time
is 1966. Brody spends his time in helicopter combat
and endless banter. There are several subplots. One
has to do with two deserters who fight with the
Vietcong. Another describes the trials of a wounded
soldier who returns to Vietnam as a civilian and
begins a romance in Saigon with a Vietnamese woman.

393. Hawkins, Jack. Chopper 1 #6: Suicide Mission. NY:
     Ivy Books, 1987. 345 pp. 87-90923.

Whoremonger, Snakeman and the other artfully nicknamed
helicopter crewmen are once again flying around the
Void Vicious. This time it is late 1966, and they are
supporting an operation by the Americal Division
northwest of Saigon. As usual in this series, there
is no real plot or structure--merely a series of
battles mixed with overwritten, slangy conversations.
One unique element in this book is the introduction of
a group of Chinese Nung mercenaries as minor characters.

394.   Helm, Eric. Vietnam: Ground Zero--The Fall of Camp
        A555. NY: Worldwide, Gold Eagle, 1987. 221 pp.
        0-373-62704-1.

In his fourth adventure, Captain Matt Gerber is lured
out of his Special Forces camp in late 1965 on a
dubious mission. During his absence, traitorous South
Vietnamese help the enemy to capture the camp. They
also bag a beautiful American reporter and a visiting
general. Alerted to the capture, Gerber marshalls
various forces and repossesses the place in a brilliant vertical envelopment.

395.   Helm, Eric. Vietnam: Ground Zero--Guidelines. NY:
        Worldwide, Gold Eagle, 1987. 218 pp.
        0-373-62708-4.

With his trusty sidekick, Sergeant Fetterman, Captain
Mack Gerber is off on another secret mission. The men
lead a hastily assembled team, which includes the
inevitable beautiful Eurasian woman, into North
Vietnam. They parachute from a B52 bomber and look
for a secret radar site. The team acquires important
information, but the mission comes apart. Gerber
manages to rescue some captured American pilots and
arrange for most of his team to be evacuated by
helicopter. Back in Saigon, some journalists who
learn of the story are suitably crass and unpatriotic.

396.   Helm, Eric. Vietnam: Ground Zero--The Hobo Woods.
        NY: Worldwide, Gold Eagle, 1987. 219 pp. 0-373
        62707-6.

After a year in the United States, Captain Mac Gerber
and his favorite suubordinate, Sergeant Fetterman,
return to Vietnam. It is probably sometime in the

late 1960s. They find a conflict between increased
enemy pressure and a political need to pretend that
the war is winding down. A pitched battle in the Hobo
Woods ends with many American casualties and unwanted
press interest. As a result, Gerber and his Special
Forces associates are in disfavor. Like earlier books
in this series, Gerber has several romantic entangle-
ments that do little for the plot.

397.   Helm, Eric. _Vietnam: Ground Zero--Incident at Plei_
       Soi. NY: Worldwide, Gold Eagle, 1987. 221 pp.

Captain Gerber and his trusted subordinate, Sergeant
Fetterman, are sent to evaluate a Special Forces camp
near the Cambodian border. During their visit, the
camp is attacked and overrun by the enemy. Gerber,
Fetterman and a few other survivors are rescued at the
last moment by friendly forces. This long battle
occupies much of the book. Back in Saigon, Gerber
recommends that the camp be rebuilt because any place
the enemy wants so badly must be important. This is
not one of the best books in the series.

398.   Helm, Eric. _Vietnam: Ground Zero--The Kit Carson_
       Scout. NY: Worldwide, Gold Eagle, 1987. 221 pp.
       0-373-62706-8.

This is one of the more fantastic novels in the
series. Captain Mac Gerber and his men are sent into
Cambodia on what they believe is a reconaissance
mission. In fact, they are bait for a trap that will
be sprung by a huge airstrike. The plan is engineered
by a careerist general and foiled by a CIA agent loyal
to Gerber. Among the various characters are two
beautiful women, one of whom accompanies the Special
Forces men into Cambodia.

399.   Helm, Eric. _Vietnam: Ground Zero--Soldier's Medal_.
       NY: Worldwide, Gold Eagle, 1987. 219 pp.
       0-373-62705-X.

This fifth book in the series about Special Forces
Captain Mac Gerber and his men has to do with a
soldier who goes crazy. A young sergeant who has seen
too much combat begins to act on his own. He gathers
a ruthless team of South Vietnamese and moves into
Cambodia to take the war to the enemy. When Gerber

and another senior officer discover the sergeant's
action, Gerber decides to assassinate him. As it
happens, the man is killed in battle and Gerber is
able to cover up the incident. Eventually the
sergeant is awarded a posthumous Congressional Medal
of Honor.

400. Helm, Eric. Vietnam: Ground Zero--The Ville. NY:
        Worldwide, Gold Eagle, 1987. 221 pp.
        0-373-62709-2.

In a change from earlier books in this series, Captain
Matt Gerber is a secondary character, and his former
executive officer, Jonathan Bromhead, is the hero.
Perhaps this is a sign of exhaustion on the part of
the two men who write as Eric Helm, or it may be an
attempt to broaden the scope of the series. Late in
the war, Bromhead is sent to command an impromptu
mission in Laos. He and two other servicemen organize
the military potential of a Meo village near the Ho
Chi Minh Trail. He is at first hampered and finally
assisted by a liberal, idealistic American woman who
is studying the villagers. After preliminary
engagements with the Vietcong, Bromhead disobeys
orders and successfully defends the village.

401. Hill, Larry. Viet Nam: Up Front. FL: Exposition
        Press of Florida, 1987. 242 pp. 86-91430.

In a preface, Hill explains that this is a barely
fictionalized account of his experiences as a civilian
newsman in Vietnam in 1967 and 1968. He was based in
Danang and went into combat with Marines, Army Special
Forces, Koreans and Vietnamese. He was on hand for
the Battle of Hue. He also found time to become
involved with civilian women and children, to witness
at least one atrocity and to arrange the murder of an
Indian moneychanger. The reporter's perspective is
unusual, but the book seems not to have been proofread
or edited.

402. Lansing, John. Black Eagles #11: Duel on the Song
        Cai. NY: Kensington, Zebra, 1987. 236 pp.
        0-8217-2048-1.

Robert Falconi, newly promoted to lieutenant colonel,
leads his select detachment in a river war in this

episode. The book includes a list of over thirty former team members killed in action and a brief review of their adventures in earlier books. There is the usual abundance of combat as well as most unusual expressions of appreciation for the efforts of rear echelon support troops. Once again, one of Falconi's men finds a romance with a beautiful woman in the midst of battle.

403. Lansing, John. Black Eagles #12: Lord of Laos. NY: Kensington, Zebra, 1987. 222 pp. 0-8217-2126-7.

In one of the more fantastic adventures of this series, Lieutenant Colonel Falconi and his eleven-man detachmennt of military supermen are sent into northern Laos. Their mission is to provide support for a former French sergeant who has supposedly been fighting a private war against the communists for fifteen years. When they discover that he is nothing more than an opium warlord they escape. After many implausible encounters, they make their way south for over five hundred miles to an allied unit.

404. Lansing, John. Black Eagles #13: Encore at Dien Bien Phu. NY: Kensington, Zebra, 1987. 238 pp. 0-8217-2197-6.

Although the Black Eagles have suffered almost seventy percent casualties since their first outing, new volunteers continue to show up. After the usual biographies, Lt. Colonel Falconi and his bold band are off to blow up a Russian communications complex in North Vietnam. They alert local troops to their presence, but nonetheless manage to finish the job after their ace scout returns from illegal leave. As usual, at least some of the Black Eagles find beautiful women available in the Vietnam War.

405. Mackenzie, Steve. SEALS #1: Ambush! NY: Avon, 1987. 181 pp. 86-92063.

The role of the Navy in Vietnam is not fully represented in fiction, so any novel about that service is noteworthy. This one, unfortunately, is a disappointment. Lieutenant Mark Tynan and his SEAL team are supposed to be trained exhaustively in irregular warfare, but they make fundamental mistakes about

clothing and equipment. They rattle around the
southern area of Vietnam, hitching rides on helicopters to join any battle that suits Tynan. In this
story, they save an Army firebase by noticing that the
enemy uses tunnels. In the novel's favor, it is
written in a very spare style. Sadly, this is only
the first of yet another adventure series.

406. Mackenzie, Steve. SEALS #4: Target!. NY: Avon, 1987.
      185 pp. 87-91595.

After two stories set elsewhere, the Seals are back in
Vietnam sometime after 1968. They are directed by the
CIA to assassinate enemy officers along the Ho Chi
Minh Trail in Laos. Lieutenant Tynan and his men have
bad luck on this mission, despite help from Laotian
irregulars. Virtually everyone in the unit but Tynan
is a casualty, and all they have to show for the cost
are a couple of dead NVA officers. Worse yet, they
miss a chance to kill General Vo Nguyen Giap.

407. McColl, Alex. Valley of Peril. NY: Tor, Tom Doherty,
      1987. 316 pp. 0-812-51213-8.

McColl is a practiced writer, and this story is based
on his own experience. His main character, Captain
Hamilton, advises a remote Vietnamese unit in 1967 and
1968. Hamilton is professional and brave. Within the
realistic limits of his situation he provides good
advice to the Vietnamese. Their war is much different
from what faces American units. Among much combat, an
account of the 1968 Tet Offensive stands out.
Occasional long patches of dialogue seem to be taken
from field manuals. Otherwise, characterization is
good.

408. Nichols, John. American Blood. NY: Henry Holt, 1987.
      338 pp. 86-25616.

Nichols did not serve in Vietnam, so his accounts of
infantry action in the first part of the book may be
suspect to some. His first-person narrator, Michael
Smith, observes and participates in a mind numbing
series of atrocities. When Smith returns home, he
cannot lose his memories and dreams of the war. He is
a deranged, violent and well-armed man, and he
associates with other, similar people. The climax

comes when another veteran, an old acquaintance from
Vietnam, murders the daughter of the woman he loves.
Nichols ably describes horrible characters; anyone who
has known a few will recognize the type.

409. Parque, Richard. Flight of the Phantom. NY:
      Kensington, Zebra, 1987. 368 pp. 0-8217-2127-5.

Vince Battaglia is a Marine Reserve Lieutenant who has
been called to active duty to fly F-4 Phantoms out of
Da Nang during the last part of the Johnson administration. He has serious doubts about the war and his
role in it. On a leave in Saigon, Battaglia befriends
two street children and a prostitute. Later, when he
is shot down and captured in North Vietnam, his
friends manage to make their way to his prison camp
and rescue him. There are good scenes of Marine
combat flying, but the plot is farfetched.

410. Pelfrey, William. Hamburger Hill. Based on the
      screenplay by Jim Carabatsos. NY: Avon, 1987.
      197 pp. 87-91495.

Pelfrey, whose The Big V (114) is an outstanding
Vietnam novel, has done a fine job with Jim Cara-
batsos' screenplay. In 1969, a squad in the 101st
Airborne Division takes part in the assault of
Hamburger Hill, a heavily fortified enemy position.
The squad includes typical military characters, and
Pelfrey lets them work out their fate in a costly
infantry battle. While the elements of a good combat
novel are not unique to this one, Pelfrey's characterization and the excellent dialogue add a special
dimension.

411. Philburn, Dennis K. Freedom Bird. NY: Tor, Tom
      Doherty, 1987. 313 pp. 0-812-51210-3.

Ryan James' year in the infantry in Vietnam passes
reasonablly well. He arrives as a frightened private
during what is probably 1970 and is assigned to the
Americal Division near Chu Lai. He leaves a year
later as a frightened but experienced sergeant. Along
the way he grows from boy to man and earns some
well-deserved medals. All the standard elements of a
Vietnam novel are here: good and bad officers and
NCOs, drugs, racial problems and futile death. James'

war is particularly bloody, and when he returns to
civilian life, he does not want to discuss it.

412. Pruitt, James N. _Striker One Down_. NY: Tor, Tom
      Doherty, 1987. 279 pp. 0-812-51217-0.

      Stories of Salt and Pepper, a biracial team of
      turncoats, appear occasionally in the literature and
      folklore of the Vietnam War. Here, they are
      associated with an evil North Vietnamese major and
      made the target of a Special Forces assassination
      team. After numerous jungle battles, including some
      in North Vietnam, virtually everyone in the novel is
      dead. If the action is relentless, the dialogue is
      completely unbelievable. Pruitt is not without
      literary skill, but his characters and their words are
      nearly as overdone as those in some Vietnam adventure
      series.

413. Raines, Jeff. _The Big Island_. NY: Beech Tree Books/
      William Morrow, 1987. 239 pp. 87-1122.

      Much of this story about a corrupt Hawaiian police
      chief takes the form of a long flashback to the
      Vietnam War. James Yamasaki was a Marine sergeant in
      1965. Taken with an elite Army unit on a secret
      mission to Laos, his job was to assist in the destruc-
      tion of a village involved in the heroin trade. The
      mission ended in disaster and Yamasaki found himself
      the prisoner of an Asian drug warlord with whom he
      ultimately came to terms. After leaving Asia through
      Bangkok in 1966, Yamasaki returned to Hawaii and began
      a career in law enforcement. In the present crime
      drama, his past is an important component.

414. Scott, Leonard B. _The Last Run_. NY: Ballantine,
      1987. 435 pp. 86-91570.

      Like Scott's earlier _Charlie Mike_ (337), this novel of
      the 75th Airborne Rangers in Vietnam is emotional but
      effective. Some characters from the earlier book
      appear here, and the military quality of the unit is
      also sustained. The story has to do with first
      training new replacements in 1970 and then leading a
      few of them on a mission to locate an enemy divisional
      headquarters. The Rangers are successful, but at
      great cost to themselves. Subplots about romances

between enlisted men and American civilian women
detract from the novel's general credibility, and
Scott works too hard to create colorful characters.
Nonetheless, he has been there and his novel shows it.

415.   Sherman, David. The Night Fighters: Knives in the
       Night. NY: Ivy, 1987. 256 pp. 86-91840.

This is a better book than its lurid title would
suggest. Based on the author's experience, it
describes a Marine Combined Action Program platoon in
a Vietnamese village in 1966. The Marines are
excellent at their jobs and highly motivated to deny
the enemy freedom of movement at night. Combat action
abounds and it is described well. Characterization is
shallow, especially for Vietnamese. Although the
Marines are somewhat larger than life, the book is an
interesting account of a program that is not well
known.

416.   Sherman, David. The Night Fighters, Book 2: Main
       Force Assault. NY: Ivy, 1987. 308 pp.
       87-90847.

In his second book about Marines in a Combined Action
Platoon in 1966, Sherman continues to write with more
realism and less hyperbole than is customary in
paperback series. Here he takes up a familiar
military theme--the education of a young lieutenant by
an experienced sergeant. There is also an excellent
account of the theft of a jeep that will amuse anyone
who knows how the military really works. These
Marines fight a serious war, and their enemies include
a corrupt South Vietnamese officer who apparently
knows how to defend himself.

417.   Sherman, David. The Night Fighters, Book 3: Out of
       the Fire. NY: Ivy Books, 1987. 241 pp. 87-
       90996.

This third book in the series about a Marine Combined
Action Program unit follows immediately the plot of
its predecessor. It is November of 1966 and the
Marines in Bun Hou village have been framed for
smuggling heroin by their enemy, a corrupt Vietnamese
officer. As they face these charges, they continue
the harsh war of patrols and ambushes against the

enemy. As always, they fight well and are successful.
Finally, with help from both Vietnamese and American
friends, the Marines are cleared of the criminal
charges. The corrupt officer comes to a bad end, and
the war can go on.

418.   Whiteley, L.S. Deadly Green. NY: New American
          Library, Signet, 1987. 285 pp. 0-451-15000-7.

Even in the wide variety of Vietnam novels, this one
is unusual. In 1969, a small group of infantrymen
decide to leave the war. Theu escape to a small
village on the seacoast where they are taken in by the
friendly inhabitants. When a helicopter crashes
nearby, the only survivor is a colonel who appears to
be involved in the black market. The men refuse to
accompany him back to the Army. Shortly afterward, he
returns with combat forces and destroys the village.
The only American survivor the Army can find is
wounded and told he will be returned to the field.
Throughout the novel, the characters talk and think a
great deal about philosophical matters.

419.   Williams, Michael. Door Gunner. NY: Tor, 1987.
          319 pp. 0-812-51202-2.

The helicopter door gunner is one of the enduring
images of the Vietnam War. This realistic and
effective novel describes the career of Carl
Willstrom, a nineteen-year-old gunner who learns his
trade in Vietnam during the time of the Cambodian
invasion. Willstrom sees a great deal of action and
is promoted to Specialist Fifth Class by the end of
his tour. Attracted by excitement, he extends for a
transfer to dangerous work in scout helicopters. In
the end, his attraction proves fatal.

420.   Zeybel, Henry. Gunship: Spectre of Death. NY:
          Pocket, 1987. 280 pp. 0-671-62867-4.

In contrast to the disgruntled and reluctant
infantrymen who populate many Vietnam novels, Zeybel's
Air Force officers are enthusiastic professionals.
His hero, Hal Zorn, is a navigator in an AC-130
gunship that flies out of Thailand to hunt trucks
along the Ho Chi Minh Trail in 1970-71. These
converted cargo planes are loaded with sophisticated

electronics and a variety of guns that enable them to
destroy thousands of enemy vehicles. The Vietnamese
fight back with antiaircraft cannons and an occasional
guided missile. Zorn is a thoughtful, bloodthirsty
man who has some penetrating and sensible thoughts
about the effects of combat on men during and after
the event. As usual in Air Force novels, machines are
major characters, and Zeybel loves the AC-130 so much
that he ends the book with an account of its role in
the invasion of Grenada.

1988

421. Lansing, John. Black Eagles #14: Firestorm at Dong
        Nam. NY: Kensington, Zebra, 1988.   256 pp.
        0-8217-2287-5.

Lansing takes a giant step toward the ridiculous with
this plot. The reader is asked to believe that the
U.S. and Soviet governments agree to a fight to the
death between the Black Eagles and a similar military
team from Soviet bloc countries. The purpose is for
the winning group to impress intelligence operatives
around the world. An appropriate venue in Vietnam is
selected, and the two teams parachute in and fight it
out. After a series of suitably bloody encounters,
the Black Eagles emerge victorious.

422. Mackenzie, Steve. SEALS #5: Breakout! NY: Avon,
        1988.   153 pp.   87-91625.

Lieutenant Mark Tynan and his Navy SEAL team capture
enemy documents and learn the location of captured
Americans. They rush to the rescue, missing the
Americans by only two hours, but liberating thirteen
South Vietnamese. Without authorization, Tynan and
his men pursue the Americans and their captors toward
Cambodia. They eventually rescue the Americans and
trick two enemy units into a battle with one another.
Tynan loses two of his own men, but manages to escape
with the former prisoners. This episode is standard
for the series.

423. Willson, David. REMF Diary. Seattle: Black Heron
        Press, 1988.   313 pp.   0-930773-05-5.

REMF Diary is unique and accurate. It makes an

important contribution to the very sparse literature
about rear echelon service in Vietnam. Anyone
familiar with the military will recognize this day-by-
day account of a clerk in an Army office in Saigon in
1966 and 1967. Willson's unnamed diarist never sees
the enemy. Instead he contends with good and bad
officers, incompetent WACs and the endless trivia of
military life. But for the location, he could be on
any Army post in the United States. In an Army where
at least five men served in noncombat roles for every
one who actually fought the enemy, the life Willson
describes is much more typical of Vietnam than the
popular novels of combat.

NO DATES

424. Baker, W. Howard. [Bill Rekab]. The Dead and the
      Damned. London: Zenith Publications, n.d.
      192 pp.

The title page gives the author's name as Baker; on
the cover he is Rekab. The story here is that a
British secret agent, working with the South Vietnamese government of Marshall Ky, foils a revolutionary plot. Among the characters are an American
civilian banker, his wife, a Chinese traitor and the
inevitable beautiful Eurasian woman. The plotters are
members of a religious sect in league with the
Vietcong. At one point the British agent penetrates
North Vietnam, is captured and escapes in a private
airplane, bringing important prisoners along. In a
nation armed to the teeth, he achieves all this with
his bare hands and a Luger pistol.

425. Crocket, Bob. Viet Cong Torture Shack. N.p.: War
      Horrors, n.d. 180 pp.

Susan Schaefer, a journalist for Newsworld magazine,
has various sexual adventures in Saigon with a variety
of partners. When she and some colleagues are
captured by the Vietcong, she is brutally tortured
with electricity. Later, there are other nonstop
sexual activities before Susan escapes.

426. HoWan, Wang. Nurse Prisoners of the Cong. N.P.: War
      Horrors, n.d. 180 pp.

A group of American nurses is captured by the Vietcong
after they bail out of a burning plane. As prisoners,
they are frequently raped and otherwise sexually
tortured. One of them, the daughter of a U.S.
senator, escapes, but she is unable to convince anyone
of the conditions being endured by women still in the
camp.

427. Sakai, Joe. <u>Sex Slaves of the Viet Cong</u>. N.p.: War
        Horrors, n.d.

Susan, a U.S. senator's daughter who escaped from a
camp for sex slaves in <u>Nurse Prisoners of the Cong</u>
(426), is recovering in Washington from her ordeal.
Back in Vietnam, her former fellow prisoners are still
raped and otherwise abused. In a variation on the
customary plot of these boring pornographic novels,
there is some sense of history here. The war is at or
near its end as some characters reach freedom.

428. Schrieber. <u>Captive Nurses of Viet Cong</u>. N.P.: War
        Horrors, n.d. 180 pp.

Two entertainers are captured by the Vietcong after
their truck is ambushed. They are Francie and Rhonda,
who may be persons of the same names in other pornographic novels by this publisher. Characteri-
zationis so shallow that one cannot be sure. The two
women join others in a Vietcong sex camp where they
are raped and debased.

429. <u>Victims of the Cong</u>. N.p.: War Horrors, n.d.
        188 pp.

Eight American civilian women, seven nurses and the
teenage sister of one of them are captured and
sexually tortured by the Vietcong. Among their
captors is a renegade American. Eventually, the
survivors escape and are awarded the Congressional
Medal of Honor.

1964

430. Kelly, F.J. "The Vietnam Circle." In <u>Alfred Hitch-
      cock's Tales to Fill You with Fear and Trembling</u>,
      edited by Eleanor Sullivan, 308-318. NY: Dial
      Press, 1980. 76-43201.

When a Special Forces trooper in a Montagnard village
uses a deadly snake to murder another soldier, he
discovers that the hill people have curious ideas
about revenge.

431. Steiber, Raymond. "The Lost Indemnity." <u>Trace</u> 53
      (1964): 166-172.

In a war that must be Vietnam, a lieutenant and an
enlisted man are on patrol at night. The enlisted man
is terrified of the enemy and the dark. He loses his
weapon, makes unnecessary noise and plans to stop the
lieutenant from killing an enemy soldier. As they
return to their own lines, the enlisted man makes his
way successfully through the perimeter barbed wire,
but the lieutenant is trapped. The enlisted man
leaves him there to die.

1965

432. Thanh Giang and Luu Ngo. "An American Sees the
      Light." In <u>The Fire Blazes</u>, 171-181. Hanoi:
      Foreign Languages Publishing House, 1965.

This is the only story with an American character of
significance in a collection from North Vietnam.
Georges Fryet, an American soldier, is captured by the

Vietcong and reeducated to understand their version of
correct political and historical ideas. Finally,
after repenting his past sins, Fryet is released. The
impression is conveyed that imprisonment by the Vietcong is a sort of pleasant political summer camp.

1966

433. Edelson, Morris. "A Mission in Vietnam." Quixote 1,
        7 (June 1966): 40-43.

An Army platoon is on patrol somewhere in Vietnam in
1966. They have just enjoyed a rest in Saigon. The
patrol encounters an old Vietnamese man with a
wagon-load of personal possessions. The man sells
them some whiskey at an exorbitant price. Afterward,
when he makes an abrupt and suspicious movement, one
member of the platoon shoots and kills him. The
Americans then take the remaining alcohol and burn the
wagon and its contents. Later, when the platoon
leader reports the events to his sergeant, he is told,
"Tell your troubles to the chaplain, kid, he just went
over the hill."

434. Moriarity, Tom H. "Murder in Saigon." The Man from
        U.N.C.L.E. Magazine 2, 2 (September 1966): 60-90.

Joe Rodriguez, a cop from Los Angeles, is activated as
a member of the Army Reserves and sent to Saigon.
There, he outwits criminals, Vietcong and corrupt
officials to solve a currency manipulation problem.
There is also an interesting subplot about prisoners
of war in this early story.

435. Moriarity, Tom H. "The Saigon Charade." The Man from
        U.N.C.L.E. Magazine 2, 5 (December 1966): 88-118.

In this adventure, Joe Rodriguez saves a secret peace
conference in Saigon and destroys an enemy spy ring.
A fascinating bit player is a World War II French
naval cannon in Vietcong hands.

1967

436. Kolpacoff, Victor. "The Room." New American Review,
        no.1 (1967): 7-27.

Also in Writing Under Fire, edited by Jerome
Klinkowitz and John Somer, 71-89. NY: Delta,
1978. 78-17682.

A former officer, now a prisoner, is forced to assist
in the interrogation of a Vietcong suspect. The room
in which the interrogation takes place is described in
detail.

437. Mayer, Tom. "Anson's Last Assignment." Playboy,
      August 1967, 97, 131-134, 136-137.
      Also in his The Weary Falcon, as "The Last
      Operation," 79-110. Boston: Houghton Mifflin,
      1971. 75-132335.

Bender, an American photojournalist, and Anson, an
English photographer, visit a Korean unit. The
Koreans are sharp, capable and motivated troops. The
visitors observe karate practice and fly to a company
in the field that has just been in combat. Anson is
killed just before he intended to return to England.

438. Moriarity, Tom H. "Condition Red in Saigon." The
      Man From U.N.C.L.E. Magazine 4, 2 (September
      1967): 106-123.

Ace CIA agent Captain Joe Rodrigues overcomes many
dangers in Hanoi and Saigon to foil a Chinese plot to
bomb Saigon with an atomic weapon.

                              1968

439. Bonazzi, Robert. "Light Casualties." Transatlantic
      Review 28 (Spring 1968): 46-51.

Specific locations are not mentioned, but this appears
to be a story of the Vietnam War. Two brothers meet
in a field hospital where one is on the staff and the
other is a wounded front line soldier. The unwounded
man describes the meeting as he plans letters to his
mother.

440. Eastlake, William. "The Biggest Thing Since Custer."
      Atlantic Monthly 222, 3 (September 1968): 92-97.
      Also in Prize Stories 1970, edited by William
      Abrahams, 17-28. NY: Doubleday, 1970.

Writing Under Fire, 58-68.

An infantry company is wiped out in northern Vietnam.
The event is compared to the massacre of Custer's
troops at the Battle of the Little Big Horn as
photographers and graves registration personnel
process the bodies.

441. Gerald, John Bart. "Walking Wounded." Harper's 237,
       1419 (August 1968): 45-50.
       Also in The Fact of Fiction, edited by Cyril M.
       Gulassa, 112-121. San Francisco: Canfield Press,
       1972. 75-184742.

Dunbar is an enlisted medical specialist at an Air
Force base hospital in the United States that receives
casualties from a battle zone that must be in Vietnam.
Some of the wounded are in terrible physical and
psychological shape. They bring the war home with
them. Dunbar is sensitive and professionally competent. He knows that he is fortunate not to be in
combat and he cannot remain unaffected by his job.

442. Grinstead, David. "A Day in Operations." The
       Literary Review 12, 1 (Autumn 1968): 103-115.
       Also in The Fact of Fiction, 86-98.

The narrator tells his story in the present tense. He
is an experienced combat soldier who has been wounded
and assigned to assist a major in battalion operations. The major, a veteran of World War II and
Korea, does not understand the military situation in
Vietnam. His insistence on classical military
operations and procedures regularly causes men in the
field to be killed. The narrator fails both in
reasoning with the major and in sabotaging his work,
so he decides to apply for a transfer back to his
original company in the field.

443. Neimark, Paul G. "The Boy Who Did a Man's Job." In
       Combo #3: An Ace Anthology, edited by John
       Cooper, 17-19. NY: Scott, Foresman, 1968.

A proud father describes how his son, a young black
soldier in Vietnam, sacrificed his life and won a
Congressional Medal of Honor.

444. Poyer, Joe. "Null Zone." Analog 81, 5 (July 1968):
        54-72.

      After an armistice in the Vietnam War, an American
      Special Forces unit blocks the Ho Chi Minh Trail with
      radioactive waste.

445. Smith, Kathleen R. "Letters from Vietnam."
        Scholastic Magazine (1968).
        Also in The Fallen Angel and Other Stories,
        155-120. NY: Scholastic Book Services, 1970.

      In this story for adolescents, a high school newspaper
      editor corresponds with a soldier in Vietnam who later
      dies in a hospital.

446. Tam, H.T. Saigon Seven. Saigon: Damson, 1968.

      Tam's English is not always precise, but his point of
      view is unique. The review copy is awkwardly punc-
      tuated and very poorly printed.

   a. "Silver Bird Slave," pp. 6-21.

      An American colonel is acquainted with the wife of a
      Vietnamese officer. She becomes pregnant after an
      encounter with an American.

   b. "Here is the Kill Road," pp. 23-41.

      A former South Vietnamese soldier is unemployed and
      broke. For a fee, he agrees to plant a bomb for the
      Vietcong.

   c. "PFC Report," pp. 43-63.

      Both American and Vietnamese employees have trouble
      with a corrupt, inefficient commanding officer.

   d. "A Footsoldier in Town," pp. 65-82.

      A Vietnamese marine on convalescent leave in Saigon,
      has an encounter with a woman who urges him to desert
      and become her lover.

   e. "The PMA Guy," pp. 83-100.

      An American officer in Saigon attempts to seduce a

Vietnamese secretary, and her husband threatens to
kill him.

f. "Black Jack Won't Make It Home," pp. 101-118.

Jackson, a black American soldier, is killed on his
last night in Vietnam during a rocket attack.

g. "Operation Hang Xanh," pp. 119-173.

American and Vietnamese ranger officers engage in
urban warfare in Saigon during the 1968 Tet Offensive.

1969

447. Chatain, Robert. "The Adventure of the Mantises."
         New American Review 7 (August 1969): 150-158.
         Also in The Fact of Fiction, edited by Cyril M.
         Gulassa, 104-111. San Francisco: Canfield Press,
         1972. 75-184742.

A group of soldiers in a rear area near Bien Hoa feed
insects to a mantis. Various men walk up and are
absorbed in the action.

448. Heinemann, Larry. "Do You Know What an Ambush Is?"
         In don't you know there's a war on?, edited by
         John Schultz, 13. Chicago: Columbia College
         Press, 1969.

In two paragraphs, Heineman tries to explain a
military ambush in terms of civilian experence.

449. Heinemann, Larry. "The Mission." In don't you know
         there's a war on?, 14-17.

A sergeant in command of a patrol makes an unwise
decision that leads to disaster.

450. Heinemann, Larry. "Suddenly the Sun." In don't you
         know there's a war on?, 18-23.

Crewmen on armored personnel carriers clean up and
attempt to reorganize after a battle. They have the
unpleasant job of handling the badly burned corpse of
a friend. Later they have an exchange of views with

visiting television cameramen.

451. Dinh Phong. "A Surgical Operation." South Vietnam:
      Giai Phong Publishing House, 1969. 22 pp.

      This product of the National Liberation Front of South
      Vietnam is dedicated "to american [sic] friends who
      are struggling against the unjust war in VietNam."
      The story has to do with the staff of an underground
      Vietcong hospital that is faced with a wounded
      American soldier. In dialogue that is measured in
      paragraphs, they seek a correct political solution.
      Although many of their family and friends have been
      killed or maimed by Americans, the staff eventually
      reaches the correct consensus, and an operation is
      performed to save the man. Members of the hospital
      staff are influenced by the fact that the American is
      a black from a working class background. His docu-
      ments show that he neither drinks nor smokes and that
      he sends all his money home.

452. Parker, Thomas. "Troop Withdrawal--The Initial
          Step." Harpers 239, 1431 (August 1969): 61-78.
          Also in The Fact of Fiction, edited by Cyril M.
          Gulassa, 67-85. San Francisco: Canfield Press,
          1972. 75-184742.
          Writing Under Fire, 90-107.
          Touring Nam, 389-411.

      In 1968, a specialist fourth class and a lieutenant
      who are long time adversaries work in an Army hospital
      near Saigon. Through able and astute use of military
      forms and regulations, the specialist manages to have
      the lieutenant declared officially dead.

453. Presley, John. "The Soldier." Kansas Quarterly 2, 1
          (Winter 1969-70): 86-101.

      Slatermore, a career Army sergeant, is a patient in a
      military hospital in the United States. After
      learning that his former unit in Vietnam had been
      badly mauled in an ambush, he got drunk and crashed a
      car, killing two women and injuring himself. As he
      undergoes treatment, he remembers scenes from his
      military career, including Vietnam.

454. Richie, Mary. "Hunt and Destroy." New American
        Review, no.6 (1969): 64-68.
        Also in The Fact of Fiction, edited by Cyril M.
        Gulassa, 99-103. San Francisco: Canfield Press,
        1972. 75-184742.

        Jimmy is an enlisted member of a Marine reconnaissance
        unit in a war among the rice paddies of what seems to
        be Vietnam. On one operation, he acquires a pet
        snake. On another, a cobra comes between him and an
        enemy soldier. Jimmy identifies with snakes. He is
        an able and unfeeling being in a war situation that is
        much more symbolic than realistic.

455. Woods, W. C. "He That Died of Wednesday." Esquire, 6
        (June 1969): 213-164.
        Also in Writing Under Fire, 152-164.

        This touching story includes a brief description of
        events in the war, but it deals mostly with reconcil-
        iation of a returning soldier with his girlfriend.
        She has been unfaithful to him and has donated money
        and blood to the enemy, but they still love each other
        and plan to be married.

                                  1970

456. Dozois, Gardner R. "A Dream at Noonday." In Orbit 7,
        edited by Damon Knight, 132-145. NY: Putnam's,
        1970. 66-15585.
        NY: Berkley Medallion, 1970. Pp. 127-139.
        Also in his The Visible Man, 119-132. NY:
        Berkley, 1977.

        A soldier observes his surroundings in detail and
        daydreams about his childhood and youth. Later,
        medics bring in the dead body of his friend.

457. Kaplan, Johanna. "Dragon Lady." Harper's 241, 1442
        (July 1970): 78-83.
        Also in Writing Under Fire, 22-34.

        A Chinese girl, brought up in Cholon, becomes a
        Vietcong assassin. Her specialty, until she is
        caught, is shooting Americans and Vietnamese from the
        back of a motorcycle. She uses a .45 pistol.

458. Ly Qui Chung, ed. <u>Between Two Fires</u>. NY: Praeger
        Publishers, 1970. 119 pp. 72-126776.

  Four of the nine stories in this collection have
  American characters or are related in some substantial
  way to Americans.

  a. Nguyen Tan Bi. "When the American Came,"
        pp. 3-14.

  A two-month stay of an American company in a Vietnamese village is viewed from the perspective of the
  villagers. They are able to see little difference
  between the Americans and the French. Nothing is
  gained militarily, and the life of the village is
  disrupted.

  b. Thanh Chau. "The Tears of Tan Qui Dong,"
        pp. 21-41.

  A resettlement village near Saigon is the scene of
  fighting in May 1968. A family is forced to evacuate.
  They observe American tanks and helicopters in combat
  against the enemy. From incidental fire, the
  villagers suffer material and human losses.

  c. Chu Thao. "Resuscitation of the Dead Earth,"
        pp. 53-61.

  In the small village of Binh Hoa, near Highway 1, an
  American unit is attacked by the Vietcong. In
  addition to more customary reactions, the Americans
  later defoliate the area. Afterward, local farmers
  find that nothing will grow in the soil. Finally,
  they import earthworms, and the soil begins to live
  again.

  d. Nguyen Pham Ngoc. "House for Rent," pp. 63-73.

  In 1969, a Vietnamese soldier searches for housing for
  his family in Danang. He finds that the city has been
  economically and socially harmed by the Americans, and
  he is unable to afford decent housing on his soldier's
  pay.

459. Major, Clarence. "We is Grunts." In <u>19 Necromancers
        from Now</u>, edited by Ishmael Reed, 177-183.
        Garden City, NY: Anchor, 1970.

Black soldiers in Vietnam are mistreated by white NCOs
and officers who also rape Vietnamese children.

460. The Mountain Trail. Hanoi: Viet Nam Women's Union,
     1970. 136 pp.

Lengthy political rhetoric characterizes all the
stories in this collection about Vietnamese women
fighting the Americans. There are a few simple black-
and-white illustrations.

a. Bich Thuan. "The Red Tie," pp. 9-24.

A North Vietnamese or Vietcong nurse treats children
injured by American planes.

b. Bich Thuan. "Women Gunners in Quang Binh,"
   pp. 25-40.

A woman in a seacoast village operates artillery
against the American Seventh Fleet.

c. Nguyen Kien. "A Moonlit-Night in the Forest,"
   pp. 41-56.

Female Vietcong work to keep a road open after
American bombing.

d. To Hoang. "The Intermediate Post," pp. 57-75.

A communication specialist works in a village that is
frequently attacked by American aircraft.

e. Ma Van Khang. "Sung My," pp. 77-99.

A young Meo woman works to maintain agricultural
production in her village.

f. Nguyen Thi Nhu Trang. "Drizzling," pp. 101-116.

A woman physician from a revolutionary family treats
men injured by the Americans.

g. Huu Mai. "The Mountain Trail," pp. 117-136.

A woman from the lowlands assists anti-American
fighters in the mountains.

1971

461. Brunner, John. "The Inception of the Epoch of Mrs.
          Bedonebyasyoudid." _Quark_, 1971.
          Also in his _From This Day Forward_, 215-222.
          Garden City, NY: Doubleday, 1972.
          NY: DAW Books, 1973. Pp. 169-175.

Although this story unfolds in a direct, linear
fashion, the Vietnamese connection is established only
at the end. In New York City, a group of young men
of several races set booby traps that kill and maim
numerous citizens. It is then revealed that they are
working for a Vietcong officer who lives under cover
in the city. Their next project is to be a mortar
bombardment of New York.

462. Chatain, Robert. "On the Perimeter." _New American
          Review_ 13 (1971): 112-131.
          Also in _Writing Under Fire_, 209-226.
          Touring Nam, edited by Martin H. Greenberg and
          Augustus Richard Norton, 302-323. NY: Morrow,
          1985.

An Army enlisted man reflects on many aspects of the
war as he stands guard on the perimeter. His numerous
thoughts are all rather brief and they change quickly.

463. Deighton, Len. "First Base." In his _Eleven Declara-
          tions of War_, 98-115. NY: Harcourt Brace
          Jovanovich, 1971. 74-13068.

Two Army truck drivers become lost in the rain
somewhere in Vietnam. After wandering for a while,
they find an abandoned American base with abundant
supplies. One of them is burned in an accident and
dies shortly afterward. The other truck driver may
still be there, eating packaged foods and listening to
popular music recordings.

464. Erhart, Stephen. "As the Hippiest Doctor Almost
          Grooved." _Harper's_ 242, 1452 (May 1971): 82-84,
          86.

This uncomfortable and effective story is told by a
casualty on a hospital ship off the coast of Vietnam.

At one point, the ship sails in company with the battleship New Jersey, but there are no other clues as to when the story takes place. The medical and social routines of the ship unfold and these seem to be the central action of the story. There is more than enough unpleasantness, and the touches of satire are refreshingly light when compared with most Vietnam fiction.

465.   Hardy, Frank. "A Friend of Today is an Enemy of
          Tomorrow." In We Took Their Orders and are Dead,
          edited by Shirley Cass, et al, 52-55. Sydney:
          Ure Smith, 1971. 0-7254-0070-6.

A legendary Australian soldier is successful in his atempt to draw first blood in Vietnam.

466.   Hauley, D. Jr. "Two Separate Men Sharing the Same
          Seat on a Train." Mirror Northwest 2 (Summer
          1971): 56-60.

A sniper shoots down two American helicopters with a machine gun. When he examines the downed aircraft, he sees but does not kill a surviving crewman.

467.   Heinemann, Larry. "By the Rule." In it never stopped
          raining, edited by John Schultz, et al, 15-18.
          Chicago: Columbia College, 1971.

After suffering casualties from command-detonated mines, members of an Army unit capture two prisoners and give serious thought to vengenance

468.   Heinemann, Larry. "Cole." In it never stopped
          raining, 9-14.

The narrator first meet Cole in a mechanized unit in Vietnam. Cole was a serious, dangerous and completely crazy soldier. When word comes to the veteran that Cole was killed in a truck accident, he remembers and describes several encounters with Cole.

469.   Huddle, David. "The Interrogation of the Prisoner
          Bung by Mister Hawkins and Sergeant Tree."
          Esquire 75, 1 (January 1971): 128-129, 156, 158,

160, 162.
Also in <u>Free Fire Zone: Short Stories by Vietnam</u>
<u>Veterans</u>, edited by Wayne Karlin, et al, 59-67.
Coventry, Conn.: 1st CasualtyPress, 1973.
72-12486.
<u>A Dream With No Stump Roots In It</u>, by David
Huddle, 17-26. N.p.: University of Missouri
Press, 1975. 74-22229.
<u>Vietnam Anthology: American War Literature</u>,
edited by Nancy Anisfield, 37-44. Bowling green,
OH: Bowling Green State University Popular Press,
1987.

An American and a Vietnamese interrogate a Vietcong
suspect, After they beat him and he supplies some
information, they release him. The prisoner returns
to his village happy that he has been able to gather
so much information for his Vietcong unit at the cost
of only a minor beating.

470. Mayer, Tom. <u>The Weary Falcon</u>. Boston: Houghton
      Mifflin, 1971. 174 pp. 75-132335.

  a. "The Weary Falcon" pp. 1-54.

  Chaney is a warrant officer flying a Cobra helicopter
  out of An Khe. He flies with Slade, a regular Army
  captain, and with Mood, a new pilot. In an active day
  which is quite revealing of the helicopter war, both
  Slade and Mood are killed. Chaney visits each of
  their rooms afterward and comes to know more about
  them. At the end of the story, he is even more weary
  than at the beginning.

  b. "A Walk in the Rain," pp. 55-57.

  An inexperienced Special Forces officer leads a patrol
  of Vietnamese over the border into Laos. They engage
  in minor and inconclusive action. The officer does
  his job well, but he is not sure whether he has the
  courage and ability for real combat. Back at his
  base, he learns that another patrol was attacked and
  that an American was wounded. Then he is told that he
  will take out another patrol soon.

  c. "The Last Operation," pp. 79-110.
          Originally published in <u>Playboy</u> 14 (August 1967)
          as "Anson's Last Assignment".

See annotation 437.

d. "Kafka for President," pp. 111-147.

Bender, an American reporter, visits a Marine Combined
Action Company outside of Danang. The company assists
with civic and defense projects in a village. On one
patrol with the Marines, Bender witnesses the capture
and later the torture of a female Vietcong. Under
pressure, she reveals that the Vietnamese girlfriend
of one of the Marines is also a Vietcong. The two
women are later taken away.

e. "A Birth in the Delta," pp. 149-174.
      Also in Writing Under Fire, 43-57.
      Touring Nam, 339-357.
An Army company in the Mekong Delta engages and
destroys a Vietcong encampment. Among the ruined
huts, they find a dead woman with a baby at the point
of being born. The company medic performs a crude
operation in an attempt to save the baby, but he is
unsuccessful, and the baby dies.

471. Moorcock. Michael. "So Long Sonn Lon: 1968: Babies."
      In his Breakfast in the Ruins, 156-166. NY:
      Random House, 1971. 73-18306.
      London: New English Library, 1975. Pp. 156-166.
      NY: Avon, 1980. Pp. 152-163.

This is actually a chapter in a science fiction novel
whose main character travels through space and time.
The chapter describes a young infantryman's participation in the slaughter of civilians.

                              1972

472. Baber, Asa. "The Ambush." The Falcon 4, 4 (Spring
      1972): 39-44.
      Also in his Tranquility Base and Other Stories,
      14-20. Canton, NY: Fiction International, 1979.
      79-89138.
      TriQuarterly, no. 45 (Spring 1979): 165-171.
      Published as "Ambush: Laos, 1960."
      Writing Under Fire, 130-135.
      Touring Nam, 94-101. "Ambush: Laos, 1960."
      Vietnam Anthology, 45-49.

A Marine officer is a patient in the hospital at Camp

Pendleton. He suffers psychological problems because
of his cowardice in an ambush in Laos which is
described briefly.

473. Haldeman, Joe. "Counterpoint." In Orbit 11, edited
      by Damon Knight, 168-178. NY: Berkley, c1972,
      1973. 66-15585.
      Also in his Infinite Dreams, 1-12. NY: St.
      Martin's, 1978. 78-3959.

Two men are born on the same day in 1943. Michael,
the son of a rich man, lives a life of ease and goes
to Vietnam in 1966 as an officer. Roger, the bastard
son of a New Orleans prostitute, leads a squalid life
and eventually goes to Vietnam as an enlisted artil-
leryman. They do not know each other. By exercise of
bad professional judgement, Roger puts an artillery
round on Michael's position. Michael is wounded, and
the remainder of his life, through 1985, is spent as a
human vegetable in hospitals. Roger returns to
America to become a successful university professor,
but he, too, meets his final fate in a suprise ending.
This is one of the most intellectually satisfying
stories of the Vietnam War.

474. Hamil, Ralph E. "The Vietnam War Centennial
      Celebration." Analog 90, 2 (October 1972):
      94-107.

In the 21st century, a greatly altered future world
celebrates the centennial of a Vietnam War that turned
out much differently from the real one. The story is
conveyed in a group of documents from the centennial
commission.

475. Hasford, Gustav. "Is That You, John Wayne? Is This
      Me?" Mirror Northwest 3 (1972): 58-59.

A Marine enlisted man wearing a peace symbol has a
confusing encounter with an officer.

476. Major, Clarence. "Dossy O." Black Creation 3, 4
      (Summer 1972): 4-5.
      Also in Writing Under Fire, 108-110.

This story has to do with the attitudes and percep-

tions of black soldiers serving in Vietnam. The
language, a sort of Black slang, is particularly
difficult to follow.

477. Pfundstein, Roy. "An Odd Coin." Ball State Univer-
        sity Forum 13, 2 (Spring 1972): 52-56.

     John, a Vietnam veteran, is insane, seemingly driven
     so by the war. One of his two selves narrates the
     story. He remembers scenes of dead bodies, heli-
     copters and his work as a sniper. He is in jail,
     apparently having used his military skills to ambush
     his mother when she harassed him too much after his
     return from Vietnam.

478. Pittman, Luther. "A Day in Camp." Mirror Northwest 3
        (1972): 60-63.

     American prisoners, kept in horrid conditions, receive
     marginal "medical" treatment and a bowl of rice with
     fish sauce on a special day.

479. Porsche, Don. "Evenings in Europe and Asia." Prairie
        Schooner 46, 2 (Summer 1972): 96-104.
        Also in Writing Under Fire, 35-42.
        Touring Nam, 20-29.

     On a visit to Europe, a young man develops and
     expresses his reservations about war and killing.
     Later he compromises in order to serve as a radio
     operator in Vietnam.

480. Shields, James. "The Candidate." Caroline Quarterly,
        Spring 1972.
        Also in Free Fire Zone, 108-117.

     Mixed together in this particularly difficult story
     are reflections about racial tension in the military
     and observations about railroad tracks in the jungle
     of Vietnam.

481. Vargas, Ernesto. "The Excuse." Mirror Northwest 3
        (1972): 53-57.

     A Navy corpsman watches as Marines beat and then

murder a young Vietnamese prisoner. He lacks the
courage to speak out or stop the Marines. Later he
writes to his parents that it was an uneventful day.

482. West, Thomas A. Jr. "Gone Are the Men." Trans-
     atlantic Review, no. 41 (Winter/Spring 1972):
     35-45.
     Also in Writing Under Fire, 136-145.

This awkward story seems to be made up of the thoughts
of a soldier during either an artillery attack or a
religious service. Among his reflections are poems
and the lyrics to songs.

483. Wongar, B. The Sinners: Stories of Vietnam. Greens
     borough, Australia: Greensborough Press, 1972.
     76 pp.

The indroduction explains that the author is a black
American deserter, but internal evidence suggests the
book was written by an Australian.

a. "The Hole," pp. 14-20.

A soldier in a village clearing operation hides in a
hole with a Vietnamese woman and her children. After
the troops leave, aircraft come to level the village.

b. "Boomerang Bullets," pp. 21-29.

A sergeant invents bullets that hit the enemy and
return to their source. In a field test, they prove
to be too effective.

c. "At Half Mast," pp. 29-38.

A soldier is imprisoned in a concrete bunker and
visited by various people.

d. "Khe Sanh," pp. 39-45.

At Khe Sanh, a journalist observes two soldiers
arguing about survival.

e. "Hot Ace," pp. 47-52.

A black pilot hears the voice of his sister, a civil
rights activist, while he is on a bombing run.

f. "The Charge at Dawn," pp. 53-59.

During an assault on a village, a soldier visualizes
his pregnant wife. He finds an infant in the village.

g. "The Soldier that Died of Glory," pp. 61-67.

After returning to a strangely unrealistic homeland,
an intelligence officer remembers his experiences in
Vietnam.

1973

484. Algren, Nelson. "Police and Mama-sans Get It All."
      In his The Last Carousel, 144-150. NY: Putnam,
      1973. 72-97289.

Although listed in a standard index as a short story,
this may well be journalism. A Vietnamese prostitute
who maintains both pride and hope despite her working
conditions is befriended by an American. After she
sees the relative luxury of his hotel room, she tries
to move into his life. Although the American admires
her sprit, he declines the proffered arrangement.

485. Algren, Nelson. "What Country Do You Think You're
      In?" In his The Last Carousel, 138-143.

Like the other Algren work listed here, this may be
journalism. An American civilian lives in a hotel in
Saigon in 1969. Among his acquaintances are a deaf-
mute Vietnamese prostitute and her teenage son. He
invites them to join him for dinner on a riverboat
restuarant. On the appointed day, the boy insists
that the American join him at a cricket fight instead.
Later, the American learns that the restuarant had
been bombed that day.

486. Anderson, S.E. "Soldier Boy." In Vietnam and Black
      America: An Anthology of Protest and Resistance,
      edited by Clyde Taylor, 195-199. Garden City,
      NY: Anchor Press/Doubleday, 1973. 72-84972.

In a firefight in 1972, a Black soldier socializes
with one of the enemy and then attacks a white
officer.

487. Clifton, Merritt. "In the Field." The Gar #19 2, 8
     (1973).

An infantryman, probably in the Army, is assigned a
new buddy on patrol. Having seen new men come and go,
he is not particularly interested in this person, who
wears a peace medallion on his neck and has two
notches on the stock of his rifle. At the end of an
uneventful patrol, the new man kills a peasant woman
who seems suspicious. Passing airplanes mask the
shot.

488. Davis, George. "From Coming Home." In Vietnam and
     Black America: An Anthology of Protest and
     Resistance, edited by Clyde Taylor, 185-194.
     Garden City, NY: Anchor Press/Doubleday, 1973.
     72-84972.

In this extract from the novel, black soldiers
socialize with prostitutes and discuss the shortcomings of white people.

489. Dempsey, Hank. "The Defensive Bomber." In Nova 3,
     edited by Harry Harrison, 93-111. NY: Walker,
     1973. 72-95775.

A North Vietnamese pilot enters the United States
disguised as a student. With the help of an unsavory
group of American radicals, he obtains an aircraft and
bombs two military installations in the San Diego
area. His plane is hit and forced to land. Then he
and a Black assistant are beaten to death by Americans
who reach the plane ahead of the Marines.

490. Grant, C.L. "Come Dance with Me on My Pony's Grave."
     The Magazine of Fantasy and Science Fiction 45,
     1 (July 1973): 72-84.

A Vietnam veteran with an adopted Montagnard son
dreams and remembers a time in Vietnam when he met the
boy and observed a supernatural event.

491. Just, Ward. "Journal of a Plague Year." The Atlantic
     Monthly 232, 2 (August 1973): 87-90.
     Also in his Honor, Power, Riches, Fame, and the
     Love of Women, 87-122. NY: Dutton, 1979.

79-10123.

The heroine of this love story is a journalist working
in Vietnam. She moves in and out of the battle zone,
back and forth between America and Vietnam, and in and
out of relationships with her lover, another journalist. She is certainly a stranger to most situations and people, and her alienation may indeed be the
result of exposure to the war.

492. Just, Ward. "Prime Evening Time." In his The
        Congressman Who Loved Flaubert, 93-114. Boston:
        Little, Brown, 1973. 73-3189.

The captain in this story is not named. Having
survived and won an important battle he is returned to
the United States and awarded the Congressional Medal
of Honor. He is then assigned to a staff job in
Washington, D. C. Under pressure from his superiors,
he agrees to an interview with a reporter who asks
about details of the action in which he won the medal.

493. Karlin, Wayne, Paquet, Basil T., and Rottmnan, Larry,
        eds. Free Fire Zone: Short Stories by Vietnam
        Veterans. Coventry, Conn.: 1st Casualty Press,
        1973. 208 pp. 72-12486.
        NY: McGraw-Hill, 1st Casualty Press, [1973].
        72-13881.

This is the most complete and well edited collection
of Vietnam short stories.

  a. McCusker, Michael Paul. "The Old Man," pp. 1-2.

An American infantryman, on a sweep through a village,
kills an old man for amusement. Afterward, he feels
nothing.

  b. Pelfrey, William. "Bangalore," pp. 3-12.

A new replacement in an Army unit is sent to join more
experienced men at an ambush site. With careful
planning and technique, the men successfully attack
and kill five Vietcong.

  c. Grajewsky, Julian. "The Meeting," pp. 14-16.

A soldier awakes in the morning and walks from his

bunker down to a nearby river to bathe. A leopard
with bloody paws and mouth drinks from the opposite
bank.

d. Karlin, Wayne. "Medical Evacuation," pp. 17-19.

A helicopter door gunner flies to a medical evacuation. At the landing site, he fires at suspected
enemy positions. After the ship returns to base, the
wounded and dead are removed.

e. Dorris, James R. "The Accident," pp. 21-27.

Temple, a sergeant, and Adams, a major, are assigned
to a support unit near Bien Hoa. They take a jeep to
a Vietnamese Army compound for a meeting. On the
return trip, while Adams is driving, they accidentally
hit and kill an old man. Over Adams's objections,
Temple insists on telling their commanding officer, a
colonel. The colonel explains that the matter is not
important enough to ruin the career of a good officer,
and it is forgotten.

f. Smith, Steve. "First Light," pp. 28-39.

After he kills civilians during a mistaken attack on a
village, a helicopter door gunner is harassed by a
rear area sergeant. He attempts to kill the sergeant,
but he is brought under control by a friend.

g. Little, Loyd. "Out with the Lions," pp. 41-50.

Two Special Forces troopers lead a party of Nung
mercenaries to an outpost on the Cambodian border. On
the way back, they are ambushed. After taking minor
wounds, they learn from shouting that their attackers
are Nungs in the employ of the Vietcong. An arrangement is made to end the battle, and each party goes
its separate way.

h. Karlin, Wayne. "Search and Destroy," pp. 51-54.

Marine helicopter crewman share quarters that are
infested with rats. After several unsuccessful
attempts, they manage to kill a mother and ten babies.

i. Karlin, Wayne. "The Vietnamese Elections,"
        pp. 56-58.

Marine helicopter crewman are ordered to kill two of

their three pet dogs. They conduct an election to make the choice and kill the two losers.

j. Huddle, David. "The Interrogation of Prisoner
        Bung by Mr. Hawkins and Sergeant Tree,"
        pp. 59-67.

    See annotation 469.

k. Kimple,John M. "And Even Beautiful Hands Cry,"
        pp. 69-79.

    A soldier living in Saigon falls in love with a
    Vietnamese bar girl. When her friend's child becomes
    ill, the soldier arranges for it to be treated in an
    American hospital. The baby dies, and the love affair
    is broken.

l. Aitken, James. "Lederer's Legacy," pp.80-96.

    Lederer and his buddies work in a unit whose job it is
    to write commendations. His legacy is a list of
    phrases in specialized military terminology describing
    the heroism or futility of men who show bravery in
    combat.

m. Bobrowsky, Igor. "The Courier," pp. 98-107.

    A Marine infantryman attempts to organize and control
    his thoughts as he drives a jeep in a convoy. He
    remembers the death and fear of battles.

n. Shields, James. "The Candidate," pp.108-117.
        Also in Caroline Quarterly (Spring 1972).

    See annotation 481.

o. Rottmann, Larry. "Thi Bong Dzu," pp. 119-125.
        Also in Vietnam Anthology, 50-55.

    Thi Bong Dzu is an adolescent rice farmer in a village
    north of Saigon. On the eve of his twelfth birthday,
    he sets out to assist his Vietcong squad and is killed
    in an ambush.

p. Pitts, Oran R. "Temporary Duty," pp.126-134.

    Three enlisted men from a medical support unit are
    sent forward to an evacuation hospital for thirty
    days. They find the situation there quite fright-

ening, and the experience helps them put their
previous problems into better perspective.

q. Karlin, Wayne.   "R & R."   pp.136-143.

During the Tet holiday in 1967, a Marine spends a
brief recreation leave in Saigon. He goes through the
usual experiences with bars, girls, and American
food, but he finds the leave unsatisfying.

r. Davis, George.   "Ben," pp. 144-146.
    Excerpt from his novel Coming Home (89).

A black lieutenant is offered a teenage Vietnamese
girl by her parents. Although he is not interested in
having sex, he takes the girl for a walk as he thinks
about the war and his part in it.

s. Tavela, John.   "The Souvenir," pp. 148-153.

A middle-aged overweight mess sergeant falls in love
with a Vietnamese woman. He offers her various gifts
and promises to take her to America with him. She
agrees, but later he learns that she has been trading
sex to another soldier for his promise, too, to take
her to America.

t. Paquet, Basil T.   "Warren," pp.154-175.

Warren is an enlisted man working with the living and
the dead at a hospital near Bien Hoa. His work and
recreation seem to be depressing and pointless. There
are explicit accounts of his relatioships with
prostitutes.

u. Karlin, Wayne.   "Extract," pp. 177-182.

Joshua, a door gunner on a helicopter, goes on a
mission to extract a group of reconnaissance Marines
in the Demilitarized Zone. He appears to be only
mildly interested in what he is doing.

v. Davis, George.   "Ben," pp. 183-186.
    Excerpt from his novel Coming Home (89).

Ben Williams, a black pilot, is on leave in Bangkok.
In a bar, he meets a black soldier who is AWOL and
plans to escape to Sweden. Ben sympathizes with the
man.

w. Currer, Barry. "The Rabbi," pp. 188-201.

The Rabbi is the nickname of Lt. Rowan, who commands a
military police detachment in Saigon. Rowan knows the
city and the language well; he is happy in his job and
has extended his tour several times. Unfortunately,
one of his subordinates makes a mistake, and the
threat of an investigation forces Rowan to leave for
the United States.

x. Mueller, Quentin. "Children Sleeping--Bombs
        Falling," pp. 202-204.

An American walks among the streets of Danang,
gathering last impressions of Vietnam on the day
before he leaves for Okinawa.

494. Perea, Robert L. "A War Story." Thunderbird 23, 2
        (December 1973): [24-25].

In the review copy, the proximity of this story to an
apparently unrelated photograph and its abrupt end at
the bottom of the page suggest that it may not be
complete. As it stands, a party of Army enlisted men
visit a whorehouse in Pleiku, where they escape
detection by military police during a raid.

495. Stone, Robert. "Fear." Place: Neon Rose III, 1 (June
        1973): 126-135.

In Saigon, sometime in the early 1970s, a freelance
writer considers becoming a dope dealer. In his
travels around the city, he encounters enough danger
and hopelessness to convince himself that there are no
moral absolutes. This story is an excerpt from the
novel Dog Soldiers (144).

496. Suddick, Tom. "The Diehard." The Berkeley Samisdat
        Review 1, 1 (June 1973): 3-12.
        Also in his A Few Good Men. Samisdat 4, 1
        (1974): 108-116.
        The Tower Anthology, 1-7. San Jose, CA: Tau
        Delta Phi Fraternity, 1974.

A lance corporal is separated from his unit, and he
survives for months, possibly years, in the jungle.
When he is finally rescued by Vietnamese troops, he

refuses to believe that the American troops have gone home. Sent to an American psychiatric hospital, he believes the staff are Russian interrogators.

1974

497. Drake, David. "Contact!" In Body Armor: 2000, edited by Joe Haldeman with Charles G. Waugh and Martin Harry Greenberg, 5-20. NY: Ace, 1986. Original copyright 1974.

A tank unit in Vietnam encounters a spaceship and its alien pilot.

498. Gains, Timothy Southerly. "The Deserter." The North American Review 259, 4 (Winter 1974): 53-60.

A deserter, working as a restroom attendant in Arizona, remembers a time in 1968 when he called in an airstrike on his own position.

499. Heinemann, Larry. "Coming Home High." Penthouse, December 1974, 92-94, 160, 175-176. Also in the story workshop reader, edited by John Schultz, 29-55. Chicago: Columbia College, 1982.

Sergeant Philip Dosier spends his last night in Vietnam drunk and stoned. Then he flies to the United States and goes through the process of separating from the Army. At home, he finds that the bad nights have begun.

500. Linhein, K.J. "A Sort of an Occultation." The Reed, Spring & Summer 1974, 23-27.

After the war, a veteran tells others in a bar how his rifle jammed in combat. Later in the story, a Vietnamese remembers the same event.

501. McDonald, Walter. "The Sendoff." In The Bicentennial Collection of Texas Short Stories, edited by James P. White, 74-80. Midland, TX: Texas Center for Writers Press, 1974. 74-81546.

Eddie, an Air Force enlisted man, is on his way to

Vietnam late in the war. On the airplane, he meets a
civilian with experience in Vietnam who entertains him
with horror stories about the war.

502.   McNamara, Brian W.   "Dust."   Assay 29, 2 (Winter
           1974): 27-28.

A patrol led by a lieutenant takes a break in the hill
country in Vietnam. Below them is a Montagnard
village. They fear they may have been seen by the
enemy and that they may be subject to mortar or
artillery attack. In a desultory fashion, they
discuss the relative merits of fighting in the jungle
versus fighting in the hills. After a while, they
move off.

503.   McNamara, Brian W.   "Swanson."   Assay 29, 2 (Winter
           1974): 5-7.

Swanson is a nineteen-year-old and he is dying in the
rain somewhere in Vietnam. Walking point on patrol,
he has stepped on a mine and he is fatally injured.
As members of his squad wait for the evacuation
helicopter, each of them thinks of the implications of
Swanson's death. The squad leader thinks how it will
affect his command; another man wants Swanson's food;
and the squad medic thinks how futile are his attempts
to keep Swanson alive. The story ends as the
helicopter arrives.

504.   Nash, Jay Robert.   "Getting the Count."   In his On All
           Fronts, 137-139. Western Springs, IL: December
           Press, 1974. 74-81911.

In 1967, a Marine platoon suffers heavy casualties
attempting to count enemy bodies in order to create a
photo opportunity for visiting reporters.

505.   Steele, Rodger.   "Just Another War Story."   Assay 29,
           3 (Spring 1974): 25-28.

An infantry radioman describes how his unit rests near
a Vietnamese hut, becomes acquainted with its occu-
pants and then burns it down.

506. Suddick, Tom. <u>A Few Good Men</u>. <u>Samisdat</u> 4, 1 (1974).
116 pp.
NY: Avon, 1978. 140 pp. 77-18336.

In his introduction to this issue of <u>Samisdat</u>, Suddick
suggests that the work may be considered a story
collection or a novel. After reading, the former
seems more reasonable. Like most <u>Samisdat</u> issues seen
for this bibliography, the reproduction is of poor
quality. The characters are Marines in the early
1970s.

a. "Caduceus," pp. 8-21.
Also in <u>Touring Nam</u>, 206-221.

A Navy corpsman attached to a Marine infantry unit
deals with the squalor of life in a bunker as well as
with his professional duties. At one point, he kills
a man too badly wounded to survive.

b. "A Hotel on Park Place," pp.21-35.

A staff sergeant in a rear area is a capable hustler
and promoter. Among other things, he is a consistent
winner of Monopoly games. He arranges to assume the
management of a large post exchange and to have a
suspicious Vietnamese medical officer killed.

c. "If Frogs Had Wings," pp.35-45.

Two enlisted Marines take a rest and recuperation
leave in Taiwan because Australia and other more
desirable places are not available. During the leave,
they devote their time to alcohol and sex, but they
cannot forget the war.

d. "It Was A Great Fight Ma," pp.46-66.

A lance corporal, new to Vietnam, is assigned as a
radioman. Before he can fully learn his trade, most
of his company is captured. He and a few other
survivors are assigned to another unit.

e. "A Shithouse Rat," pp. 68-78.
Also in <u>The Berkeley Samisdat Review</u> 2, 2 & 3
(Summer/Fall 1974): 25-36.
<u>Touring Nam</u>, 325-336.

A group of enlisted men is assigned to burn human
waste. They steal the private files of a senior NCO

and throw them into the burning pit. As the NCO
orders them to dig the files out with their hands, a
rocket attack kills him.

f. "Totenkopf," pp. 79-89.

After returning from Vietnam, a former Marine continues his business of selling war souvenirs,
including human skulls. Once, he uses the skull of a
dead Marine, and that man's brother seeks him out and
tries to kill him. Instead, the salesman beheads the
brother and plans to sell his skull, too.

g. "The Two Hundredth Eye," pp.89-107.

A lieutenant in a psychiatric hospital believes his
eye is missing as the result of capture and torture by
the enemy. The scenes the lieutenant remembers are
quite realistic and horrible.

                              1975

507. Ellison, Harlan. "Basilisk." In his Deathbird
            Stories, 94-113. NY: Dell, c1975, 1976.
            Also in Study War No More, edited by Joe
            Haldeman, 7-23. NY: St.Martin's, 1977.
            NY: Avon, 1978, 7-25.
            In the Field of Fire, edited by Jeanne Van Buren
            Dann and Jack Dann, 350-369. NY: Tor, 1987.
            86-50955.

Vernon Lustig, a Marine Lance Corporal, is injured by
pungi stakes then captured by both the enemy and a
supernatural being. After torture, rescue and court
martial, Lustig returns to the U.S. where he finds
that both his captivities bring him many problems.

508. Grant, John. "Polyorifice Enterprises." Penthouse,
            January 1975, 64-66, 146-148.

This strange and interesting piece of writing seems to
be part of at least two stories, and perhaps three.
One has to do with a Vietnamese prostitute; another
with a delightful old Vietnamese woman who, in effect,
buys the souls of orphans; and a third with Tex
Buchanan, a soldier who goes home to finish his life
in a wheelchair. A case could be made for a theme

that ties these fragments together, but in fact they
are arranged in an awkward and surprising, but not
unpleasant, manner.

509. Hannah, Barry. "Midnight and I'm Not Famous Yet."
          Esquire 48, 500 (July 1975): 58-60, 134, 136.
          Also in his Airships, 105-118. NY: Knopf, 1978.
          77-90938.
          NY: Vintage, 1985. Pp. 105-118.

An Army captain meets an old friend who is in Vietnam
as an official photographer. That man joins the
captain's unit and photographs a captured enemy
general. Later, the photographer is killed, and the
captain kills the general as he tries to escape.
After the war, the captain is finally able to obtain a
copy of the photograph of the general from the
Pentagon.

510. Heinemann, Larry. "The Firefight." Penthouse,
          October 1975, 100-102, 115-117.

Heinemann's ability to describe combat is fully
apparent in this fine story about armored personnel
carriers in action. The setting is near the Cambodian
border, and the characters are well drawn.

511. James, Joseph. "Back in the World." Penthouse,
          April 1975, 65-66, 92, 94, 108.

An artillery forward observer is wounded in Vietnam.
He moves through the military hospital system back to
the United States. He then makes a rather uncomfortable adjustment to civilian life. His family and
friends want to know how it was in Vietnam. In a
Veterans' Administration Office, he observes a callous
attitude on the part of the civil servants toward
veterans. A feeling is conveyed to the reader that
Vietnam veterans are separated from other Americans by
differences that are almost impossible to understand
or overcome.

512. McDonald, Walter. "New Guy." In New and Experimental
          Literature, edited by James P. White, 43-50.
          Midland, TX: Texas Center for Writers Press,
          1975.

An Air Force officer is sent to Vietnam on temporary
duty near the end of the war. He lives through a
rocket attack on his base and wonders how anyone can
stand the war for very long.

513. McDonald, Walter. "Snow Job." Quartet 7, 51-53
     (Summer-Fall-Winter 1975-1976): 75-84.

An Air Force officer on temporary duty in Vietnam is
assigned to write a history of the war. While a
passenger on an operational Phantom flight, he assists
in the defense of a Special Forces camp, and then the
plane attempts but fails to save the survivor of a
radar station that has been overrun. The officer has
an interesting and impressive reaction to his first
experience of air combat.

514. O'Brien, Tim. "Landing Zone Bravo." Denver Quarterly
     4, 3 (August 1975): 72-77.

American infantryman fly into an assault in a helicopter. The door gunners fire incessantly. As the
aircraft takes ground fire, one man freezes. Later he
must be forced out. As he wanders aimlessly in a rice
paddy, the door gunners shoot at him. He returns
their fire as the helicopter flies away.

515. O'Brien, Tim. "Where Have You Gone, Charming Billy?"
     Redbook 145, 1 (May 1975): 81, 127-132.
     Also in Phoenix Country, edited by Nigel Gray,
     80-86. A special issue of Fireweed (September
     1976).
     Prize Stories, 1976: The O. Henry Awards,
     edited by William Abrahams, 211-219. Garden
     City, NY: Doubleday, 1976. Published as "Night
     March."
     Prize Stories of the Seventies from the O. Henry
     Awards, edited by William Abrahams, 257-265. NY:
     Doubleday, 1981. 80-22790.
     NY: Pocket Books, Washington Square Press, 1981.
     Pp. 318-328.

An Army private first class is on patrol. He remembers the recent death of a friend. The man had lost a
foot to a mine and then died of a heart attack. The
surviving PFC is oppressed by the war, not very good
at his job and terrified.

516. Porsche, Don. "The Hump." <u>Samisdat</u> 4, 4 (Summer
          1975): 72-78.

      An experienced, capable sergeant in a combat unit is
      arrested by CID agents in 1968. Thhe sergeant serves
      time in prison and receives a dishonorable discharge.

517. Sayles, John. "Tan." In his <u>The Anarchists' Conven-
          tion</u>, 257-281. Boston: Little, Brown, 1975.
          78-78036.
          Also in <u>Soldiers and Civilians</u>, edited by Tom
          Jenks, 107-125. Toronto/NY: Bantam, 1986.
          86-47574.

      Tan, a Vietnamese girl, survives the Battle of Hue and
      spends two years as the mistress of an American Army
      sergeant. He arranges for her to go to San Francisco,
      where she becomes a bar girl. After some time in the
      U.S., she decides to have an eye operation to reduce
      her Asian appearance.

                              1976

518. Belanger, Charles A.   "Once Upon a Time When It Was
          Night." In <u>Angels in My Oven</u>, edited by John
          Schultz, 76-86. Chicago: The Columbia College
          Press, 1976. 75-33527.

      An Army helicopter pilot, on his second tour in
      Vietnam, is in the shower at his base when a rocket
      attack occurs. Although he is unwilling to seem
      afraid, the situation becomes serious and he joins
      others in a bunker. After the attack, the men drink
      beer on the roof of their quarters and discuss aspects
      of the war, including their fear, their hatred of the
      antiwar movement in the United States and their
      chances of survival.

519. <u>Distant Stars</u>. Hanoi: Foreign Languages Publishing
          House, 1976.

      According to introductory material, all of the stories
      in this collection were written after the American
      escalation of the war against North Vietnam in 1965.

   a. Le Minh Khue. "Distant Star," pp. 9-34.

A young woman works on a road crew repairing damage
caused by American planes.

b. Nguyen Thi Nhu Trang. "Rain," pp. 35-51.

A North Vietnamese army doctor returns on leave to her
home and remembers recent events in her struggle
against the Americans. Her comrades were especially
vulnerable to cluster bombs.

c. Chu Van. "The Perfume of the Areca Palm,"
        pp. 52-73.

With the men away fighting, a young woman and her
sister-in-law struggle to lead an agricultural
production brigade.

d. Ma Van Khang. "The Young Meo Wife," pp. 74-95.

A young woman in the highlands rises above her origins
and overcomes the resistance of her husband to earn a
high political post.

e. Xuan Trinh. "On the Long Road," pp. 96-108.

A truck driver ignores American bombing to deliver
needed supplies to fighters.

f. Do Chu. "The Wind in the Valley," pp. 109-127.

A medical worker visits home and remembers a friend
who wanted to be an artist.

g. Vu Le Mai. "The Heart of a Mother," pp. 128-142.

A young woman fighter rescues a child from an American
massacre in the Demilitarized Zone. Later, she
surrenders the child to another woman who claims to be
its mother.

h. Xuan Cang. "The Sparks," pp. 143-155.

Members of a revolutionary entertainment troupe
undergo U.S. bombing.

i. Nguyen Minh Chau. "Moonlight in the Forest,"
        pp. 156-176.

A soldier tells his comrades of his experience driving
a truck and enduring American bombing.

j. Tran Kim Thanh. "Story on the Bank of the River," pp.
    177-191.

A photographer is fascinated by a young woman he meets
at a construction site.

k. Vu Thi Thuong. "The Drama of the Director of a
    Cooperative," pp. 192-223.

A rising bureaucrat brings success to an agricultuural
cooperative.

520. Drake, David. "Firefight." In Frights, edited by
      Kirby McCauley, 181-204. NY: St. Martin's Press,
      1976. 75-40798.

An armored unit sets up a night position in the
highlands near a grove of trees that is sacred to the
local people. After dark, supernatural beings emerge
from one of the trees and engage the troops.

521. Jorgensen, Erik. "Typhoon." In Angels in My Oven,
      edited by John Schultz, 294-312. Chicago:
      Columbia College Press, 1976. 75-33527.

This is a fine and comprehensive story of Marine
infantry at war. The time is 1968, and the narrator
is a nineteen year old enlisted man. Somewhere near
An Hoa, he and his platoon stand guard, engage in a
firefight, murder some prisoners, walk back to base,
endure a typhoon and finally find a place to rest in
camp. In this relatively short story, Jorgensen
brings up and deals with such matters as race relations, personal fear, differences between career
sergeants and privates and other differences between
rear area troops and those actually engaged in combat.
This is all done in a convincing manner, and the
story moves at a fast pace.

522. Jorgenson, Kregg P.J. "Red, White, & Tutti Frutti."
      Stonecloud, no. 6 (1976): 61-65.

A Vietnam veteran in Logan, Utah, remembers how he won
a Silver Star in Vietnam.

523. Koons, George. "Extra Man." In <u>Angels in My Oven</u>,
        edited by John Schultz, 140-144. Chicago:
        Columbia College Press, 1976.

      The narrator is the leader of a deep penetration
      patrol in Laos in 1968. The five-man squad is
      watching a large group of North Vietnamese soldiers
      when the extra man, a news photographer, pops a
      flashbulb and reveals their position. In the ensuing
      attack, the squad is nearly overrun and one man is
      wounded. On a helicopter after a successful evacu-
      ation, the narrator beats the photographer in the face
      with a pistol and must be restrained from throwing
      him out of the aircraft. Afterward, he sees the
      photographer in the hospital, but they cannot communi-
      cate.

524. McDonald, Walter. "Lebowitz." <u>RE: Artes Liberales</u> 3,
        1 (Fall 1976): 75-80.

      Lebowitz, a pilot, believes he may have accidentally
      attacked a Vietnamese schoolyard. In despair, he
      later drops his bombs deliberately on an empty field.
      This begins a feud between Lebowitz and his navigator
      that causes serious problems.

525. McDonald, Walter. "The Track." <u>Sam Houston Literary
        Review</u> 1, 1 (April 1976): 45-48.

      Two officers are running on an athletic track at their
      base in Vietnam. Moose is newly arrived, and Lebowitz
      is an old hand. It is late in the war, and everone is
      just trying to stay alive until the end.

526. McDonald, Walter. "Waiting for the End." <u>Descant</u> 20,
        4 (Summer 1976): 2-10.

      A pilot is shot down somewhere in Vietnam. He spends
      a harrowing and dangerous time on the ground, wounded,
      before being rescued. He is evacuated to a hospital,
      where he meets an old friend. Then he is sent on to
      Japan on a medical plane. He carries graphic memories
      of combat.

527. Moore, Robin. "Combat Pay." In his <u>Combat Pay</u>, 13-
        41. NY: Manor, 1976.

N.p.: Weedhill, 1977.

Early in the war, a Special Forces sergeant in Saigon falls in love with a beautiful Eurasian woman. When he is killed on an operation, she learns that he has left her enough money to go to college in the U.S.

528. Moore, Robin. "We Have Met the Enemy." In his Combat Pay, 181-186.

An American patrol is ambushed in the Vietnamese jungle. As the terrified survivors escape, they kill a young Vietnamese girl.

529. Nam Ha. "The Land That is Ours." In Phoenix Country, edited by Nigel Gray. A special issue of Fireweed (September 1976): 62-69.

A Vietcong digs his two hundredth bunker since the beginning of the war and then joins his unit to successfully repel an American attack.

530. Nguyen Sang. "The Ivory Comb." In Phoenix Country, 2-15.

A young female revolutionary leader receives, indirectly, an ivory comb that her father had made for her many years before.

531. Nguyen Trung Than. "The Village in the Forest." In Phoenix Country, 132-145.

The visit of a Communist soldier to his home village is the occasion for telling heroic stories about revolutionary deeds in the past.

532. O'Brien, Tim. "Going After Cacciato." Ploughshares 3, 1 (1976): 42-65.
      Also in The Best American Short Stories 1977, edited by Martha Foley, 256-274. Boston: Houghton Mifflin, 1977. 16-11387.

In this first chapter from the novel of the same title, Cacciato's personality is established. He

begins his walk from Vietnam to Paris, and the third
squad goes after him.

533. O'Brien, Tim. "Keeping Watch by Night." Redbook 148,
          2 (December 1976): 65-68.

A group of soldiers establishes an ambush site along a
trail. As they organize themselves and their weapons,
one of them relates an act of Christian faith he
witnessed in Africa.

534. O'Brien, Tim. "The Way It Mostly Was." Shenandoah
          27, 2 (Winter 1976): 35-45.

A group of fifty-nine soldiers, perhaps a very
depleted company, marches toward a battle in the
mountains. The unit commander, a captain, and one of
the soldiers reflect independently on the nature of
the war and their parts in it. Despite differences in
rank and perspective, they reach the similar conclusion that there is no central idea motivating the
American forces.

1977

535. Bejarano, Arthur T. Bring Back the Boys--U.S. Armed
          Forces in Indo-China. NY: Vantage, 1977. 141
          pp. 553-02639-3.

Two of the three stories here are set in Southeast
Asia. They make their points with awkward irony.

  a. "Tom, Dick and Harry--U.S. Armed Forces in Indo-
          China," pp. 7-76.

U.S. pilots talk at great length and come to grief
over North Vietnam.

  b. "Dionna--U.S. Withdraws from Vietnam," pp. 77-141.

Two persons, apparently peace activists, fly from San
Francisco to Hanoi. On the return trip, they accompany released American prisoners and question one of
them at length.

536. Garry, Allan. "Two Looks at the Funeral Business."

Red Fox Review 1, 5 (1977): 51-56.

A funeral home worker contrasts his experiences in Vietnam and in civilian life.

537. McDonald, Walter. "Bien Dien." _Sam Houston Literary Review_ 2, 2 (November 1977): 46-53.

A group of pilots sets off to take a gift of medicine to a Vietnamese village called Bien Dien. One of them is let off to fish in a nearby stream. At the village, the others learn that a schoolyard was attacked by what the Vietnamese believe were American rockets. The Vietnamese are furious. The pilots believe the attack was made by Vietcong mortars. They leave and on the way back they pick up the fisherman, who has had an uneventful day.

1978

538. De Grazia, Emilio. "The Sniper." _Samisdat_ 17, 1 (Spring 1978): 29-42.
        Also in his _Enemy Country_, 121-132. St. Paul, MN: New River Press, 1984. 84-060334.

The narrator is an Army sniper, chosen for the job because he volunteered for special duty. "It reminded me that in the Army I could only do the things I didn't want to do." In addition to his work, which is described in minute detail, the sniper writes to a girl back home, considers a scheme to buy rifles as counterfeit souvenirs and plans for his forthcoming leave in New Zealand. Toward the end of the story, he no longer shoots at available targets. Instead, he tries only to survive. Reproduction in the review copy of this periodical is poor, and in some places the text is impossible to read.

539. Gibson, Margaret. "All Over Now." In her _Considering Her Condition_, 53-67. NY: Vanguard Press, 1978.

Until he is killed on April 21, 1969, Calvin, a Marine in Vietnam, corresponds with his girlfriend in Toronto. Their letters comprise the entire story. Calvin's experiences are contrived to express the feelings that Gibson, a Canadian woman, has about the war.

540. Klinkowitz, Jerome and Somer, John, eds. <u>Writing</u>
     <u>Under Fire</u>. NY: Delta, 1978. 274 pp. 78-17682.

     This collection includes nonfiction and critical
     pieces as well as stories that are not set recog-
     nizably in Vietnam. Those stories that fit the scope
     of this bibliography are annotated below.

a.   Kaplan, Johanna. "Dragon Lady," pp. 22-34.

     See annotation 457.

b.   Porche, Don. "Evenings in Europe and Asia,"
     pp. 35-42.

     See annotation 480.

c.   Mayer, Tom. "A Birth in the Delta," pp. 43-57.

     See annotation 470e.

d.   Eastlake, William. "The Biggest Thing Since
     Custer," pp. 58-68.

     See annotation 440.

e.   Kolpacoff, Victor. "The Room," pp. 71-89.

     See annotation 436.

f.   Parker, Thomas. "Troop Withdrawal--The Initial
     Step," 90-107.

     See annotation 452.

g.   Major, Clarence. "Dossy O," pp. 108-110.

     See annotation 477.

h.   Baber, Asa. "The Ambush," pp. 130-135.

     See annotation 473.

i.   West, Thomas A. Jr. "Gone Are the Men," pp. 136-
     145.

     See annotation 483.

j.   Woods, W.C. "He That Died of Wednesday," pp. 152-
     164.

See annotation 455.

k. Chatain, Robert. "On the Perimeter," pp.209-226.

See annotation 462.

541. Perea, Robert. "Dragon Mountain." De Colores 4, 1 &
          2 (1978): 33-41.
          Also in The Remembered Earth: An Anthology of
          Contemporary Native American Literature, edited
          by Geary Hobson, 358-365. Albuquerque: Univer-
          sity of New Mexico Press, 1981. 80-54561.

At a remote radio relay station, one of two American
enlisted men mistakenly shoots two ARVN soldiers.
Then he vanishes. The remaining American and a loyal
Vietnamese sergeant negotiate with the other Vietnamese soldiers and agree to pay an indemnity as
ransom for the incident. Perea writes well, and his
characters are believable.

542. Scott, L.E. "Three Hearts." In his Time Came Hunting
          Time, 38-50. Cammeray, Australia: Saturday
          Centre Books, 1978.

A black Army sergeant, Don Evans, is assisted by other
black enlisted men to arrange a transfer to a rear
area after receiving three Purple Hearts. There is
considerable emphasis on race relationships.

543. Scott, L.E. "Vietnam--April 4, 1968." In his Time
          Came Hunting Time, 51-55.

Williams, a black Army sergeant who is recovering from
wounds in a hospital, is visited by several friends.
He learns that he is going home and that Martin Luther
King has been killed.

1979

544. Abbott, Lee K. "The Viet Cong Love of Sgt. Donnie T.
          Bobo." North American Review 264, 3 (Winter
          1979):43-47.
          Also in his The Heart Never Fits Its Wanting, 26-
          34. Cedar Falls: North American Review, 1980.

80-83374.
Touring Nam, 181-192.

Lee K. Abbot is successful at the very difficult
business of writing a funny story about the Vietnam
War. The narrator, Leon Busby, and his lifelong
friend Donnie Bobo are all over Vietnam in 1967 and
1968 practicing their specialty of coaxing Vietcong
out of tunnels. They use the English language and
such blandishments as Otis Redding records. A female
Vietcong resists Bobo, but after she is captured, he
falls in love with her and finds a Korean priest to
marry them. Then they disappear. Back in the United
States after the war, Busby hears from Bobo that the
couple are happly settled in Ho Chi Minh City.

545. Anderson, Kent. "Sympathy for the Devil." *Tri-
        Quarterly*, no. 45 (Spring 1979): 99-150.
        Also in *Touring Nam*, 117-179.

Sergeant Hanson and the other Special Forces NCOs in
his unit have adapted well to the war. They treat
each other with a balance of affection and off-hand
brutality. In their camp among the Montagnards, they
fight the enemy with a frightened professionalism that
is entirely convincing. Hanson survives, and on the
airplane home he loads a souvenir pistol so he will be
comfortable.

546. Baber, Asa. "How I Got Screwed and Almost Tattooed,
        by Huck Finn." In his *Tranquillity Base and
        Other Stories*, 95-108. Canton, NY: Fiction
        International, 1979.

Huck and Tom consider disfigurement and try bribery to
avoid the draft, but Judge Thatcher sends them to
Vietnam anyway. In Vietnam, the dope is plentiful and
potent, but life as an infantryman includes no
guarantees.

547. Coleman, Charles A. Jr. "In Loco Parentis." *Tri-
        Quarterly*, no. 45 (Spring 1979): 189-197.

The setting here is a military psychiatric hospital in
Texas, but the lengthy flashback explains how a
patient, Eddie Sailor, broke down in a battle and was
sent to the hospital. Most of the dialogue occurs

between Eddie and a psychiatrist who is attempting to prepare him for a review board that has the power to decide his future.

548. Ehrhart, W. D. "I Drink My Coffee Black." Tri-Quarterly, no. 45 (Spring 1979): 172-177. Also in Vietnam Flashbacks: Pig Iron No. 12, edited by Jim Villani, et al, 42-43. Youngstown, Ohio: Pig Iron Press, 1984. 84-061225.

Bill Ehrhart brings the fine touch of a poet to this tight story of a Marine in Hue in 1968. His character, an experienced infantryman, thinks about home and many other things as he fires an occasional shot out of a window in a building where he has taken refuge. He is also making a cup of coffee. In his preoccupation, he forgets the essential rule of combat that one should never fire twice from the same place, and he pays the price for his neglect.

549. Elonka, Stephan Michael. "Marmy's Etched Teeth." In his Marmaduke Surfaceblow's Salty Technical Romances, 75-77. Huntington, NY: Krieger, 1979. 79-14107.

A supply unit in Saigon returns damaged generator parts to a manufacturer who decides the harm was caused by termites.

550. Flanagan, Robert. "A Game of Some Significance." Phoebe 8, 3 (July 1979): 52-57.

A sergeant, awaiting evacuation after being wounded, remembers playing at war when he was a child.

551. Heinemann, Larry. "The First Clean Fact." TriQuarterly, no. 45 (Spring 1979): 178-188. Also in The Best American Short Stories, 1980, edited by Stanley Elkin and Shannon Ravenel, Boston: Houghton, 1980. 16-11387. Best of TriQuarterly, edited by Jonathan Brent, N.p.: Washington Square Press, 1982. Vietnam Anthology, 66-74.

This first person account is in what seems to be black street patois. It is a rambling account of the

experiences and attitudes of the black soldier in
Vietnam. It is difficult to follow, and the surprise
at the end is that the narrator is dead, having been
killed in an air strike.

552. Howe, John F. "Danang to An Hoa." Hair Trigger III:
       A Story Workshop Anthology, 23-25. Chicago:
       Columbia College, 1979.

       Marines encounter mines and hostile villagers on a
       Vietnamese highway.

553. Howe, John F. "KIA." Hair Trigger III: A Story
       Workshop Anthology, 20-22.

       Marines loading bodies onto a helicopter are harassed
       by a colonel.

554. Ireland, David. "The Wild Colonial Boy." In Winter's
       Tale 25, edited by Caroline Hobhouse, 71-84. NY:
       St. Martin's, c1979, 1980. 55-13894.

       Ten years after returning home, an Australian Vietnam
       veteran describes his war experiences including an
       encounter with a booby trap that cost him a foot.

555. Ivey, Ross. "Major Little's Last Stand." Penthouse
       11, 2 (October 1979): 144-147.

       Major Little commands a helicopter unit that is based
       at several places in Vietnam in 1967 and 1968. The
       major has grandiose notions about war and his own
       heroism. He puts his troops into a number of dan-
       gerous and stupid situations. Then he causes himself
       to be awarded several medals. Subsequently, his men
       capture him and tie him beneath the enlisted men's
       latrine. Shortly after that, a general inspects the
       unit, and Major Little is subsequently assigned to a
       meaningless job in a rear area.

556. Just, Ward. "Dietz at War." In his Honor, Power,
       Riches, Fame, and the Love of Women, 73-86. NY:
       Dutton, 1979. 79-10123.

       Dietz is a journalist based in an unnamed country

covering an unnamed war. The specifics of his
circumstances point unquestionably to Vietnam. Dietz
has been there for three years. He has lost both his
desire to return home and his journalistic obligation
to seek out and report the hard facts of the war.
However, he has made a comfortable adjustment to his
environment, and he intends to remain indefinitely.

557. Oestreich, Jerry. "Perimeter Guard." In Hair Trigger
     III: A Story Workshop Anthology, 27-28. Chicago:
     Columbia College, 1979.

Soldiers on perimeter guard endure discomfort and
boredom as they do their jobs badly.

558. Oestreich, Jerry. "Poetry at Parade Rest." In Hair
     Trigger III, 29-33.

During a briefing in Vietnam, a soldier fantasies
about a training film he had seen at military police
school.

559. Oestreich, Jerry. "Tu Do Street." In Hair Trigger
     III, 26.

Tu Do Street in Saigon is a bastion of wealth and
privilege, well protected from the reality of war.

560. Suddick, Tom. "China Beach." Samisdat 23, 3 (Fall
     1979): 21-26.

China Beach, near Danang, is a huge recreation
facility. Maxwell and other Marines there enjoy the
commercialism of the place and wonder how it was
named.

1980

561. Flanagan, Robert. "An Ordinary Imperative." Phoebe
     10, 1 (Fall 1980): 68-73.

Two Americans join a crowd of Vietnamese in Saigon.
When they reach the center of the group, they watch a
Buddhist monk burn himself to death.

562. Heinemann, Larry. "Good Morning to You, Lieutenant."
     Harper's June 1980, pp. 59-60, 64, 66-69.
     Also in Soldiers and Civilians, edited by Tom
     Jenks, 155-168. Toronto/NY: Bantam, 1986.
     86-47574.

     This excellent story is set initially among the
     problems and sexual fantasies of Paco, an alcoholic
     Vietnam veteran in a city in the United States. Its
     substance, however, is a long flashback about a gang
     rape in Vietnam. Paco and others who are almost
     certainly Army enlisted men capture a female member of
     the Vietcong. Paco remembers precisely the physical
     and emotional circumstances of the rape. A lieutenant
     carefully ignores the event. Finally, they kill the
     women and move off. If Heinemann's purpose is to
     illustrate the hardening effect of war on men's souls,
     he ably succeeds.

563. Herd, Dale. "Girls." In his Wild Cherries, 33-34.
     Bolinas, CA: Tombouctou, 1980.

     A soldier accidently kills a girl who is running from
     a hut. Later he has trouble understanding American
     women.

564. Howe, John F. "Impaled Man." Hair Trigger IV: A
     Story Workshop Anthology, 147-150. Chicago:
     Columbia College, 1980.
     Also in Best of Hair Trigger, edited by John
     Schultz, 389-393. Chicago: Columbia College,
     1983.

     An infantry platoon enters a deserted village where
     the Vietcong have impaled several persons on stakes.
     At night, one of the men removes gold teeth from the
     corpses.

565. Howe, John F. "The Land." Hair Trigger IV, 145-146.
     Also in Best of Hair Trigger, 387-389.

     An infantryman describes the elusiveness of the
     Vietcong. To him they have supernatural qualites.

566. Kidder, Tracy. "In Quarantine." Atlantic Monthly
     246, 3 (September 1980): 92-100.

In this fantastic account of a homecoming from
Vietnam, a lieutenant comes under the influence and
control of Pancho, an enlisted man. Pancho induces
him to desert, and they find their way to a strange
quarantine island. After that interlude, they board a
freighter bound for Seattle. Pancho abandons the
lieutenant, who has assumed the identity of another
officer. The lieutenant finds himself accepted by
that officer's parents into their home, and they will
not let him go.

567. Laufer, William. "Prospects and Abysses." North
       American Mentor Magazine 18, 1 (Spring 1980):
       47-54.

In Danang in 1963, the life of an American advisor is
saved by a Eurasian woman. She knows his billet is to
be bombed and keeps him with her for the night.

568. Perea, Robert L. "Small Arms Fire." In Cuentos
       Chicanos, edited by Rudolfo A. Anaya and Antonio
       Marquez, 43-47. Albuquerque, NM: New America,
       1980.
       Albuquerque: University of New Mexico Press,
       1984. Pp. 119-124. 84-13066.

At the time of the invasion of Cambodia, two American
enlisted men come upon an ARVN truck that has hit a
mine. They call a helicopter to assist with the
wounded, but the officer in the aircraft refuses to
help because he has an important meeting. Later, the
men hear that the officer was killed by small arms
fire while assisting another ARVN group.

569. Suddick, Tom. "On Making the Same Mistake Twice."
       Samisdat 26, 2 (1980): 18-23.
       Also in Tour of Duty, edited by Cranston Sedrick
       Knight. Samisdat 46, 2 182nd release (1986):
       13-23.

A Marine squad returning from a medical visit to a
village near the Demilitarized Zone comes under mortar
fire from both friendly and unfriendly forces. It
develops that part of the problem is reliance on an
old French map. One of the men in the squad reflects
on the similarities between the French and American
occupations of Vietnam.

570. Wolff, Tobias. "Wingfield." Encounter, no.55 (July
          1980): 3-5.
          Also in his In the Garden of the North American
          Martyrs, 101-105. NY: Ecco Press, 1981. 81-880.
          Vietnam Anthology, 75-78.

      Wingfield, a sleepy soldier, survives basic training
      and the Vietnam War. Later a former buddy sees him
      asleep in a railway station.

                                 1981

571. Baber, Asa. "The French Lesson." Playboy 28, 3
          (March 1981): 98-100, 108, 202, 205-206, 208.

      The narrator is a Marine officer who has just resigned
      his commission after losing three men on a clandestine
      mission near the Plain of Jars in Laos. The time is
      1961, and as he waits in Vientiane for orders, he
      learns the identity of a Frenchman who may have been
      involved in the deaths of his men. The former officer
      kills the man. He is immediately returned to the
      U.S., where he is debriefed and released from the
      Marine Corps.

572. Boyd, William. "On the Yankee Station." In his On
          the Yankee Station. Np: Hamish Hamilton, 1981.
          Middlesex, England: Penguin Books, 1983.
          Pp.111-134.
          NY: William Morrow, 1984. Pp.104-129. 84-60480.

      Lydecker, a Navy enlisted man on a carrier off the
      coast of Vietnam, nurses a hatred for a pilot who has
      bullied and abused him. Eventually, he achieves a
      suitable revenge.

573. De Grazia, Emilio. "Brothers of the Tiger." In
          Likely Stories: A Collection of Untraditional
          Fiction, selected by B.R. McPherson, 9-46. New
          Paltz, NY: Treacle Press, 1981. 81-12927.
          Also in his Enemy Country, 58-94.

      In 1967, a peasant from North Vietnam travels slowly
      south to visit his sick brother who lives near Saigon.
      Along the way he encounters soldiers from both sides.

574. Flanagan, Robert. "Mayday." Phoebe 10, 4 (Spring
          1981): 71-75.

      A sergeant, the only survivor of a downed aircraft,
      waits for either rescue or capture. While he waits,
      his wounds cause him to hallucinate about his child-
      hood.

575. Heinemann, Larry. "God's Marvelous Plan." Harper's,
          August 1981, 54-60.

      Heinemann writes some of the best Vietnam fiction.
      This story of a medic who finds the only survivor of
      an infantry company is up to his usual standard.

576. Henschel, Lee Jr. Short Stories of Vietnam. Guthrie,
          MN: Guthrie Publishing Co., 1981. 154 pp.
          81-85593.

  a. "The First Day," pp. 1-4.

      A veteran remembers his first day in Vietnam.

  b. "The Game," pp. 6-9.

      A sergeant and a captain plan a patrol to recover an
      unexploded artillery round. They discuss whether to
      take along a soldier who had recently failed to kill a
      snake at point-blank range with two magazines of
      ammunition.

  c. "The 'Reb,'" pp. 11-14.

      Duke, a soldier from Tennessee, is so boastful about
      his past that he becomes caught up in destructive
      behavior while in Vietnam

  d. "The 5:30 News," pp. 16-19.

      Gulch, an infantryman, purchases a portable television
      set while in the rear area. Before his unit leaves
      for the field, a friend destroys it.

  e. "Ferguson and the Old Mama-san from Song Mao,"
          pp. 21-25.
      Ferguson, an artilleryman, attempts to marry an
      elderly Vietnamese woman in an effort to prove he is
      crazy.

f.   "Psychedelic 'Nam: The World," pp. 27-38.

On a rest and recreation leave in Australia, an
American soldier encounters experiences and individuals who cause him to question the war. On his return
to Vietnam, he brings his buddies some LSD.

g.   "The Desertion of Wiley Blooms," pp. 40-107.

Blooms, an American Indian, is a drunken troublemaker
in an artillery unit near Dalat. A friend, Lopez, is
ordered to take Blooms to jail at Long Binh. After
various adventures in Na Trang, Lopez is killed.

h.   "Yobo Shibo," pp. 109-126.

Members of an American artillery section gamble and
otherwise interact with soldiers in a Korean unit to
which they have been temporarily attached.

i.   "Psychedelic 'Nam: Karma," pp. 128-145.

Three soldiers on guard duty take LSD and engage in a
firefight.

577. Lake, Larry. "Dumb Slumbo." In his 5000'and Closing,
       13-27. Denver: Bowery Press, 1981.

Saluigman, a signalman who went bad, finds himself in
a rear area camp in Vietnam where he earns the
nickname Dumb Slumbo. When things heat up in the
supposed noncombat zone, he paints a target on his
chest and shoots himself. Several black-and-white
drawings illustrate this story.

578. O'Brien, Tim. "The Ghost Soldiers." Esquire 95, 3
       (March 1981): 90-100.
       Also in Prize Stories, 1982: The O. Henry Awards.
       NY: Doubleday, 1982.
       Great Esquire Fiction: The Finest Stories from
       the First Fifty Years, edited by Rust Hills.
       NY: Viking, 1983. 83-47877.
       Soldiers and Civilians, edited by Tom Jenks,
       182-201. Toronto/NY: Bantam, 1986. 86-47574.

A particularly frightening aspect of the Vietnam War
is evoked in this story of Army enlisted men turned
against one another for revenge. The narrator, Herb,

had nearly died because a medic, Jorgenson, had been too afraid to come to him in combat and treat his wound. Later Herb and a friend attempt to scare Jorgenson to death, but Jorgenson reacts to the situation with maturity and military professionalism. The game of fright, however, has become more important to its players than the reason that gave it birth. In the end, Herb and Jorgenson, former enemies, are allied in a new plan to terrify or kill another man.

579. Zackly, Rock. "Vietnam." N.p., 1981. 55 pp.

Professionally printed and bound, this story is identified as a chapter from a forthcoming novel. It has to do with supernatural adventures of a very unlikely infantry squad on a rescue mission in the northern part of South Vietnam.

1982

580. Dawson, Fielding. "Straight Lines." In his Krazy Kat & 76 More, 209-211. Santa Barbara, CA: Black Sparrow Press, 1982.

A soldier relates a poem he has heard to an experience in combat.

581. Dawson, Fielding. "The Triangle on the Jungle Wall." In his Krazy Kat & 76 More, 278-283.

After seeing the death of a friend in combat, a soldier later tries to explain the circumstances of his death to his parents.

582. Hasford, Gustav. "The Short-Timers (Excerpt)." In Yesterday's Tomorrows, edited by Frederick Pohl, 425-430. NY: Berkley, 1982. 0-425-05648-1.

This brief excerpt from Hasford's excellent novel describes a rat hunt that is followed by an enemy rocket or mortar attack.

583. Mann, Ted. "Vietnam Vets." National Lampoon, April 1982, 47-53.

This cynical and occasionally humorous story is profusely illustrated. It has to do with Army veterinarians in Vietnam.

584. Prager, Emily. "The Lincoln-Pruitt Anti-Rape Device: Memoirs of the Women's Combat Army in Vietnam." In her A Visit from the Footbinder and Other Stories, 103-180. NY: Simon & Schuster, 1982. 82-6977. NY: Wyndham, 1982. London: Chatto-Windus, Hogarth Press, 1983. NY: Berkley, 1984. Pp. 99-179. 0-425-06597-9.

Near the end of the war, a group of former prostitutes in the U.S. Army attempts to kill Vietcong men with vaginal weapons. The attempt fails, in part because of affection between the women and men involved.

585. West, Paul. "He Who Wears the Pee of the Tiger." TriQuarterly, no. 55 (Fall 1982): 5-13.

On Operation Dewey Canyon Two in Loas, an infantryman and a captain survive an enemy rocket attack. Later, the infantryman lives through a helicopter crash and saves a door gunner from the wrecked aircraft.

1983

586. Drake, David. "The Dancer in the Flames." In Whispers IV, edited by Stuart David Schiff, 151-158. Garden City, NY: Doubleday, 1983. 82-45337.

A lieutenant in an armored unit is haunted by the demonic image of a Cambodian girl.

587. Landis, John. "Bill." In Twilight Zone: The Movie, edited by Robert Block, 7-55. NY: Warner Books, 1983.

Bill, a racist bigot, is supernaturally transported back to Vietnam where he served as a soldier. He is mistaken for an enemy by American soldiers and driven to other adventure.

588. Mitcalfe, Barry. "Black Cat." In <u>The Oxford Book of</u>
      <u>New Zealand Writing Since 1945</u>, chosen by Mac-
      Donald P. Jackson and Vincent O'Sullivan,
      446-448. Auckland, N.Z.: Oxford University
      Press, 1983.

      A New Zealand infantryman compares killing Vietcong to
      killing animals at home. He has contempt for the
      American and ARVN forces.

                              1984

589. De Grazia, Emilio. <u>Enemy Country</u>. St. Paul, MN: New
      River Press, 1984. 145 pp. 84-060334.

      The same characters and the same setting, an infantry
      unit late in the war, occur throughout these stories.
      De Grazia is an excellent, complex writer, and his
      work has unquestionable literary merit.

   a. "The Death of Sin," pp. 9-19. Originally in
         <u>Carleton Miscellany</u>, n.d.

       A few dogs are lost and the commanding officer is
       served a special dinner at an American base somewhere
       in Vietnam.

   b. "The Mask," pp. 20-29. Originally in <u>Green River</u>
         <u>Review</u>, n.d.

       A pilot who seems to be a forward air controller bails
       out after his aircraft is hit. He is captured by the
       enemy and put to death.

   c. "The Girl and Two Old Men," pp. 30-41. Originally
         in <u>Colorado Quarterly</u>, n.d.

       After he is wounded, and before he dies, an infantry-
       man remembers parts of his past life.

   d. "The Enemy," pp. 42-48. Originally in <u>North</u>
         <u>Count[r]y Anvil</u>, n.d.

       In an assault on a village, a soldier misbehaves with
       two prisoners, an old woman and a boy.

   e. "Enemy Country," Originally in <u>Touchstone</u> as
         "Gooks," n.d.

After suffering combat fatigue in Vietnam, a veteran
finds much to be frightened of after he returns home.

f. "Brothers of the Tiger," pp. 58-94.

    See annotation 573.

g. "The Cat Hater," pp. 95-108.

    William, a cook in Vietnam, finally catches and kills
    a cat he has long hated.

h. "Zabel's Choice," pp. 109-115.

    A veteran in a bar remembers combat experiences in
    Vietnam.

i. "The Man Who Cursed and the Good Lutheran Boy,"
    pp. 116-120.

    An extremely foulmouthed soldier is killed in combat.

j. "The Sniper," pp. 121-132.

    See annotation 538.

k. "The Light at the End of the Tunnel," pp. 133-145.

    An infantryman is obsessed with the death of a friend
    in battle. He continues to ask questions of the
    survivors until he learns the details of how his
    friend died.

590. Guidera, Mark. "Tiger in the Rain." The North
        American Mentor Magazine 22, 1 (Spring 1984):
        22-29.

      On a patrol in the jungle, a young infantryman from
      Kansas encounters an old Vietnamese man with a yin and
      yang tattoo. Later, elsewhere in the jungle, the old
      man reappears and tells the soldier of a safe place to
      sleep.

591. Heinemann, Larry. "Gallagher's Old Man." Chicago,
        edited by Reginald Gibbons, 380-385. A special
        edition of TriQuarterly, no. 60 (Spring/Summer
        1984).

As a group of infantrymen rests in camp, one of them
describes the pain and futility of his father's life.
He compares his father's expression to that of a
recently wounded man.

592. Hollenbeck, Peter. "Chapter from a Forthcoming Novel
     on Vietnam, The Lotus and the Night." In
     Vietnam Literature Anthology: A Balanced
     Perspective, edited by J. Topham, 67-77. NY:
     American Poetry and Literature Press, 1984.

A new soldier is processed into his unit while an old
Vietnamese man meditates on Buddhist phantoms.

593. Leonardy, Peter. "The Dust Off." In Hair Trigger
     6 & 7, 171-173. Chicago: Columbia College
     Writing Dept., 1984.

A medic lands from a helicopter to tend a man with a
sucking chest wound. Despite his best efforts, the
man dies and the medic jams a dog tag between the
corpse's teeth.

594. Shedivy, Charles. "The Kid and Victor Charlie." In
     Hair Trigger 6 & 7, 31-38.

A new replacement to a Navy SEAL unit watches a Korean
Marine torture a Vietcong.

595. Shedivy, Charles. "The Virgin French Nurse." In
     Hair Trigger 6 & 7, 23-30.

Huey, a practical joker, obtains an inflatable sex
doll. He convinces the other men in his compound that
the doll is actually the ghost of a French nurse who
killed herself years ago to avoid being raped by the
Vietminh.

596. Villani, Jim, et al, eds. Vietnam Flashbacks: Pig
     Iron No. 12. Youngstown, Ohio: Pig Iron Press,
     1984. 96 pp. 84-061225.

This valuable issue includes photographs, graphics,
nonfiction, poetry and short stories. There are
thirty poems by different authors. The appropriate

short stories are annotated below.

a. St. Denis, Bake. "With Only One Shot," pp. 6-16.

    In 1964, a Marine sniper is assigned by the CIA to
    kill an official in North Vietnam who has tortured
    American prisoners. The actions of the sniper and his
    victim are specific and convincing.

b. McCord, Howard. "Sharing a Little Heat With the
        Pathet Lao," pp. 18-19.

    Covert American operatives ambush a Pathet Lao patrol
    in 1965.

c. Ferrandino, Joseph. "Saddleback Ridge," p. 26.

    In what became the fifteenth chapter of his novel,
    Firefight (387), Ferrandino provides a good story
    about airborne troops arriving and fighting in a very
    hot landing zone.

d. Palladino, Michael P. "Khong Biet," pp. 30-35.

    In their words and thoughts, an American Marine and an
    elderly Vietnamese villager attempt to communicate and
    wonder about each other. Then the war intrudes and
    people are killed and injured.

e. Viorel, George. "The Haint," pp. 37-39.

    A new soldier on an Army patrol sees the ghost of a
    woman killed earlier.

f. Ehrhart, W.D. "I Drink My Coffee Black,"
        pp. 42-43.

    See annotation 548.

g. Dubbs, Chris. "My Fear in Little Cages," pp. 44-
        45.

    A Marine in Con Thien has a few problems, including
    enemy action and the family of his dope connection,
    but he keeps them all in perspective.

h. Hogdin, D'Wayne. "Interrogation," pp. 46-47.
    A helicopter door gunner observes an American officer
    and an interpreter interrogate and murder captives.

i. Flynn, Robert. "The Killer," pp. 48-49.

A black soldier who has killed a man on his first
patrol receives questions and comments from various
people after he returns to camp.

j. Juvik, Tom Millier. "Pulling Guard," pp. 51-53.

The memories and pressures of combat affect a man who
will return home in twenty-three days.

k. Meisinger, Richard Jr. "Taps," pp. 56-60.

A soldier who did not serve in Vietnam imagines combat
experiences.

l. Lupack, Alan. "Miss America and the Strippers,"
        pp. 67-69.

A base camp in Vietnam enjoys performances by two
strippers and Miss America. The men have different
reactions to the two types of entertainment.

1985

597. Greenberg, Martin H. and Norton, Augustus Richard,
          eds. <u>Touring Nam: The Vietnam War Reader</u>. NY:
          Morrow, 1985. 416 pp. 84-62022.

The works of fiction in this anthology are cited
below.

a. Abbott, Lee K. "The Viet Cong Love of Sgt. Donnie
        T. Bobo," pp. 181-192.

See annotation 544.

b. Anderson, Kent. "Sympathy for the Devil," pp. 117-
        179.

See annotation 545.

c. Baber, Asa. "Ambush: Laos, 1960," pp. 94-101.

See annotation 473.

d. Bunting, Josiah. "The Lionheads," pp. 223-260.

In this chapter from his book of the same title,

Bunting contrasts the lives of the generals who plan
battles and the infantrymen who fight them.

e. Chatain, Robert. "On the Perimeter,"
      pp. 302-323.

   See annotation 462.

f. Mayer, Tim. "A Birth in the Delta,"   pp.339-357.

   See annotation 470e.

g. Parker, Thomas. "Troop Withdrawal--The Initial
      Step," pp. 389-411.

   See annotation 452.

h. Porche, Don. "Evenings in Europe and Asia," pp.
      20-29.

   See annotation 480.

i. Suddick, Tom. "Caduceus," pp. 206-221.

   See annotation 506a.

j. Suddick, Tom. "A Shithouse Rat," pp. 325-336.

   See annotation 506e.

598. Mort, John. "Called of God." Gentlemen's Quarterly
         55, 3 (March 1985): 299-301, 323, 324.
         Also in his Tanks, 7-15. Kansas City, MO: BkMk
         Press, 1986.

   A new infantryman, assigned as point man on a patrol,
   kills his first enemy soldier. Afterwards, he
   refuses, from religious conviction, to carry a weapon.
   This introduces lively conflict in the platoon.

599. Mort, John. "The New Captain," Missouri Review 8, 2
         (1985): 45-51.
         Also in his Tanks, 61-68.

   A newly arrived captain, commanding an infantry
   company, finds that his character and emotions are not
   suitable for his aggressive military goals.

600. Perea, Robert. "Trip to Da Nang." The Bilingual
     Review 12, 1 & 2 (January-August 1985): 97-102.

     On a trip to Da Nang, some soldiers stop to watch
     Marines torture prisoners. The entertainment proves
     costly to one of them.

601. Shiner, Lewis. "The War at Home." Isaac Asimov's
     Science Fiction Magazine 9, 5 (May 1985): 74-76.
     Also in Third Annual Year's Best Science
     Fiction, edited by Gardner Dozois, 522-525. NY:
     Bluejay, 1986.
     In the Field of Fire, edited by Jeanne Van Buren
     Dann and Jack Dann, 325-328. NY: Tor Books,
     1986.

     Flashbacks to combat are a staple feature of much
     fiction about Vietnam veterans, but in this brief,
     interesting story, it is nonveterans who imagine
     scenes of combat.

                              1986

602. Abbott, Lee K. "I'm Glad You Asked." In his
     Strangers in Paradise, 225-231. NY: Putnam,
     1986. 86-8139. 0-399-13196-5.

     A mad, humorous infantryman in Vietnam has the habit
     of carrying a tape recorder to battles and other
     interesting events.

603. Abbott, Lee K. "Rolling Thunder." In his Strangers
     in Paradise, 225-231.

     In 1968 at the siege of Khe Sanh, a black Marine
     decides to leave and seek a medical discharge. Later
     he changes his mind.

604. Abbott, Lee K. "We Get Smashed and Our Endings are
     Swift." In his Love is the Crooked Thing.
     Chapel Hill, NC: Algonquin Books of Chapel Hill,
     1986. 0-912697-30-X

     Herkie Walls and Zion T. McKinney are trained to kill
     with everything from guns to bombast. They murder

various miscreants in Vietnam and elsewhere in the
late 1960s. When McKInney deserts, Walls and their
commanding officer track him down in Saigon, but Walls
refuses to kill his former friend.

605. Banks, Russell. "The Fish." In his Success Stories,
         40-48. NY: Harper & Row, 1986. 85-45617.
         NY: Ballantine, 1987. Pp. 43-51.

In a Southeast Asian country that is almost certainly
Vietnam, Colonel Tung, Lieutenant Han and their men
try various methods to destroy a huge fish in a
village pond. Only when they have decided that they
want to keep the fish alive do they finally kill it.

606. Barrus, Tim. "Tunnel Rats." Christopher Street 9,
         issue 105, pp. 22-30.

A group of soldiers enters Cambodia to search for a
"black box" from a downed U2 aircraft. The story has
a homosexual element.

607. Boswell, Robert. "The Right Thing." The Antioch
         Review, n.d.
         Also in his Dancing in the Movies, 127-144. Iowa
         City: University of Iowa Press, 1986. 85-13966.

Hagget, a Vietnam veteran, has frequent and very
confusing mental flashbacks to events in the war.
Apparently he delivered a child from the body of a
dead woman in a village.

608. Clodfelter, Michael D. "The Mountain." In Tour of
         Duty. Samisdat 46, 2 (1986): 93-95.

Near the beach at Tuy Hoa, an Army patrol is sent on
an exhausting, meaningless climb up a mountain.

609. Cole, Duff. "Got Some Religion." In Tour of Duty,
         27-28.

A machinegunner changes his nickname and inadvertently
also changes his luck.

610. Haldeman, Joe. "The Monster." In Cutting Edge, 56-

66, edited by Dennis Etchison. NY: St. Martin's,
1986. 86-8854.

The only survivor of a patrol in Vietnam is accused by
a Vietnamese deserter of killing and sexually
mutilating two Americans. The survivor claims the
deed was done by a huge, humanoid monster.

611. Mort, John. "Incubation Period." Gentlemen's
      Quarterly 56, 7 (July 1986): 172-174, 184, 186,
      188.

Lansing, an enlisted man, has sex with a Cambodian
prostitute and contracts gonorrhea. While the
infection causes him certain military difficulties, it
also takes him to a medical facility for treatment at
a time when his unit suffers heavy casualties in a
battle.

612. Mort, John. Tanks: Short Fiction. Kansas City, MO:
      BkMk Press, 1986. 85-73391.

  a. "Called of God," pp. 7-15.

      See annotation 598.

  b. "Human Wave," pp. 17-26.

      A new soldier at a firebase near the beach encounters
      some strange characters and deals with bodies left
      over from a recent battle.

  c. "Tanks," pp. 27-54.   Also in Soldiers and
          Civilians, edited by Tom Jenks, 169-181.
          Toronto/NY: Bantam, 1986. 86-47574.

      Near the Cambodian border, a combined infantry and
      armor unit sets an ambush then attacks a bunker
      complex. They are successful, but victory is not
      without cost.

  d. "Hot," pp. 55-60. Originally published in
          Missouri Short Fiction, n.d..
      An infantryman deals with a hot landing zone, a boil
      on his chin and his dreams.

  e. "The New Captain," pp. 61-68.

See annotation 599.

613. O'Brien, Tim.   "The Things They Carried."   Esquire
     106, 2 (August 1986):   76-81.
     Also in The Bread Loaf Anthology of Contemporary
     American Short Stories, edited by Robert Pack and
     Jay Parini, 227-246.   Hanover, NH: Univ. Press of
     New England, 1987.   86-40387.
     Vietnam Anthology, 79-94.

     By describing the military equipment, personal
     possessions and psychological baggage of an infantry
     platoon, O'Brien crafts a fine short story.

614. Perea, Robert L.   "The Battle of Engineer Hill."
     The Americas 14, 2 (Summer 1986): 15-20.

     In a well-crafted short story, Perea describes a
     battle that occurs a year after the 1968 Tet Offen-
     sive.   Because of the anniversary, much is made of
     little and a minor skirmish is bloated into a major
     engagement.

615. Pitzen, Jim.   "The Village."   Fiction Network,
     Spring-Summer 1986, pp. 13-17.
     Also in Prize Stories of 1987: The O. Henry
     Awards, edited by William Abrahams, 132-143.   NY:
     Doubleday, 1987.

     After an infantry company destroys a village, one of
     the men is accidently shot.

616. Scotellaro, Robert.   "Ti-Ti."   In Tour of Duty, 77-89.

     Near Tay Ninh a young medic joins an experienced
     sergeant on a drive to dump dispensary garbage.   Then
     he has an unsettling encounter with a Vietnamese
     prostitute.

617. Tipton, Paul W.   "A Day for No Letters."   In Tour of
     Duty, 44-46.

     After an uneventful trip for water, a young soldier
     barely escapes when the truck he used is destroyed by
     a charge planted by village children.

1987

618. Dann, Jeanne Van Buren and Dann, Jack, eds. <u>In the</u>
      <u>Field of Fire</u>. NY: Tor, 1987. 86-50955.

      Although only ten of the twenty-two stories in this
      collection are set among Americans fighting in
      Vietnam, it is included here as a story collection
      because of its general focus on the Vietnam War. Like
      some other collaborations between husband and wife, it
      is notably self-indulgent.

   a. Shepard, Lucius. "Delta Sly Honey," pp. 25-43.

      A soldier with many problems recieves unwanted but
      irresistible help from members of a ghost patrol.

   b. Strete, Craig Kee. "The Game of Cat and Eagle,"
           pp. 44-69.

      An American Indian lieutenant with supernatural powers
      visits Vietnam to discover whether America can win the
      war.

   c. Frazier, Robert. "Across the Endless Skies,"
           pp. 90-94.

      An infantryman uses drugs to cope with surreal
      experiences in Vietnam.

   d. Russo, Richard Paul. "In the Season of the
           Rains," pp. 107-121.

      An alien spaceship takes an infantryman away from a
      patrol in the jungle.

   e. Bova, Ben. "Brothers," pp. 212-223.

      Twin brothers, one an astronaut and the other a navy
      pilot in Vietnam, make telepathic contact.

   f. Malzberg, Barry N. "The Queen of Lower Saigon,"
           pp. 238-246.
      The Queen, who may be a prostitute or a metaphor for
      Vietnam, muses on many subjects.

   g. Cross, Ronald Anthony. "The Heavenly Blue
           Answer," pp. 258-269.

In Vietnam, a soldier witnesses the accidental explosion of a booby trap. Later, he discovers that his war experiences have followed him back to the U.S.

h. McAllister, Bruce. "Dream Baby," pp. 271-304.

A nurse in Vietnam has extrasensory perception.

i. Shiner, Lewis. "The War at Home," pp. 325-328. See annotation 601.

j. Ellison, Harlan. "Basilisk," pp. 350-369.

See annotation 507.

k. Haldeman, Joe. "DX," pp. 394-401.

This appears to be a prose poem about the dangers of making personal friendships in wartime.

619. Fabian, Stephen E. "Dat-Tay-Vao." *Amazing Stories* 81, 6 (March 1987): 16-33.

Dat-tay-vao, the miraculous healing touch, is passed from an old Vietnamese man to a venal U.S. Army cook. After being wounded, the American finds a way to pass the ability to an Army medic.

620. Gibson, John. "Nothing Could Happen." Burnsville, NC: AMS/RGW, 1987. 41 pp.

The point of view of a Navy enlisted man is almost unknown in Vietnam literature, so this story is unusual and revealing. It is an account of life on a destroyer off the coast of Vietnam in 1966. In addition to firing on shore targets, the men endure typical military harassment and enjoy a good deal of shore leave in the Philippine Islands and Taiwan.

621. O'Brien, Tim. "How to Tell a True War Story." *Esquire*, October 1987, pp. 208-215.

O'Brien at his best is very good indeed. In and around a story about an infantryman dying from a booby trap he weaves a discussion of the methods and credibility of war stories.

622. Weaver, Gordon. "Under the World." <u>Western Humani-</u>
         <u>ties Review</u> 41, 3 (Autumn 1987): 193-257.

      A soldier of small stature is recruited by a gung-ho
      lieutenant for a special tunnel-clearing unit. After
      the war, the soldier remains behind, living in an
      enemy tunnel stocked with supplies.

1965

623. Alley, Rewi. <u>The Mistake</u>. Christchurch, NZ:
    Caxton Press, 1965. 19 pp.

The eleven poems in this booklet were written in
Peking and elsewhere in China in 1965. They are all
anti-American. Many describe American bombing of
North Vietnam and emphasize its affect on the civilian
population.

1966

624. <u>Quixote</u> 1,7 (June 1966).

This "Peace Issue" of the literary magazine of the
University of Wisconsin contains many brief poems set
in Vietnam as well as many more with themes of protest
and anti-militarism. One pertinent short story,
Morris Edelson's "A Mission in Vietnam," is cited
elsewhere in this bibliography.

1967

625. Bly, Robert and Ray, David, eds. <u>A Poetry Reading
    Against the Vietnam War</u>. Madison, MN: The
    Sixties Press, c1966, 1967. 63 pp. 66-4861.

It is not always the case that collections of protest
or antiwar poetry include anything actually set in
Vietnam. In this instance, along with the work of
such persons as Adolf Hitler, I.F. Stone and Walt
Whitman, there are a number of Vietnam poems.

626. Lowenfels, Walter, ed. <u>Where is Vietnam?</u> Garden
      City, NY: Anchor Books, 1967. 160 pp.

      Among the eighty-seven poets represented in this
      anthology are James Dickey, Hayden Carruth, Lawrence
      Ferlinghetti and Denise Levertov. Most are new poems,
      and some were written for various anti-Vietnam
      readings in the 1960s.

627. Nhat Hahn. <u>Viet Nam Poems</u>, 3d ed. Santa Barbara, CA:
      Unicorn Press, c1967, 1972. 0-87775-030-0.

      This is a remarkably fine edition of poems in English,
      all of which appear in the author's <u>The Cry of Vietnam</u>
      (630).

628. Shea, Dick. <u>Vietnam Simply</u>. Coronado, CA: The Pro
      Tem Publishers, 1967.

      Shea was a Navy lieutenant involved in underwater
      operations in Vietnam, and the poems here reflect his
      tour. They are untitled, and the book is unpaged. At
      the rear is a list of what may be the titles of the
      poems "in order of appearance." This arrangement is
      quite awkward.

                            1968

629. Connell, Robert. <u>Firewinds: Poems on the Vietnam War</u>.
      Sydney: Wentworth Press, 1968. 21 pp.
      68-141365.

      There are eight poems, ranging in length from a few
      lines to two pages. Also included are eight black and
      white drawings. The illustrators are identified as
      David Ogg and Chris Amitzboll.

630. Thich Nhat Hahn. <u>The Cry of Vietnam</u>. Santa Barbara,
      CA: Unicorn Press, 1968. 57 pp.

      This is an essential book of Vietnamese poetry in
      English. Fine illustrations enhance a finely made
      book.

631. Tuck, Alfred David. <u>Poems of David</u>. NY; Carlton

Press, 1968.   79 pp.

Many of Tuck's poems have to do with the military
hospital system in Vietnam and Japan. Others describe
the city of Qui Nhon and infantry combat. He is
obviously not a practiced poet, but he clearly feels
grateful to U.S. medical personnel.

1969

632.   Kimler, Forest L., comp. and ed.   Boondock Bards.   San
         Francisco: Pacific Stars and Stripes, 1968.
         122 pp.

Virtually all the poets here were American servicemen
in Vietnam who sent their poems to the Pacific Stars
and Stripes in the mid-1960s. They are not all good
poets, but their honesty and sincerity are unmistakable. Location or unit designation is given for all.

1970

633.   Balaban, John.   Vietnam Poems. Oxford: Carcanet
         Press, 1970.   16 pp.

Several of these poems are set in Vietnam. Prefatory
material states that six hundred copies of this work
were published.

634.   Clover, Timothy.   The Leaves of My Trees, Still
         Green.   Chicago: Adams Press, 1970.   99 pp.

Clover was killed in Vietnam in 1968. Many of the
poems here were written long before his military
service, but more recent ones relate to Vietnam and to
the Army. The copy in hand was reproduced from a
typescript with corrections entered in pen and pencil.

635.   Eastlake, William.   A Child's Garden of Verses for the
         Revolution.   NY: Grove Press, 1970.   240 pp.
         72-121419.

About a third of the poems and brief prose pieces in
this collection relate to Vietnam, where Eastlake
visited as a journalist. The poems touch on a number
of subjects related to the war, including racial

matters, American values in the war and the prospect
of death. The prose pieces appear to be nonfiction
accounts of Eastlake's experiences in Vietnam.

636. Larsen, Earnest and Larsen, Bill. And Tomorrow We...
          Liguori, MO: Liguorian Books, 1970. 185 pp.
          78-116045.

      One of a series of inspirational books for adoles-
      cents, this reflects the experiences of a combat medic
      in the Vietnam War.

637. Martin, Earl E. A Poet Goes to War. Bozeman, MT: Big
          Sky Books, 1970. 78 pp.
          Bozeman, MT: Big Sky Books, 1977. Rev. ed.

      The untitled poems are grouped in several headings and
      reflect Martin's military training, sevice in Korea,
      sevice in Vietnam during the 1968 Tet Offensive, and
      homecoming. The information "About the Poet" reveals
      that Martin was wounded while serving in an Army
      armored unit.

                              1971

638. Livingstone, Richard N. Speak in Shame and Sorrow.
          Hampton, NH: Hampton House, 1971. 16 pp.

      Very much a work of protest literature, this volume
      combines stark photographs with antiwar poetry.

639. Luce, Don; Schafer, John C.; and Chagnon, Jacquelyn,
          eds. We Promise One Another. Washington, D.C.:
          Indochina Mobile Education Project, 1971.
          119 pp.

      This broad collection of Vietnamese poetry includes a
      number of war poems. Unfortunately this useful book
      is in an odd-sized, fragile format.

640. Moore, Daniel. Burnt Heart. San Francisco: City
          Lights, 1971. 62 pp. 78-164496.

      Some images of death and destruction in Vietnam appear
      in this long, rambling, lurid poem about death and

religion. A few black-and-white drawings of burning
and tortured human hearts appear on apparently random
pages. There is no question about the truth of the
author's introductory statement that the poem was
"written in a hurry."

1972

641. Berry, D.C. saigon cemetery. GA: University of
      Georgia Press, 1972. 50 pp. 78-169949.

      The brief, spare poems in this collection are un-
      titled, but they are clearly separate, rather than
      chapters of a single long poem. The jacket indicates
      that Berry was a medical officer in Vietnam.

642. Casey, Michael. Obscenities. New Haven, CT: Yale
      University Press, 1972. 68 pp. 78-179470.
      NY: Warner Books, 1972. 93 pp.

      The poems combine to form a sort of narration of
      Casey's experience as a rear area military policeman
      in Vietnam. Thoughtful definitions of obscure
      military terms and slang are provided at the bottom of
      various pages.

643. Rottman, Larry; Barry, Jan; and Paquet, Basil T., eds.
      Winning Hearts and Minds. Brooklyn, NY: 1st
      Casualty Press, 1972. 119 pp.
      NY: McGraw-Hill, 1972. 116 pp. 72-5875.

      The publisher is a company formed of members of the
      Vietnam Veterans Against the War, and that organi-
      zation also assisted in collecting the works of the
      thirty-three poets represented. The works are
      arranged to reflect a sort of tour in Vietnam. An
      index provides each poet's former military rank and
      unit as well as any decorations awarded.

1973

644. Kiley, Fred and Dater, Tony, eds. Listen, the War.
      Colorado Springs, CO: Air Force Academy
      Association of Graduates, 1973. 157 pp.

      This is certainly the most important book of Air Force

poetry to emerge from the Vietnam War. The editors,
assigned to the U.S. Air Force Academy, sought poems
from many sources and originally considered three
thousand from which the contents of this book were
selected. Most, but not all, of the poems relate to
Air Force subjects.

645. Layne, McAvoy. How Audie Murphy Died in Vietnam.
          Garden City, NY: Anchor Books, 1973. 72-96279.

The lack of page numbers, a table of contents or an
index of any kind makes this book rather awkward. It
seems to be a novel in verse. The poems take Murphy
into Marine boot camp and through various combat and
rear area experiences. Most of the poems occupy less
than one page, and many are much shorter than that.

1974

646. Balaban, John. After Our War. Pittsburgh: University
          of Pittsburgh Press, 1974. 84 pp. 73-13313.

Balaban appears to be a particularly sensitive and
able poet. Many of the poems and prose pieces in this
collection relate to Vietnam, although not always to
military matters.

1975

647. Berkhoudt, John C. Vietnam: A Year Before the
          "Peace". NY: Carlton Press, 1975. 48 pp.

Berkhoudt served in Vietnam as an infantry officer.
His poems are of various lengths and styles.

648. Ehrhart, W.D. A Generation of Peace. NY: New Voices
          Publishing, 1975. 49 pp. 74-18995.

The dust wrapper explains that this work was done as
an undergraduate thesis at Swarthmore College. The
poems, however, seem mature and capable. Well over
half of them relate to the poet's experience in the
Vietnam War.

649. Jordan, William Reynier. In the Darkness and the
         Shadow. Philadelphia: Dorrance, 1975. 44 pp.
         0-8059-2129-X.

      Most of these varied poems are about the Vietnam War,
      and many reveal the author's education and consider-
      able wit.

                                 1976

650. Barry, Jan and Ehrhart, W.D., eds. Demilitarized
         Zones. Perkasie, PA: East River Anthology,
         1976. 182 pp. 76-17200.

      The subtitle is "Veterans After Vietnam," but many of
      these poems are directly about the war. The editors
      are both qualified and well placed to do their job,
      and they make a fine selection of the work of many
      poets. This is an important anthology of Vietnam War
      poetry.

651. Floyd, Bryan Alec. The Long War Dead: An Epiphany.
         NY: Avon, 1976. 95 pp. 75-27440.
         Sag Harbor, NY: Permanent Press, n.d. 95 pp.
         83-063243.

      Each poem is titled with the rank and name of a Marine
      and serves as his description or, in some cases, his
      epitaph. Descriptions of the circumstances of death
      in combat are both graphic and wry. There is a
      continuity to this book that is lacking in much
      Vietnam War poetry.

652. Gray, Nigel, ed. Phoenix Country. Fireweed, 6
         (September 1976). 188 pp.

      This special issue of the English literary journal
      Fireweed is dedicated to the British Hospital in
      Vietnam, and everything in it has something to do with
      that country or with the war. There are black and
      white photographs, many poems, songs and both fiction
      and nonfiction prose pieces. The fiction is annotated
      elsewhere. Notable is the inclusion of some work by
      Vietnamese authors.

653. McDonald, Walter. Caliban in Blue and Other Poems.
         Lubbock, TX: Texas Tech Press, 1976. 51 pp.

The title poem is divided into a number of shorter
poems that all seem to emerge from the experiences of
a fighter pilot in Vietnam. The subjects vary from
tiger attacks to post exchanges to hospitals.
McDonald is a capable poet.

654. Oldham, Perry. Vinh Long. Meadows of Dan, VA: North-
      woods Press, 1976. 56 pp.

These brief poems deal with many aspects of a soldier's life in Vietnam. Their format and style vary
widely. The copy in hand is unfortunately rather
badly made, with margins that in some cases cut into
the text and with uneven inking throughout.

1977

655. Ehrhart, W.D. A Generation of Peace. Samisdat 14, 3,
      54th release, 1977. 32 pp.

This is a limited selection of the poems printed in
Ehrhart's earlier work of the same title. There are
also a few new poems here. Ehrhart's work fills this
whole issue of the periodical Samisdat.

656. McCarthy, Gerald. War Story. Trumansburg, NY: The
      Crossing Press, 1977. 69 pp. 77-23320.

The poet was a Marine in Vietnam. Many of the poems
in the first half of the book describe his experiences
and impressions there and upon his return to the
United States.

1978

657. Scott, L.E. Time Came Hunting Time. Cammeray, Aus-
      tralia: Saturday Centre Books, 1978. 56 pp.

According to preliminary material, Scott is a black
American who lives in New Zealand. His text includes
poems, brief prose pieces and short stories. The
poems and miscellaneous prose are all brief--usually
less than a page. The short stories are described
elsewhere in this bibliography.

1979

658. Hollis, Jocelyn. Vietnam Poems: The War Poems of
      Today. NY: American Poetry Press, 1979. 38 pp.
      Philadelphia: American Poetry Press, 1983. 33
      pp. 80-65621.

All of the poems are about the war, and some are set
in Vietnam. The images and narration are not particularly realistic. A biographical note about the
author says nothing about any firsthand experience in
Vietnam.

659. Johnson, G.P. I Was Fighting for Peace, but, Lord,
      There Was Much More. Hicksville, NY: Exposition
      Press, 1979. 88 pp.

Johnson served as an infantryman in Vietnam in 1968
and 1969. The first section of poems relates to that
experience, describing his reaction to a new country
and, for example, to his first act of killing. The
poet's strong Christian faith is apparent in his work.

1980

660. Baker, Richard E. Shell Burst Pond. Tacoma, WA:
      Rapier Press, 1980. 26 pp.
      Tacoma, WA: Vardaman Press, 1982. 28 pp.
      0-942648-02-1.

Baker served as an infantryman in Vietnam. Some of
the poems describe in grisly detail his experiences
and his impressions. Others touch on philosophical
and romantic topics.

661. Cantwell, James M. Highway Number One: A Vietnam
      Odyssey in Verse. Smithtown, NY: Exposition
      Press, 1980. 64 pp. 0-682-49595-6.

A note on the back cover says that Cantwell served in
the Marine Corps Reserve. His long poem describes the
experiences of Vietnamese refugees from 1946 through
1975. During the war years, they encounter American
troops.

662. Currey, Richard. Crossing Over: A Vietnam Journal.
          Cambridge, MA: Apple-wood Press, 1980. 46 pp.
          0-918222-22-2.

      The author's indentification of this work as a "poetic
      documentary" is appropriate for these dense, austere
      prose poems. They convey the awful experiences of a
      Navy corpsman serving with Marine infantry.

663. Ehrhart, W.D. The Awkward Silence. Stafford, VA:
          Northwoods Press, 1980. 41 pp. 79-92943.

      As a poet and editor, Bill Ehrhart is clearly one of
      the major figures in Vietnam War literature. He
      served as a sergeant in the Marines in Vietnam in 1967
      and 1968, often as a scout in combat. This collection
      includes poems that appear in earlier works.

664. Ehrhart, W.D. The Samisdat Poems of W.D. Ehrhart.
          Samisdat 24, 1, 93rd release (1980). 72 pp.

      In this collection are many poems, sometimes revised,
      that appear in other works Ehrhart has written and
      edited. The typeface, legibility and other physical
      qualities of this work are much superior to earlier
      Samisdat publications. Most of the poems here emerge
      from Ehrhart's experiences as a Marine sergeant in
      Vietnam.

665. Hamilton, Fritz. A Father at a Soldier's Grave. NY:
          Downtown Poets, 1980. 63 pp. 0-917402-16-2.

      In each of fifty-six poems, a different father
      addresses his buried son at a gravesite. Many of the
      poems are biting and ironic. Often the circumstances
      of the son's death in Vietnam are described in the
      poem.

666. [Hollis, Jocelyn]. Poems of the Vietnam War. Edited
          by J. Topham. NY: American Poetry Press, 1980.
          80-65621. 48 pp.
          Philadelphia: American Poetry & Lit. Press, 1985.
          49 pp. 85-1292.

      The story told by these poems takes a soldier from
      home through training, battle, wounds and return to

home. There are poems on other subjects as well,
including submarine disasters. Always more intro-
spective than realistic, Hollis is listed as author on
the 1985 edition. The 1980 version lists only J.
Topham as editor.

1981

667. Barry, Jan, ed. <u>Peace is Our Profession</u>. Montclair,
      NJ: East River Anthology, 1981. 294 pp.
      80-70115.

The subtitle, "Poems and Passages of War Protest,"
accurately describes this work. There are photographs
and prose pieces, but the work is primarily a collection of poetry. Included are works by W.D. Ehrhart,
Don Duncan and other Vietnam veterans. A substantial
number are set in Vietnam.

668. <u>Deros</u>. Alexandria, VA.

This quarterly journal takes its name from the Army
initialism that stands for "date of estimated return
from overseas." A major outlet for poetry about the
war, <u>Deros</u> began publication in December 1981.

669. Ransome, Donald F. <u>Nothing but the Boo</u>. Portland,
      OR: Skydog Press, 1981. [24 pp].

These poems describe an infantryman's war. Well made
for a small press product, publications like this were
more common in earlier decades.

670. Schlosser, Robert. <u>The Humidity Readings</u>. <u>Samisdat</u>
      29, 1 (1981). 14 pp.

These brief poems describe what Schlosser saw and felt
during his service as a military policeman in Thailand
in 1969 and 1970.

1982

671. Topham, J., ed. <u>Vietnam Heroes: A Tribute</u>. Claymont,
      Delaware: American Poetry Press, 1982. 19 pp.
      82-3955.

Vietnam Heroes II: The Tears of a Generation.
Claymont, Deleware: American Poetry Press, 1982.
38 pp. 82-11465.
Vietnam Heroes III: That We Have Peace. Philadelphia: American Poetry Press, 1983. 32 pp.
83-6400.
Vietnam Heroes IV: The Long Ascending Cry.
Philadelphia: American Poetry & Literature Press,
1985. 57 pp. 85-9008.

These short anthologies are characterized by the poems
of Vietnam veterans and "friends of the veterans,"
including the editor. Not all of the poems are set in
Vietnam, but they all relate to the war in some way.
There are some brief prose pieces.

1983

672. Barry, Jan. Veterans Day. Samisdat 36, 1, 141st
      release (1983). 12 pp.

The eight poems in this brief pamphlet convey Barry's
memories of the war as well as his reflections on its
cost and aftermath.

673. Barry, Jan. War Baby. Samisdat 39, 2, 154th release
      (1983). 12 pp.

A sequel to his earlier Veterans Day (672), this
pamphlet contains six war poems.

674. Barth, R.L. Forced Marching to the Styx: Vietnam War
      Poems. Van Nuys, CA: Perivale Press, 1983.
      20 pp. 0-912288-21-3.

Barth served as a Marine in Vietnam in the late 1960s.
His sensitive, erudite poems describe some of his
experiences there. This Perivale Poetry chapbook is a
remarkably well printed paperback edition.

675. Hope, Warren. An Unsuccessful Mission. Florence, KY:
      Robert L. Barth, 1983. 0-941150-15-1.

There are no poems about combat in this short collection. They appear to describe the observations of an
enlisted ambulance driver.

676. Le, Nancylee. <u>Duckling in a Thunderstorm</u>. Colorado
        Springs, CO: Rong-Tien Publishing, 1983. 241 pp.

      The title is apt. Le's life as a Vietnamese housewife
      of American origin appears fascinating in these poems.
      The cursive print is, unfortunately, distracting.

                              1984

677. Baka, Steve, ed. <u>Thunder Silence</u>. Annapolis, MD:
        Annapolis Works, [1984]. 32 pp. [approx.]

      Most of the eighteen poems here are by the editor.
      Each poem is accompanied by a facing page of photo-
      graphs. Topics include typical combat experiences and
      one particularly biting comment about a famous
      American actress and other war protesters.

678. Ehrhart, W.D. <u>To Those Who Have Gone Home Tired</u>. NY:
        Thunder's Mouth Press, 1984. 72 pp. 84-91.

      Many of the poems in this collection are set in the
      war, and most of them have previously appeared
      elsewhere. This is a welcome gathering of Ehrhart's
      work. He is, deservedly, one of the best known
      Vietnam War poets.

679. Sinke, Ralph E.G. Jr. <u>Don't Cry For Us</u>. N.p.: REGS
        Enterprises, 1984. 124 pp.

      The author is a serving Marine major and Vietnam
      combat veteran. His book combines poems of varying
      lengths, numerous drawings, some photographs and a few
      prose pieces that seem to be factual rather than
      imaginative. While combat is the principal subject,
      Sinke also deals with the veteran's experiences and
      feelings.

680. Topham, J., ed. <u>Vietnam Literature Anthology: A
        Balanced Perspective</u>. NY: American Poetry &
        Literature Press, 1984. 83 pp. 84-11029.
        Philadelphia: American Poetry & Literature Press,
        1985. Rev. ed. 67 pp. 85-3948.

      Topham is a talented editor and each poet in this
      anthology has a different perspective and a unique

voice. The prose section appears to be the first
chapter from a proposed novel.

681. Villani, Jim, et al, eds. Vietnam Flashbacks: Pig
      Iron No. 12. Youngstown, Ohio: Pig Iron Press,
      1984. 96 pp. 84-061225.

      This valuable issue includes photographs, graphics,
      nonfiction and short stories, which are annotated
      elsewhere in this bibliography (596). There are
      thirty poems by different authors.

                            1985

682. Ehrhart, W.D., ed. Carrying the Darkness, American
      Indochina: The Poetry of the Vietnam War. NY:
      Avon/Bard, 1985. 288 pp. 85-90824.

      This excellent anthology reflects the abilities and
      wide association of its editor. Ehrhart has written
      widely on Vietnam and is personally acquainted with
      many of the authors whose poems appear. This should
      become the standard academic text.

683. Hertzler, Terry. The Way of the Snake and Other
      Poems: Writings from the War in Vietnam. San
      Diego, CA: Caernarvon Press, 1985.

      Hertzler seems to have drawn on experiences as an
      infantryman, probably in 1970, for these poems. Other
      pieces, including some prose, describe rest and
      recreation in Australia and events after the war.

                            1986

684. Andrews, Michael. A Telegram, Unsigned. Samisdat 45,
      1, 177th release (1986).

      Several long poems in this collection are on Vietnam
      themes. "Body Bags" is particularly good. The review
      copy is very badly printed.

685. Bauer, Bill. The Eye of the Ghost. Kansas City, MO:
      BKMK Press, 1986. 47 pp. 86-71527.

The section of "Vietnam Poems" is the larger of the
two in the book. Bauer's poetry is based on his war
experiences in 1969 and on his subsequent memories.

686. Cross, Frank A. Reminders. Big Timber, MT: Seven
        Buffaloes Press, 1986. 20 pp. 916380-43-2.

These brief poems describe the author's experience
with the Americal Division in I Corps. A preface
recounts his Vietnam service in a reconaissance
platoon during 1969 and 1970.

687. Hollis, Jocelyn. Collected Vietnam Poems and Other
        Poems. Philadelphia: American Poetry & Litera-
        ture Press, 1986. 168 pp. 85-20013.

Many of the Vietnam poems in this collection are
reprinted from the author's earlier works. They
amount to about a third of the total.

688. Knight, Cranston Sedrick, ed. Tour of Duty. Samisdat
        46, 2, 182nd Release (1986).

The particular strength of this anthology is that
Knight includes works of lesser known poets, as well
as pieces by such established poets and writers as
Bill Ehrhart, Tom Suddick and Richard Parque. The few
short stories are cited elsewhere in this
bibliography.

689. Larsen, Wendy and Tran Thi Nga. Shallow Graves. NY:
        Random House, 1986.
        NY: Perennial Library, Random House, 1987. 287
        pp.

The authors knew each other first in Vietnam and later
in the United States. The poems describe events and
impressions, including those related to the war. This
is a moving and insightful collection.

690. Mason, Steve. Johnny's Song. NY: Bantam, 1986.

Unrhymed poems that vary from a few lines to several
pages address both combat experience and the cir-

cumstances of Veterans. Each of several sections has
an explanatory preface.

1987

691. Fletcher, Harvey D. Visions of Nam. Raleigh, NC:
        Jo-Ely Publishing, 1987. 63 pp. 86-091432.

      Fletcher is older than many Vietnam writers. He
      served first in Korea and later retired from the
      Marine Corps. His descriptive poems range in length
      from a few lines to several pages.

692. Fletcher, Harvey D. Visions of Nam, Vol. 2. Raleigh,
        NC: Jo-Ely Publishing, 1987. 66 pp. 87-82291.

      This second volume of Fletcher's poetry is similar to
      the first in that it reflects more honest emotion and
      accurate memory than polished skill.

693.. Vietnam in Poems. Mclean, VA: POW-MIA Common Cause,
        [1987]. [16 pp.].

      This large-format collection includes poems by dif-
      ferent authors written between 1969 and 1987. Many
      are set in Vietnam; others deal with the POW-MIA
      issue.

NO DATES

694. Gray, Nigel. Aftermath. Lancaster, England: Lan-
        caster University Student's Union, n.d. 24 pp.

      The seventeen poems here all relate in some way to the
      Vietnam War. They seem rather less descriptive than
      most poems by Americans. The book includes several
      black-and-white drawings.

695. Kiemi, John. What's a Vietnam? N.p., n.d.

      In simple, sentimental verse, the author gets some
      things out of his system.

696. <u>Vietnam Poetry</u>. Fullerton, CA: Union of the Viet
         namese in the United States, n.d.   83 pp.

      Most poems in this anthology are written in the
      context of the war, and several mention the American
      military.   English and Vietnamese text are on facing
      pages, and there are a few black-and-white illustra-
      tions.   Readability is hampered in places by the light
      italic type.

1966

697. Terry, Megan. "Viet Rock." <u>Tulane Drama Review</u> 11, 1
      (Fall 1966): 196-227.
      Also in her <u>Viet Rock</u>, 19-110. NY: Simon and
      Schuster, 1967. 67-17889.

This parody of the Vietnam experience emphasizes
action rather than individuals. Scenes in the United
States and in Vietnam feature soldiers' parents, U.S.
senators, and the Madonna. Continuing characters are
a Sergeant, who mouths simpleminded pro-American and
promilitary slogans, and a group of his men who seem
to represent all American soldiers. The Sergeant
trains his men and leads them into combat in Vietnam,
where they suffer both wounds and death. North
Vietnamese characters, including the broadcaster Hanoi
Hannah, appear to speak lines representing their point
of view about the war. In an alternative final scene,
presented at the end of the ordinary script, Americans
are captured, tortured and murdered by North
Vietnamese. In a performance, all of this action
would probably convey an appropriate sense of diver-
sity and confusion about the war.

1967

698. Kupferberg, Tuli. <u>Fuck Nam</u>. NY: Birth Press, 1967.
      35 pp.

Very much an icon of the antiwar movement, <u>Fuck Nam</u>
makes up in crude sex what it lacks in subtlety.
There is no plot. Scenes take place in the village of
Phoc Nam and in American aircraft. Many of the
characters are nude, and sexual intercourse occurs

often. It is interesting to imagine how this play
might be staged.

699. Ribman, Ronald. The Final War of Olly Winter. NY:
         CBS Television Network, 1967.   91 pp.

This finely printed script includes still photographs
from the 1967 CBS television production. The play is
set in the jungle of Vietnam in 1963. Ollie Winter is
a black U.S. Army master sergeant who is the sole
survivor of a Vietnamese patrol he advised. As Winter
runs from the pursuing Vietcong, he picks up a
Vietnamese girl, a baby, and a prisoner along the way.
Flashbacks relate to Winter's harsh youth in the
United States and help establish his empathy with the
poor people of Vietnam. After a stop in a village,
Winter and the girl are finally caught and killed by
the Vietcong. This play offers a notably sympathetic
view of the American effort in Vietnam.

1968

700. Kustow, Michael and others, eds. US. London: Calder
         and Boyars, 1968.   214 pp.
         Indianapolis: Bobbs-Merrill, 1968. Published as
         Tell Me Lies.   214 pp.   68-13223.

The text of the play US amounts to about half of this
publication. The remainder includes an exhaustive
account of the background, production, and critical
reaction to the play. The strong and articulate
feelings of everyone involved with this play about the
Vietnam war are stated often. The play itself is in
two acts: the first seeks to depict American involvement in the war; the second appears to be focused on
reaction to the war in England. The book is laid out
so that the script is mixed with lengthy footnotes,
songs, cartoons, photographs and other peripheral
items in a manner that leads to some confusion.
American characters are stupid, brutal and venal,
while the Vietnamese are heroic patriots. It is
interesting to see such a virulent anti-American theme
in an English play.

1969

701. Rabe, David. The Basic Training of Pavlo Hummel and

Sticks and Bones. NY: Viking Press, c1969, 1973.
226 pp.   72-75746.
Middlesex, England: Penguin, 1978.

A substantial introduction explains something of the
creative background and production history of both
works and includes a cogent statement of Rabe's
opinion of "antiwar" drama.

a. The Basic Training of Pavlo Hummel begins with
Hummel's death from a terrorist's grenade in Vietnam.
Pavlo then finds himself back in Army basic training.
This, and indeed the rest of the play, may occur in
the dying Pavlo's mind. After experiences with both
cadre and other trainees that are typical for an Army
recruit, Pavlo Hummel returns to Vietnam in the second
act. He serves as a medic until he is killed again by
another grenade, thrown this time by an American.
Throughout the play, Pavlo's innocence is gradually
replaced by toughness in a sensitive revelation of the
affect of war on men.

b. In Sticks and Bones, David, a veteran blinded in
the war, is delivered by truck to the home of his
parents, Ozzie and Harriet, and his brother, Ricky.
David and the specter of his Vietnamese girlfriend,
Zung, destroy the complacent and ordinary life of the
household and particularly upset and challenge Ozzie.
In the end, his parents and his brother help David to
slash his wrists.

                              1972

702. Balk, H. Wesley. The Dramatization of 365 Days.
          Minneapolis: University of Minnesota Press, 1972.
          148 pp.   72-85756.

This play is based on 365 Days, by Ronald J. Glasser
(Braziller, 1971), a nonfiction account of an Army
doctor at a hospital in Japan. In the introduction,
Balk explains how the original work was adapted for
chamber theater. The characters are Speaker 1,
Speaker 2, etc., and they describe and portray events
both in the hospital and in Vietnam. Accounts of
combat and of wounds are especially graphic and
brutal. Dispassionate medical language is used to
convey the harm done to men's bodies by weapons of
war. Balk includes photographs from a production of
the play, staging plans, and a helpful glossary.

1973

703.   Patrick, Robert. <u>Kennedy's Children</u>. NY: Random
          House, c1973, 1976. 66 pp. 75-35959.

It is Valentine's Day, 1974, in a theatrical bar in
New York City. The few characters speak their
thoughts aloud without much interaction. A Vietnam
veteran, Mark, reads aloud from never-mailed letters
and a diary. Mark's readings, which comprise a
substantial part of the play, describe his experiences
with, and reactions to, both combat and drugs and his
relationship with a friend that finally results in
murder. The last entry in Mark's diary reports that
he is being sent home for methadone treatment.
Sections of this play were performed in 1970 under the
title <u>A Bad Place to Get Your Head.</u>

1975

704.   Berry, David. <u>G.R. Point</u>. NY: Dramatists Play
          Service, c1975, 1980. 60 pp. Originally titled
          <u>Spiders Talk upon the Lawn</u>.

The initials in the title stand for "graves registration," a facility where soldiers process the bodies
of their dead comrades. They also talk together about
their circumstances and occasionally fight and die.
The time is 1969 and the location is near the
Cambodian border.

1977

705.   Jack, Alex. <u>Dragonbrood</u>. Brookline, MA: Kanthaka
          Press, 1977. 102 pp.

Jack is to be admired for creating an epic drama about
Americans in Vietnam. It is a unique, substantial
effort. The result, however, is contrived and
labored, with a multiplicity of characters, a complex
plot and heavy-handed attempts at symbolism that
frequently fail. It is set in Vietnam in 1967.

1979

706.   Gray, Amlin. <u>How I Got That Story</u>. NY: Dramatists

Play Service, c1979, 1981. 55 pp.
Also in Coming to Terms: American Plays and the
Vietnam War, introduction by James Resoton, Jr.,
78-117. NY: Theatre Communications Group, 1985.

Gray has described his notional country of "Am-bo
Land" as an analogue to Vietnam. The two characters
are a wire service Reporter and the Historical Event,
an individual who portrays various government
officials, Americans, Vietnamese civilians, Vietcong
and other parties to the war. When the Reporter
arrives in Am-bo land directly from East Dubuque, he
is bewildered by a land plagued by war, suffering and
death, but without honesty or truth. After numerous
adventures, the Reporter sinks into the culture of
Am-bo land; he loses his journalistic objectivity and
purpose and becomes instead part of the story. At the
end, an American photographer takes his picture as an
illustration of the locale.

1980

707. Reich, Dale. The War That Never Ends. Whitewater,
      WI: typescript, 1980. 22 pp.

For Dusty, a Vietnam veteran with a missing leg, the
war is still very much a part of life some twelve
years after his discharge. The amputation affects his
job, his attitude, and his marriage. Also, he is
haunted by explicit dreams of Vietnam in which persons
he has killed return to speak to him. In conversations among Dusty and other Vietnam veterans, the idea
emerges that they are much less understood and
appreciated by society than were the veterans of
earlier wars. However, Dusty's growing relationship
with a patriotic World War II veteran ends the play on
an optimistic note. The five characters and straightforward action suggest that this would be a good play
for a small company, although the going is a bit heavy
when the characters quote statistics to one another.

1982

708. King, Bruce. Dustoff. Santa Fe, NM: Institute of
      American Indian Arts Press, 1982. 58 pp.

In a medical evacuation unit around 1970, there is a
conflict between the old top sergeant and the lower

ranking troops who ride the helicopters. The men use
drugs and wait to return to the U.S. The old sergeant
remembers better times.

1983

709. Clark, Sean. Eleven-Zulu. NY: Samuel French, 1983.
         64 pp. 0-573-61945-X.

In the mountains of Vietnam in 1971, a squad of
infantrymen is left to guard a disabled armored
personnel carrier. As they wait, women they know from
civilian life appear to them. Four of the men are
killed in unusual circumstances, but the Army does not
investigate.

710. DiFusco, John, et al. Tracers. NY: Hill and Wang,
         c1983, 1986. 105 pp. 86-295.

The script emerged originally from experimentation by
the actors who first performed it in 1980. Some
internal evidence suggests that the men are Marines.
In Vietnam they have the usual experiences in the
field and in rear areas. Several of the men recount
their fate as veterans after the war.

711. George, Rob. Sandy Lee Live at Nui Dat. Sydney,
         Australia: Currency Press, 1983. 74 pp.
         0-86819-072-1.

Very much a product of the Australian antiwar movement, this play takes place there and in Vietnam in
1970. The characters include Australian soldiers,
peace activists and a country and western singer.
There are some scenes set during patrols and in a
military hospital, and one at a concert. The antiwar
theme predominates in a manner that is neither subtle
nor sophisticated.

712. Hare, David. Saigon: Year of the Cat. London: Faber
         and Faber, 1983. 77 pp.
         Also in his The Asian Plays. London: Faber and
         Faber, 1986. 86-11470.

The frantic and unprepared nature of the American
evacuation of Saigon provides the plot here. Charac-

ters include military men, CIA agents and an American
ambassador who is unwilling to believe that South
Vietnam is falling.

1985

713. McNally, Terrence. Botticelli. In Coming to Terms:
      American Plays and the Vietnam War, 67-76. NY:
      Theatre Communications Group, 1985.

      Two infantrymen play Botticelli, a game of memory,
      while they wait for another man to emerge from an
      enemy tunnel.

714. Stone, Oliver and Boyle, Richard. Oliver Stone's
      Platoon and Salvador: The Original Screenplays.
      NY: Vintage, c1985, 1987. 254 pp.

      Bound with the screenplay of Salvador, Platoon is
      recognizable as both the motion picture and as the
      basis for Dale Dye's novel (351). The story of the
      experiences and conflicts of young men whose business
      is killing belongs among the best known accounts of
      the war.

715. Pielmeier, John. The Boys of Winter. NY: Typescript,
      c1985, 1986.

      During a few days over the Christmas holiday of 1968,
      a squad of Marines destroys itself in the jungle of
      Quang Tri Province. Standard Vietnam characters
      include the young lieutenant, the old sergeant, the
      medic, the black and the barely-trusted interpreter.
      There is little contact with the enemy, but the group
      suffers heavy casualties. Dialogue is quite realistic
      and the men's conclusions about the futility of war
      are handled with a relatively deft touch in this
      original play.

1987

716. Kubrick, Stanley; Herr, Michael and Hasford, Gustav.
      Full Metal Jacket. NY: Knopf, 1987. 129 pp.
      87-45979.

      This script includes many color photographs from the

motion picture. The story is recognizable as a
version of Hasford's <u>The Short-Timers</u> (195), a superb
novel of Marines in training and at war.

1965

717. Burrows, Ken. "Vietnam Speak-Out or, How We Won the War." Monocle 6, 4 (1965). Entire issue.

The very crude drawings in this document are captioned with quotations from senior American officials to the effect that the Vietnam War is being won. The quotations date between 1954 and 1965.

718. Heroes and Heroines of South Vietnam. Peking: Supplement to China Reconstructs, July 1965. 19 pp.

The sixteen plates in this loose portfolio are in various media, including paintings, drawings and woodblock prints. Accompanied by brief captions, they show scenes of heroic peasants and workers defeating imperialist American aggressors or their South Vietnamese puppet soldiers.

719. Moore, Robin. Tales of the Green Berets. Illustrated by Joe Kubert. NY: New American Library, Signet, c1965, 1966. 144 pp.

This is essentially a comic book in the format of a mass market paperback. Based on the author's experiences, the story takes a journalist through Special Forces training and into combat in Vietnam.

720. Zidek, Tony. Choi Oi!: The Lighter Side of Vietnam. Rutland, VT: Charles E. Tuttle, 1965. 127 pp. 65-19807.

The artwork in these cartoons shows more detail and
sophistication than other, similar books. Also, the
lettering is uniformly clear and readable.

1966

721. Melvin, Ken. "Be Nice!" Tokyo: The Wayward Press,
         1966. 100 pp.

In this sequel to their earlier Sorry 'Bout That, the
two persons who write as Ken Melvin present another,
very similar collection of Vietnam cartoons, jokes,
verse, clippings and short prose pieces.

722. Melvin, Ken. Sorry 'Bout That! Tokyo: The Wayward
         Press, 1966. 103 pp.

The book jacket explains that Ken Melvin is a name
chosen by Ken Sams and Melvin Porter, both with
extensive experience in Vietnam. They combine black-
and-white cartoons with jokes, captioned photographs,
verse and other elements of thought to be humorous.
Most of the drawings are the work of a single artist.

723. West, Richard. Sketches from Vietnam. London:
         Jonathon Cape, c1966, 1968. 159 pp.

The text is an account of the author's travels through
Vietnam in the 1960s. The twenty black and white
illustrations by Gerald Scarfe are mostly caricatures
of Vietnamese and Americans.

1967

724. Abood, Ken and Ranfone, Tony. How to Live in Vietnam
         For Less Than 10 Cents a Day. Tokyo: The Wayward
         Press, 1967. 104 pp.

These cartoons follow a typical tour in Vietnam,
beginning with arrival, including combat, leaves,
etc., and ending with departure. There are also some
views of civilian life and of the enemy.

1968

725. Abu, ed. <u>Verdicts on Vietnam</u>. Introduced by James
      Cameron. London: Pemberton Publishing, 1968.
      128 pp.

This internatonal collection of antiwar and anti-
American cartoons is divided into several sections
which reflect the beginning and growth of American
participation in the Vietnam War.

726. McIntyre, William, ed. <u>Armed Farces: Military
      Cartoons by VIP</u>. Greenwich, CN: Fawcett, c1968,
      1969.

Although the cartoons here cover all aspects of
American military life, the timing of the book assures
that many reflect the Vietnam War.

727. Stewart, George. <u>What's So Funny About Vietnam?</u>
      Tampa, FL: Tampa Art and Publishing Co., 1968.

Stewart finds a good deal that is funny about Vietnam.
Probably because of the early origin of many of these
cartoons, they seem to belong more to the era of World
War II than to Vietnam. However, the setting is
unmistakable.

728. <u>Vietnam Combat Art</u>. NY: Cavanagh & Cavanagh, 1968.
      86 pp.

This selection from the Marine Corps Combat Art
Collection is introduced by H. Lester Cooke of the
National Gallery. The works are in various media and
styles. Most are black and white. The book's large
format and excellent physical qualities enhance
reproduction. The explanatory captions by Raymond
Henri are accurate, substantial and informative. The
work narurally emphasizes the U.S. Marine Corps in
Vietnam.

729. Waterhouse, Charles. <u>Vietnam Sketchbook</u>. Rutland,
      VT: Charles E. Tuttle, 1968. 127 pp. 68-21114.

Many of the black-and-white sketches are set in the

area of the Mekong Delta. Waterhouse visited there in
1967, and his work reveals his obvious affection for
the American servicemen who are most often his
subjects.

1969

730. Grant, Vernon. Stand By One! Cambridge, MA: n.p.,
          1969.

These cartoons appear to be based on Grant's service
in Vietnam in 1966 and 1967. The drawing shows
talent, but the captions are not particularly successful humor.

731. Nielson, Jon with Nielson, Kay. Artist in South
          Vietnam. NY: Julian Messner, 1969. 64 pp.

The book is divided into seven sections, such as "The
People," "Old Vietnam," and "The United States in
South Vietnam." The numerous drawings seem to date
from 1967 or 1968. They are accompanied by both text
and captions.

1970

732. Hodgson, Michael T. With Sgt. Mike in Vietnam.
          Washington D.C.: Army Times Publishing Company,
          1970. 119 pp.

Hodgson is the "Sgt. Mike" of the title. He served
with the Marines in Vietnam, and the several continuing characters in these often humorous cartoons are
also Marines. Many of the cartoons are reprinted from
civilian and military periodicals.

733. Kissam, Edward. Vietnamese Lessons. London: Anvil
          Press Poetry, 1970.

This fan-folded single sheet is offered as a parody of
an American manual on Vietnam. The humor is so subtle
that it easily eludes an American reader in this
decade.

734. Schuffert, Jake. No Sweat . . . More 'n More.

Washington, D.C.: Army Times Publishing, 1970.
160 pp.

These cartoons originally appeared in the Army, Navy
and Air Force _Times_ and reflect all three of those
services as well as the Marine Corps. Many are
specific to Vietnam, while others are based on general
aspects of military life.

735. Tauber, Burton R.   "Preliminary Prospectus: The War
in Vietnam." NY: Workman Publishing, 1970.
16 pp.

This is one of the most subtle and sophisticated
pieces of Vietnam War humor. With a light and gentle
touch, Tauber offers a high risk investment with such
dangers as pacification, Cambodian operations and
aggressive competition. Everything is in the form of
a typical common stock prospectus.

736. Waterhouse, Charles. _Vietnam War Sketches_. Rutland,
VT: Charles E. Tuttle, 1970. 127 pp. 71-109410.

The work here is similar to Waterhouse's earlier
Vietnam Sketches (729). Realistic and engaging black-
and-white drawings have captions of one or two
sentences. Waterhouse renders military subjects with
effective accuracy.

1971

737. Adair, Dick. _Dick Adair's Saigon_. NY: Weatherhill,
1971. 144 pp. 78-157268.

The focus of this large and well-printed book is
almost entirely upon the city of Saigon. Most of the
subjects of Adair's black and white drawings are
people. Settings include the city streets, commercial
enterprises, the port and military backgrounds.

738. Trudeau, G.B. _Bravo for Life's Little Ironies_. NY:
Popular Library, 1971. 80 pp. [approx.] 72-
91561.

This is a selection of cartoons from Trudeau's _But
This War Had Such Promise_. Most of the cartoons

selected reflect the war, rather than the other
subjects in the larger work.

739. Trudeau, G.B. But This War Had Such Promise. NY:
        Holt, Rinehart and Winston, 1971. 100 pp.
        [approx.] 72-91561.

The "Doonesbury" cartoon series is well known to many
Americans, and the cartoonist's political and social
ideas are as clear as his great talent. The principal
characters in this collection are B.D., the gung ho
former football player, and Phred, the Vietcong
terrorist. Their acquaintance and relationship is
developed in numerous delightful, almost classic,
panels. Cartoons on Kent State, ecology, race
relations, politics and other subjects from the period
of the war complete the collection.

740. Tuso, Joseph F., ed. Folksongs of the American
        Fighter Pilot in Southeast Asia, 1967-1968.
        Folklore Forum, Bibliographic and Special
        Services, n.7, 1971. 28 pp.

Tuso provides a responsible and scholarly introduction
as well as a useful glossary. The mimeographed
typescript is a modest format for this important
collection of lyrics to pilot's songs. Notes for most
songs indicate the tune to which they are sung.

                            1972

741. Aument, Shary. Unforgettable Faces. Kalamazoo, MI:
        Leaders Press, 1972. 216 pp.

In 1971 and 1972, Aument, a private individual, worked
through POW and MIA organizations to obtain photographs of American prisoners and men missing in action
in Vietnam. The drawings based on those photographs
are all black and white, full face, head and shoulder
poses. Each drawing is accompanied by a letter from a
member of the man's family. Many are quite touching.

742. I Didn't Raise Our Son To Be a Soldier. Chicago:
        Playboy Press, 1972.

These cartoons date from 1955 through 1972, so a great

many have to do with Vietnam-era military. Popular
themes of the cartoonists are encounters between
Americans and Vietnamese and the credibility problems
of the military command.

743. Lee, Ron, ed. <u>Absolutely No U.S. Personnel Permitted
      Beyond This Point</u>. NY: Delta, 1972. 100 pp.
      [approx.]

      This collection of cartoons is introduced by Jules
      Pfeiffer, and the editor is identified as a member of
      the National Peace Action Coalition. Sources of the
      cartoons are newspapers and journals worldwide. Most
      are critical of the U.S. role in Vietnam. while others
      express anti-American themes more generally.

                             1978

744. Carroll, Tod and O'Rourke, P.J.   "Born Again on the
      Fourth of July: Vietnam Combat Veterans Simulator
            Kit." <u>National Lampoon</u>, July 1978, pp. 65-70,
            96.

      For the nonveteran, this humorous piece provides
      adequate background information to lie convincingly
      about combat experience.

                             1980

745. Foster, Tad. <u>The Vietnam Funny Book</u>. Navato, CA:
            Presidio Press, 1980. 81-13935.

      This collectiion of cartoons was begun by the author
      in Vietnam in 1969. The humor is often grim.

                             1981

746. Skypeck, George L. <u>Ghosts of a Forgotten Era: The
            Combat Art of George L. Skypeck</u>. N.p., 1981.

      The artist served in Vietnam, and the fifteen black
      and white reproductions here are taken from larger,
      original paintings. The subjects, usually men in
      combat, are accompanied by lengthy captions on each
      facing page.

1984

747. Pratt, John Clark, compiler. Vietnam Voices: Perspec-
      tives on the War Years, 1941-1982. NY: Penguin,
      1984. 706 pp. 84-11172.

      Pratt's anthology includes both imaginative and
      factual documents, excerpted and sorted into chrono-
      logical sections. The attempt to convey a picture of
      the whole war from so many parts is successful because
      of Pratt's ability and his sound knowledge of Vietnam
      writing. A better table of contents would have been
      welcome. This is the major anthology of its kind and
      it belongs in most collections.

1985

748. Smith, Richard R. Reflexes and Reflections: Vietnam.
      Tennyson, IN: 1985. 50 pp.

      Simple black-and-white drawings are captioned briefly
      with a few words or occasional brief verses. The
      review copy includes three postcards with Vietnam
      related illustrations.

1986

749. Anzenberger, Joseph F., ed. Combat Art of the Vietnam
      War. Jefferson, NC: McFarland, 1986. 133 pp.
      85-43570.

      Drawn primarily from originals in official military
      collections, the reproductions here show evidence of
      broad scope and wise selection. The book is arranged
      in several thematic sections, each supported by
      helpful narrative. More color would be welcome, but
      Anzenberger and his publisher deserve much credit.

750. Smith, Richard R. Visions and Voices: Vietnam.
      Tennyson, IN: n.p., 1986.

      The portraits of Vietnamese people here are accom-
      panied by very brief captions. The review copy is
      badly reproduced; it appears to have been made on a
      copy machine. A preface conveys the author's doubt-

less sincerity, but it is difficult to find the
purpose of this awkward volume.

1987

751. Anisfield, Nancy, ed. Vietnam Anthology: American War
        Literature. Bowling Green, OH: Bowling Green
        State University Popular Press, 1987.   150 pp.
        87-71030.

This limited selection of Vietnam literature includes
excerpts from six novels and two plays, as well as
reprints or excerpts of twenty-five poems and seven
short stories, which are cited elsewhere in this
bibliograpgy; it could not have been difficult to
compile, but it serves as a good basic introduction to
the literature.

NO DATES

752. The "Raven". Texas: Edgar Allan Poe Literary Society
        of Texas, n.d.   73 pp.

These songs of fighter pilots indicate origins through
Southeast Asia. For most, there is a note on the
popular tune to which they should be sung.

DATE DUE

GAYLORD			PRINTED IN U.S.A.